William John Ansorge

Under the African Sun

A Description of Native Races in Uganda, Sporting Adventures and Other Experiences

William John Ansorge

Under the African Sun
A Description of Native Races in Uganda, Sporting Adventures and Other Experiences

ISBN/EAN: 9783743386501

Manufactured in Europe, USA, Canada, Australia, Japa

Cover: Foto ©Andreas Hilbeck / pixelio.de

Manufactured and distributed by brebook publishing software (www.brebook.com)

William John Ansorge

Under the African Sun

UNDER THE AFRICAN SUN

UNDER
THE AFRICAN SUN

A DESCRIPTION OF NATIVE RACES IN
UGANDA, SPORTING ADVENTURES
AND OTHER EXPERIENCES

BY

W. J. ANSORGE

M.A., LL.D., M.R.C.S., L.R.C.P.
LATE SENIOR PROFESSOR AT THE ROYAL COLLEGE OF MAURITIUS
MEDICAL OFFICER TO HER MAJESTY'S GOVERNMENT
IN UGANDA

*WITH 134 ILLUSTRATIONS FROM PHOTOGRAPHS BY THE AUTHOR
AND TWO COLOURED PLATES*

NEW YORK
LONGMANS, GREEN, AND CO.
1899

This Edition is for sale in the United States of America only, and is not to be imported into countries signatory to the Berne Treaty.

NOTE.

In the Appendix, Mr. Ernst Hartert, Director of the Tring Museum, has given an interesting account of my collection of African birds, and his description of rarities and novelties forms an important contribution to science.

The Honourable Walter Rothschild has kindly contributed to ch. xxii. a description of some new species of African lepidoptera. In the same chapter some valuable hints to collectors will be found in an extract from a letter from Dr. Karl Jordan.

Mr. W. E. de Winton, F.Z.S., the authority on "Small Mammals" at the South Kensington Museum, has courteously added to ch. xx. a scientific list of those captured by me.

W. J. ANSORGE.

London, December, 1898.

CONTENTS.

CHAP.		PAGE
I.	INTRODUCTORY . . .	1
II.	ZANZIBAR AND MOMBASA . .	4
III.	CARAVAN LIFE . . .	15
IV.	THE UGANDA PROTECTORATE . . .	41
V.	THE RAVINE DISTRICT . . .	46
VI.	KAVIRONDO .	61
VII.	USOGA	79
VIII.	THE WAGANDA . .	90
IX.	AT KAMPALA	120
X.	THE SOUDANESE . .	142
XI.	UNYORO	167
XII.	OUR STATIONS ON THE NILE . . .	181
XIII.	ON THE SHORES OF LAKE ALBERT .	198
XIV.	ELEPHANT-HUNTING . . .	220
XV.	THE "MAN-EATER" . . .	227
XVI.	RHINOCEROS-SHOOTING . .	240
XVII.	HIPPOPOTAMUS-SHOOTING .	249
XVIII.	GAZELLES .	257
XIX.	ANTELOPES .	262
XX.	SMALL MAMMALS .	279
XXI.	REPTILES	285
XXII.	BUTTERFLIES, MOTHS, AND BEETLES	299

APPENDIX

BIRDS	.	323

LIST OF PLATES.

The "Man-Eater's" Career Ended	*Frontispiece*	
His Highness Seyyid Hamud, Sultan of Zanzibar	*To face page*	10
(Reproduced, with permission, from a photograph by Coutinho Brothers, of Zanzibar.)		
The Euphorbia Tree	,, ,,	22
Village Headman in Uganda bringing a supply of Food for the Caravan	,,	32
A Family Group in Kavirondo		62
Entrance to a Kavirondo Village	,, ,,	66
A Family Group in Usoga	,, ,,	80
In the Stocks	,,	92
Waganda Muenge-Sellers	,, ,,	96
A Lendu Mother with her Baby	,, ,,	130
Open-Air Doctoring at Fovira	,, ,,	158
Entrance of Fort Hoima	,, ,,	176
A Falua Family	,, ,,	190
A Lur Family at Mahaji	,, ,,	208
Dug-Out Canoe on Lake Albert	,, ,,	220
A Crocodile of the Victoria Nile	,, ,,	296

COLOURED PLATES.

I. New Species of African Insects	*To face page*	302
II. New Species of African Birds	,, ,,	344

LIST OF TEXT ILLUSTRATIONS.

	PAGE
MASAI	1
A STATION ON THE SUEZ CANAL	6
WASIN	11
THE ENGLISH CHURCH AT MOMBASA	14
MID-DAY HALT ON THE MARCH	16
BURCHELL'S ZEBRA	19
A SPOTTED HYENA	21
FAN-PALMS IN UNYORO	23
A WHITE-ANT HILLOCK	25
MY FOUR "BOYS" ON THE MARCH	27
CAMP-COOKERY	29
A FRIENDLY CHIEF PAYS A CALL	31
THE CHURCH MISSION SOCIETY'S STEEL-BOAT ON LAKE VICTORIA NYANZA	33
A KIBANDA, OR GRASS-THATCHED REED-HUT	35
THE TRAVELLER'S REST-HOUSE AT FAJAO	37
MASAI WOMAN WITH GOURD-BOTTLE	46
WAKIKUYU MEN	47
WAKIKUYU WOMEN	49
AT A MASAI KRAAL	51
GUINEA-FOWL AND IBIS	53
ANDEROBO WOMAN	54
KWAVI	59
A KAVIRONDO MINSTREL	61
THE KAVIRONDO CHIEF NGIRA	64
A BLACKSMITH'S PARAPHERNALIA IN KAVIRONDO	68
KAVIRONDO BELLOWS, WOODEN SHIELD, AND WAR-HELMET	70
NATIVE BRIDGE OVER THE SIO RIVER IN KAVIRONDO	73
A KAVIRONDO VILLAGE-FORGE	77
USOGA HUBBLE-BUBBLE	79

	PAGE
Usoga Boats	82
The New Fort at Luba's in Usoga	85
Pigmies of the Great African Forest	87
Usoga Drinking-Cup	89
Uganda Shield	90
Waganda Peasants	91
A Waganda Family	93
Waganda Mat-Makers	95
Bark-Cloth Manufacture	97
Waganda Soap-Sellers	98
Waganda Potters	99
Upper-Class Waganda	101
Mugwanya, the Roman Catholic Prime Minister of Uganda	103
Waganda Musicians	104
Uganda Harp	106
Uganda Drums	107
Waganda Labourers	108
Mtesa's Tomb	110
In a Wahima Kraal	111
Wahima Herdsmen	113
The Roman Catholic Princes Augustine and Joseph of Uganda	115
Ex-King Mbogo, Princess Fatima, and Prince Ramazan of Uganda	117
Uganda Spears	119
Native Fish-Creel	120
Kampala seen from Nakasero Hill	121
Arab and Swahili Ivory Traders	123
Kampala Police	125
A Chain-Gang at Kampala	126
A Fishmonger	128
Front of Protestant Cathedral on Namirembe Hill	130
Rubaga Hill seen from Namirembe	132
An Albino-Negro	133
The East African Rifles	135

LIST OF TEXT ILLUSTRATIONS xiii

	PAGE
Fort Kampala seen from the Native Market	136
Waganda Spearmen	138
Main-Entrance of Fort Kampala	140
Military Watch-Tower at Kibero	144
Soudanese	146
In a Soudanese Village	149
Soudanese Corporal Spinning Cotton-Thread	151
The Soudanese Settlement at Kibero	153
The Soudanese Captain, Surur Effendi, and his Family	155
Bekamba, the Wanyoro Chief, in his State-Carriage	159
The Medical Officer's Residence at Masindi	161
Three of the Wounded	164
At the Entrance of Fort Masindi	169
The Infant Ajaka, the youngest Chief in Unyoro	170
Wanyoro Women with Native Hoes	171
A Hospital-Hut at Masindi	173
Patients at the Hospital Dispensary	175
A Makraka Family	177
My Hut at Hoima	179
Shuli Natives	181
River Scenery at Fovira	182
Drawbridge of Fort Fovira	184
The Wanyoro Chief Lejumba	186
The Lango Chief Amien	187
Sem-Sem Drying-Stack	189
A Falua Dwelling	191
The Hospital at Fajao	194
Natives on the March	196
Lur Children	198
In the Native Village at Kibero	199
The Salt-Industry at Kibero	200
My Quarters at Kibero	202
Her Majesty's Steel-Boat "Alexandra" on Lake Albert Nyanza	204
Afternoon Tea at Mahaji	206
Lur Woman carrying a Load of Wood	208

LUR CORN-STORES	210
MY TENT	212
LUR PLAYING THE NATIVE GAME "SORO"	214
COLOBUS MONKEYS	216
WANYORO CANOE-MEN OF LAKE ALBERT WEARING REED EYE-SHADES	218
THE DAUGHTERS OF TUKWENDA	219
A LUCKY SHOT	225
THE CAGE FOR THE LION	232
THE LION-TRAP COMPLETED	233
THE LIONESS AT FAJAO	236
A RHINO HEAD	241
TWO RHINOS	247
SOUDANESE SOLDIER WITH THE FAJAO PADDLE	249
LANDING-PLACE AT FAJAO	253
A HIPPOPOTAMUS	255
GRANT'S GAZELLE ♀	260
THE IMPALLA ANTELOPE ♂	263
A PAH ANTELOPE ♂	265
THE KOBUS THOMASI ANTELOPE ♂	266
THE NSWALLAH ANTELOPE ♀	268
NEUMANN'S STEINBOK ♂	277
LOPHUROMYS ANSORGEI	279
(From "Proceedings of Zoological Society of London," 19th May 1896.)	
CROCODILE-POOL AT FAJAO	295

CHAPTER I.

INTRODUCTORY.

MASAI.

MY first journey, March 1894, to Uganda was made in the days prior to the proclamation of a British Protectorate over these regions. Caravans then had to be fitted out at Zanzibar, though Mombasa, on the mainland, was the actual starting-point. The transport, whatever the nature of the goods, depended on the efficiency of natives drawn from the mixed coast-races known collectively as Swahilies.

The caravan route from Mombasa to Port Alice, a distance of 800 miles, was practically a mere footpath. Not a few hardships and dangers had then to be faced, where the journey now has become comparatively a pleasure-trip. Barely three years ago two caravan parties were massacred by hostile natives; now, a gentleman boasted in my hearing that he could travel the whole distance of 800 miles in absolute safety armed with nothing but his walking-stick. Then, it took eighty-three days from Mombasa to Kampala; now, barely half that time. Formerly, the traveller spent eighteen days to cross the Taru desert and the fever-belt beyond it; now, he enters the train at Mombasa one day, and finds himself next day safe beyond this trying region. From Kikuyu to Kabras then, meant twenty-one days' journey without the caravan meeting another human being, except perchance some wandering Masai warrior wearing a pigtail wig and armed with a long-bladed spear. Now, three Government stations at Lake Naivasha, Eldoma Ravine, and Nandi respectively, complete the chain of forts. Where Bishop Hannington failed to pass and lost his life, mission ladies now travel safely and comfortably. At Kikuyu, where we were warned not to venture out of sight of the fort, and never to go about unarmed or without an armed escort, three families of English settlers have built themselves homes, and three chubby infants, the first Europeans born in this distant region of Africa, have made their appearance.

Zanzibar too has felt the effect of these changes. It used to be the great emporium, Mombasa being merely a geographical name as regards importance; now, with the railway an accomplished undertaking for the first 200 miles, Mombasa as its coast-terminus is every day increasing in importance, and Zanzibar is gradually but steadily sinking into the shade.

The old caravan route presented to the traveller interesting variations in scenery and surroundings :—Mombasa, with its cocoa-nut palms and mango-trees; the waterless Taru desert, with its clumps of thorn-bush and euphorbia; the Maungu, Ndara, and Ndi hills, with giraffes and elands in the adjoining plains; Kibwezi, with its huge baobab trees; the Makindo and Kiboko river-camps, with rhinos and zebras, gazelles and antelopes in their neighbourhood; the shallow Kilungu river winding through fertile and populated regions; the Athi plains, the most magnificent game country in the whole world, with its lions and ostriches, hartebeests and wildebeests; Kikuyu forest, with its glades and clearings; the extinct volcano Longonot, with the huge crater on its summit; Lake Naivasha, with its myriads of waterfowl of every description; Lake Nakuru, with its thousands of flamingoes; the virgin forest-belt of Subugo, with its noble timber; the cold Mau escarpment, nearly 9000 feet above the sea-level, with scattered patches of waving bamboos; the treeless regions of Kavirondo; the garden of Usoga, with its grey parrots and vast banana plantations; the Nile, where it forms the exit of that mighty lake the Victoria Nyanza; finally, Uganda, with its hills and valleys, its wild date-palms and twenty-feet high elephant-grass.

It fell to my lot to accomplish this journey six times, besides spending nearly a year in the more remote parts known as Unyoro and crossing Lake Albert four times. There is an indescribable fascination in African travel and adventure, which draws one again and again to the Dark Continent, though not a few Europeans have found it their grave. Within the last four years a score have passed off the scene; those personally known to me were:—Mr. Purkiss, Dr. Chartres, Mr. Muxworthy, Capt. Dunning, Mr. West, Mr. Dick, Monseigneur Guillemin, Mr. Godfrey, Capt. Sclater, Major Thruston, Mr. N. Wilson, Mr. Scott, Mr. Pilkington, and the Rev. Mr. Hubbard. The majority of these met with a violent death; only two or three fell victims to the climate. British supremacy, called "Protectorate," is slowly and steadily establishing itself over these vast realms. It has abolished slavery, compelled native races to live at peace with each other, and opened up uninhabited regions, larger than the whole of England, for skilful and willing settlers to found homesteads and farms.

On my first arrival in Uganda, we were but twelve European officials, including every one from the highest to the lowest; and only seven remain of these pioneers, the thin end of the wedge made use of by the British Government in the great work of opening up these remote regions to further British enterprise. Perhaps some of my experiences "under the African sun" may be of service to others.

CHAPTER II.

ZANZIBAR AND MOMBASA.

THE traveller to Uganda has to reach first of all Mombasa; and to do this, he may go either by French steamer and change at Zanzibar, or by English steamer and change at Aden. By the former he misses seeing Aden, and by the latter seeing Zanzibar. There are no mails at present running direct from England to Mombasa.[1]

Those who prefer to embark in London, who object to second-class passengers sharing the steamer's deck with the first-class, who dislike French cookery, and who are absolutely ignorant of the French language, should not go by the French steamer. Those, however, who wish to save themselves the long sea-voyage through the Bay of Biscay and round by Gibraltar, who prefer the passage-money to include a certain free-allowance of wine and beer on board, and who have to cut down their expenses, may prefer the French line.

If the traveller selects the English line, and money is no consideration, he may save himself the Bay of Biscay by going overland and catching up his steamer at Brindisi. If the traveller chooses the French route, he has to embark at Marseilles[2] on one of the Messageries Maritimes Company's steamers bound for Zanzibar.

From London to Marseilles takes twenty-four hours. Those who prefer crossing the Channel during the day should leave London via Dover and Calais in the morning. Those who do not mind crossing the Channel at night, and would like to see something of the scenery of France as they travel along, should leave London in the evening.

In travelling through France, the passenger should bear in

[1] Steamers of the German "Ost-Afrika-Linie" run direct from Hamburg to Mombasa, touching at Naples.
[2] P. and O. steamers now call also at Marseilles.

mind that even with a first-class ticket only 56 lbs. of luggage can be taken free, and that a very exorbitant freight is charged for every pound over weight. One small trunk for the cabin usually represents the 56 lbs. allowed free. But there is no need for any one to burden himself unnecessarily by taking the whole lot of his belongings across France. The agent in London of the French Company will take charge of all the luggage, if delivered to his care a full fortnight before the date fixed for the departure of the mail from Marseilles. The luggage is then sent on by sea, and the passenger will find it waiting for him at Marseilles when he arrives there.

The journey from Marseilles to Zanzibar takes eighteen days; this includes the unavoidable loss of time due to coaling at Port Said and Djibouti. The French steamers are noted for their remarkable punctuality as regards the advertised dates of departure and arrival. There have been considerable changes in the mail-service, since I first journeyed down the Red Sea prior to the opening of the Suez Canal. In those days we went by steamer from Marseilles to Alexandria, then by train from Alexandria *via* Cairo to Suez, and from there once more by steamer to our destination. When the Suez Canal was opened, the Messageries Maritimes boats touched at Aden, Messina, and Naples; but they do not do so now.

From Marseilles to Port Said takes five days. Port Said has become a busy centre; it has attracted wealth and at the same time the scum which caters for every evil passion. The steamer coals here; and as coaling implies dirt and discomfort, the passenger takes refuge on shore. Whether one has seen the place already or not, it is always a pleasant change, and breaks the monotony of a long sea-voyage, to take a stroll on shore.

The Suez Canal is traversed in fifteen hours. There are pretty bits of scenery and quaint glimpses of Eastern life revealed, as the vessel steams slowly past the interminable expanse of sand.

In passing through the canal, notwithstanding the apparent sameness of the surroundings, the traveller may meet with very different experiences. On one journey we traversed the canal during the night. There were many English passengers, including a good many Australians going to England for a holiday. A charming and graceful fancy-dress ball was promptly organised and enlivened the occasion. On another journey we steamed down the canal during the day. A fierce sandstorm was raging, and all the ports were tightly closed, yet the fine sand found its way somehow into everything. We were boxed up in the saloon, and the heat was stifling.

More commonly the apathetic passenger simply "kills time." To his *blasé* eye the pretty canal stations are uninteresting; to him the Egyptian ragged urchins scrambling for an orange or a coin are an absolute bore, and the white cloud of ibis, the single file of camels, the sand dunes, the salt lakes, are of supreme indifference.

A STATION ON THE SUEZ CANAL.

It is a curious fact that on board a ship every traveller becomes much more chummy; and when he does throw off the crusty shell of prejudice, he is ready to take to anybody. On board ship one meets, one parts, perhaps never to meet again; yet many a kindly word or action lingers in the recesses of memory, and is treasured for years. It does not take much to call forth a laugh when everybody is in a mood for it.

At the Suez end of the canal the steamer only stops to land mails; there is no time nowadays to go on shore and visit the Well of Moses and other sights of the neighbourhood. Industrious hawkers, however, come on board the homeward-bound ships to have their innings before the passengers reach Port Said.

From Suez to Djibouti takes six days. The steamer generally anchors very far from shore, consequently the long journey in an open boat under the broiling sun is too uninviting to tempt many passengers to land, and there is very little to see if one does go. On my last journey most of us remained on board, and we had some mild excitement in watching a monster ray disporting itself round the ship, till two of the sailors went off in a boat and successfully harpooned it. It had a filiform tail several feet long, and two remarkable blue flappers a foot long near its monster jaws. It is on occasions like these that one would like to have a few spare pounds to secure such a curiosity for a museum. I have not seen anything like it in any museum; and, for all I know to the contrary, it may have been an unknown species. It was soon chopped up, the greater part of its body being thrown overboard as "waste." The flesh was considered too coarse for the passengers' table, and was handed over to the sailors.

At Djibouti the traveller hears the same familiar cry of " Ever dive !—Ho! ho!—Ever dive!—Ho! ho!" as at Aden. A number of natives come in their tiny dug-outs to the steamer's side, jump into the water, and with hoarse cries invite the idle spectator to chuck them a coin to dive for in the clear translucent water.

From Djibouti to Zanzibar takes six days. Flying-fish occasionally drop on to the deck. It is a pretty sight when a shoal of flying-fish skims the surface of the water, clipping through the crests of the waves with the sunbeams glinting from their silvery sides. Sometimes, but not often, one sees the outlines, as if sculptured, of the "sleeping lion" presented by the rock-bound coast of Cape Guardafui.

Seen from the ocean, as the steamer nears the island, Zanzibar presents a dense growth of cocoa-nut palms and green verdure; but the town itself is a mass of buildings huddled together anyhow. The narrow tortuous streets, the crowded native bazaar, the Sultan's palace, the British Consulate, have already been described by different travellers.

Part of the wealth of Zanzibar is derived from its clove plantations, and it would be a mistake not to visit one of them

The clove-trees, most of them old, are planted in straight rows of considerable length, and form picturesque groves.

Passing through the native quarter, I came across an Arab school. Teacher and pupils were sitting cross-legged on mats; each pupil was using, instead of a slate, a scapula or shoulder-blade of some animal.

By the roadside I saw a native doctor cupping a patient, and two women were waiting for their turn. He used a goat-horn, perforated at the top with a small aperture which he blocked with a piece of wax. Having made two or three tiny incisions on the skin of the patient, the practitioner passed the mouth of the horn over a flame and then clapped it over the wound. After a few minutes, by removing the plug of wax, the horn was withdrawn, and in most cases a large clot of blood came away with it.

Apparently everybody in Zanzibar, who can possibly afford it, keeps a carriage. Arabs and Indians may be seen taking daily their afternoon drive along the Nazimoja road in a variety of elegant vehicles.

On my second visit to Zanzibar the island had just been visited by a severe epidemic; the German doctor had succumbed to it, and the English doctor was ill. I happened to take my watch to a shop to be repaired. The watchmaker, a European, was covered with boils from head to foot. He did not know that I belonged to the medical profession, when he explained to me that he was treating himself, having found in some old obscure pamphlet an excellent prescription for drawing out the bad blood! "What's the good of going to doctors?" he said, "they can't even cure themselves; there's the German doctor dead, and the other doctor very ill!" He assured me, in proof of the efficacy of his own treatment, that he had not a single boil till he began to treat himself; "and now look!" he exclaimed, pointing triumphantly to his blotched face which might have done credit to a severe attack of small-pox. He was not satisfied apparently at the success on his own person, but had tried the treatment also on his unfortunate wife and child, who were summoned to show themselves to me. Allowing that he represented the superlative degree of an exodus of boils, his family represented a very good comparative and positive stage respectively. The next time I visited Zanzibar he and his family had disappeared; possibly he went somewhere to take out a patent for a pill "warranted to draw out the bad blood."

There are a number of hotels and restaurants at Zanzibar; but most of them are simply drinking-saloons. The great drawback to all lies in their very unpleasant domestic arrangements for meeting certain imperative laws of nature.

In one of these hotels, in 1894, I met some strange customers. A troupe of performers, anxious to give an exhibition of a balloon ascent before the late Sultan, had arrived from India. The Sultan, however, declined to pay the sum they asked. Their leader was a powerful young man, but addicted to drink, and the worse for it every night. As the partitions separating the bedrooms were only thin planks, I became the unwilling listener to nightly conjugal altercations between him and his wife. The partner in this show volunteered to me the information that the lady was already the fourth wife, her three predecessors having come to an untimely and unfortunate end by dropping from the balloon. The fourth wife was then training to perform her balloon ascent and, let us hope, more successful descent. The troupe left Zanzibar within a few days—destination unknown.

Enjoying Sir Arthur Hardinge's courteous hospitality at the British Consulate, I had an opportunity of being present at a very grand Arab dinner given by him, in honour of the Queen's birthday, to all the Arab nobility and élite. The Sultan was represented by his brother, the heir-apparent to the throne. Etiquette forbids his Highness from eating in public with his subjects. The famous slave-dealer Tippoo-Tib was also present. Though there were but forty guests, over three hundred dishes loaded the table in Arab fashion with Arab delicacies. Roasts, pastry, rice, sweetmeats, fruit, were lavishly jostling each other for elbow-room. For the Europeans knives and forks were laid; but the Arabs used Adam's fork, helping themselves indiscriminately to anything within reach. They drank sherbet. Arab etiquette demands that the guest should eat very little; consequently all this profusion went to their attendants who rushed in after the guests had left the table, and *then* the eatables disappeared in a twinkling.

A very imposing ceremony was the investiture of his Highness Seyyid Hamud, Sultan of Zanzibar, with the insignia of the Order of Grand Commander of the Star of India. The investiture took place in the Victoria Hall, a first-rate building for public ceremonies of this sort. It is in the Sultan's gardens, where the slave-market used to exist in days prior to the British Protectorate. Sir Arthur Hardinge, K.C.M.G., C.B., her Britannic Majesty's Consul-General and Diplomatic Agent, sat at the Sultan's right; and Brigadier-General A. E. Raikes, commanding his Highness the Sultan's army, was at the Sultan's left. The others in sequence were Basil S. Cave, Esq., C.B., the Consul; Henry C. C. Dundas, Esq., the Vice-Consul; and next to the latter sat Captain P. F. Tillard, R.N., of H.M.S. *Magicienne*. Behind the Captain sat Mrs. Basil Cave.

Sir Arthur is deservedly popular throughout both Protectorates. His genial manners and flow of conversation cover the erudite classical scholar of Oxford and the distinguished Arabic linguist.

Mr. Basil Cave is well known, owing to the prominent part he played in the suppression of the usurper who endeavoured to seize the Sultanate when the late Sultan died.

Zanzibar is one of the bishoprics of the Universities Mission; their death-roll is appalling. I was sorry to find that of four of their number who were fellow-passengers with me in 1896 only one is left; one died, two have been permanently invalided: no comment is needed. In 1893 I visited the island of Likoma in Lake Nyassa, another of their bishoprics, where the list of dead and invalided is even heavier; the Bishop, who showed us friendly hospitality, was succeeded by his Archdeacon; when the latter died, the medical missionary became the bishop.

The English Club in Zanzibar is a very popular institution, and famous for its "Sabbath-Calms" and other mysteries, which, however, must not be divulged to the uninitiated; the stranger-guest soon learns them.

From Zanzibar to Mombasa means about fifteen hours by steamer. At present there is rather an uncertainty how long one may have to wait at Zanzibar for a steamer to cross over to Mombasa. There is, however, a monthly communication by means of the German line and the British India. In addition, the Protectorate steamer the *Juba* plies between the two islands. Last time I crossed from Mombasa to Zanzibar it was in the *Juba*, and we had an Arab dhow in tow as far as Wasin (written also Wassein).

Wasin is the southern extremity of the coast-line of the

HIS HIGHNESS SEYYID HAMUD, SULTAN OF ZANZIBAR

Investiture of his Highness with the Insignia of Grand Commander of the Star of India by Sir Arthur Hardinge, K.C.M.G., C.B.

British East African Protectorate. Opposite to it is a large island, said to be a favourite residence of pious and wealthy Arabs and a seat of Arab learning.

Mombasa is the capital of British East Africa. The island is also named Mombasa, and nestles close against the mainland which throws a protecting arm round it in the shape of a promontory, called "English-Point," on the north-east. The space between English-Point and the island forms Mombasa harbour. Coral reefs narrow the mouth of the harbour, and every now and then some vessel comes to grief. There is another harbour

WASIN.

at Kilindini, which is said to be better. The island is separated from the mainland by a narrow strip of the sea, which at low water can be forded by wading across it.

The coral rocks supply excellent building material, and the Government is raising handsome and imposing structures to serve as residences for the different Departmental Chiefs. Instead of using limekilns, the natives burn their lime in the open air. They construct a circular stack of faggots several feet high, according to the quantity of coral to be burnt. On and about it lumps of coral are piled, the stack is then fired, and the coral calcined.

Dark and grim the old Portuguese fortress frowns at the water's edge and commands the entrance of Mombasa harbour.

What sinister scenes these old walls must have witnessed, when slavery and tyranny were rampant, when it required six months to circumnavigate Africa *via* Cape of Good Hope to Lisbon, when the Portuguese governor held the life, honour, and property of residents at his mercy, and ruled with more absolute sway than the Autocrat of all the Russias! Looking at crumbling portions of the old defences and at the rusting dismantled cannons strewn about, some lapped by the restless tides, some resting in the dismal casemates, Scott's noble lines in "Marmion" are recalled—

> "The ire of a wrathful king
> Comes riding on destruction's wing!"

The littleness of human greatness is emphasised! The petty tyrant, raised by the inscrutable decree of Providence to rule a province in these distan' regions, forgets that he is as insignificant as a bubble of spray on the mighty crest of storm-tossed ocean waves; his name and word supreme to-day, to-morrow are forgotten, as the ceaseless ages roll along with their thousand years counting but as a day in the eternal history of time!

The narrow winding streets of the older portion of Mombasa town are not very inviting. With regard to the newer portion, where the Wali (the Arab governor or magistrate of the town) is erecting rows of native buildings to accommodate the rapidly-increasing native population, a wide straight road is left open for traffic, and leads to cocoa-nut plantations and copses of magnificent old mango-trees.

Swahili ladies delight in having the tiny amount of wool on their heads elaborately plaited by a professional hair-dresser. The height of fashion with them is to have the wool parted in longitudinal streaks from the forehead to the occiput, so as to give the skull the resemblance to a ribbed melon. Instead of being satisfied with one hole through the lobe of the ear, they punch a series of holes, arranged in a semicircle along the whole of the outer rim of the ear. Ear-rings in the shape of small buttons are then inserted, and a similar button worn as a nose-ring in the cartilage of the right or left nostril completes the head-toilet. As regards dress, the louder the pattern and the more glaring the colours of the cotton cloth which forms her one garment, the more is the Swahili pleased.

The traveller may see one wearing a brilliant yellow cloth with a flaring red sun radiating from the centre, or another lady sporting a huge geometrical pattern visible a couple of miles off.

The Mombasa Club deserves every success; it has supplied a great want in offering bedroom accommodation to travellers to or from Uganda. For though there are a number of second or third rate hotels, kept chiefly by Greeks, the tendency of all is to degenerate into drinking-saloons for the shady class of men met with in all seaports. Until quite recently the Uganda Government official arriving at Mombasa had to depend on the kindness of a personal friend to put him up for the night. I had a room at the hospital, owing to the courtesy of Dr. Macdonald, the chief medical officer. "A friend in need is a friend indeed," all the world over; and if it had not been for him, I would have had to pitch my tent, like a gipsy, on a piece of waste land, when I arrived at Mombasa, in the spring of 1895, from Uganda with a patient who had been invalided home. This happened in the days of the ephemeral Imperial British East Africa Company. Now a Sub-Commissioner, Mr. Cranfurd, is permanently settled here; and it was owing to his kindly assistance, when last I went up-country, that the Government was saved the expense of any considerable delay at Mombasa.

A conspicuous feature of the island is the baobab tree with its aldermanic girth among trees. When it has shed its leaves, it stands bare and gaunt, and looks as if stretching out gouty fingers in apoplectic uncertainty. It has a curious hard-shelled fruit which, when cut through and emptied of contents, furnishes bowls for drawing water, much in the same way that the coco-de-mer supplies dispensing-scoops to some of the Arab retail dealers.

A very tiny species of dwarf antelope is still occasionally met with on the island; but this pretty and graceful little creature is dangerously near extermination. Birds and insects are well represented; but it is obviously difficult to get anything new, where every collector starts his collection from, and where he finally ends it.

A good deal of mission activity prevails in Mombasa, and there are several mission societies. It is a pity that the native convert so often brings disgrace on the religion he professes to have embraced. In many cases he learns to read, write, and speak English more or less fluently, but becomes on the strength of it insufferably conceited. Bishop Tucker, the esteemed and conscientious Bishop of both Protectorates, has indeed a hard task to prevent these human canker-worms from destroying the fruit of his mission-fields.

The new little English church at Mombasa looks prim and primitive.

On my last journey to the coast I had, for the first time, the benefit of travelling by the Uganda Railway. The line was completed as far as Kinani, 170 miles from the coast; but only open for traffic as far as Voi, 100 miles from the coast, and then only on certain days of the week. To avoid delay, I accepted accommodation offered in a goods-van. We left Kinani at 9.30 P.M. and arrived at Voi at 3.30 A.M.; here we had to wait till 8.30 A.M., arriving at Kilindini Station, in the island of Mombasa, at 4.30 P.M.

This lift saved us the wearisome march through the Taru desert; but travellers to Uganda, though saved a most unpleasant part of the caravan route, have still to experience more or less of caravan life before they reach their destination.

THE ENGLISH CHURCH AT MOMBASA.

CHAPTER III.

CARAVAN LIFE.

CARAVAN life in Africa is a healthy life, owing to the constant outdoor exercise and the necessarily frugal fare. It is an ideal life for a man able to rough it, satisfied with leading a more or less solitary existence, fond of sport, and capable of culling pleasure from the gifts of Nature which a bountiful Providence strews along his path. If, in addition, the traveller has a good outfit and a well-arranged transport service, he will find the few troubles he is likely to encounter reduced to a minimum. With each journey one gains some new experience, and in proportion learns to adapt oneself better to the altered circumstances of such a life. Of course, what suits one man does not suit everybody. As a simple illustration take the routine of meals. Some travellers can stow away a very hearty breakfast in the early morning just before they march. I, for one, am unable to partake of a heavy meal at a very early hour; a plate of porridge is all I require, and it suits me best. I do not hold that a caravan should be driven, as if it were an express train or a slave gang, with scarcely a pause on to the next camping-ground. I prefer to treat them as human beings carrying heavy loads and doing hard work; I therefore always give them half-an-hour's rest during the march, if possible near some running water where they can refresh themselves. The break in the march I utilise by having a sort of breakfast and lunch combined. This midday meal consists of the cold remains of last night's dinner, a saving of labour to the cook who has to march along with the caravan like the rest of us.

Sometimes the halt occurs at a spot like a shady bower in a leafy avenue. Then, again, there are some men who cannot stand either sun or heat, and who require a mid-day siesta on arrival at camp. For them it is important to get the march over as early as possible, and they do not mind marching when the dew lies heavy on the grass, and perhaps is still falling. I, for my part, can stand dry heat a great deal better than the chilling dew; and those who have had fever, know how easily a chill may bring on an attack. It is, therefore, impossible to lay down hard and fast rules applicable to everybody under all circumstances.

With perfect weather, running streamlets at intervals along the march, a good road, no illness in the caravan, and a good supply of provisions, the march is the very opposite of a hardship; it is purely and simply a pleasure-trip. And there are many such days on the journey.

MID-DAY HALT ON THE MARCH.

Shooting "for the pot" adds additional zest to the day's enjoyment. Partridges and guinea-fowls are pretty frequently met with, and are a very delicious and acceptable addition to one's fare. The very last I shot—and meat or no meat for dinner depended on it—were a partridge and a brace of guinea-fowls. I got them on the wing with No. 5 shot, which is a good all-round article, when one has not the means of carrying a variety of cartridges like No. 4 for guinea-fowls or No. 8 for snipe. The different species of partridges are very interesting. It is worth while to skin the bird and to preserve the skin; one may thus collect some very rare specimens. The bird certainly tastes better with the skin on; but it is a mistake to imagine that the bird is not fit for food because it has been skinned. On Christmas Eve, 1896, I shot a partridge at "Mondo" in Uganda. The bird I had for my Christmas dinner. The skin I sent home to England; it turned out to be a very rare species and only the second specimen of the sort ever sent home. A similar thing happened with a very handsome partridge I shot one day near the Samia Hills in Kavirondo. The skin is now at the South Kensington Museum, and the second one there of another rare species, the first of which was shot near Mount Elgon. At Campi-ya-Simba I shot sand-grouse, and at Kikuyu spur-fowl.

But the wild guinea-fowl is *the* bird for the traveller's table. It is surprising what varieties of wild guinea-fowl are met with along the caravan route, to mention but three: the "horned," the "crested," and the "vulturine." This bird gives the best return for the shot expended on it; there is a good deal of meat on it, and what there is is good. Snipe and quail are very tasty, but yield so little that very few travellers can afford to waste a shot on them. Egyptian goose fills a big dish, but, as a rule, it is tough and therefore not a favourite.

The "horned" guinea-fowl is perhaps the variety best known in England, as it is the only one which has been domesticated and reared for the market. But there are a great many different species even amongst these; some, like the "Hildebrandti," have enormous horns; others, like the Uganda species, have a very tiny horn and a tuft of bristles in front of it; those at the Kiboko river are comparatively small birds; those near Lake Nakuru are exceptionally large.

But a far handsomer bird is the "crested" guinea-fowl, having instead of the horn a tuft of feathers like a crest. Its call is not the noisy "takák-takák-takák" of the horned bird. Swahilies call it the "kororo," in imitation of its cry.

The "vulturine" has neither a horn nor a crest; it has a bald pate like a vulture, with a semi-ring of soft feathers like a bald man's occipital patch of hair.

The guinea-fowl has a noisy and heavy flight. With a broken wing the bird may yet escape by running, but with a broken leg it cannot escape as easily by flying. It is almost sure to betray its presence by the noisy call in the early morning or towards dusk, when it roosts on some high leafy tree and falls an easy prey to the pot-hunter. Partridges roost by preference in the branches of some moderate-sized bush; they too betray their presence at dawn and sunset with their "ká! kaká!" scream. I have seen guinea-fowls clustering together by the hundred; for instance at Kariandus and on the north-west shore of Lake Naivasha, where I bagged three with one shot.

At Kariandus the guinea-fowl—it was on my third journey— gave us once a useful warning of the approach of a man-eating lion which infested the neighbourhood at the time and had carried off more than one porter from some of the other caravans. The scream of the frightened birds attracted our attention to the spot, some four hundred yards off, on the slope of the hill. I only caught a glimpse of a huge tawny animal disappearing with a bound behind some bushes, whilst a few more of the frightened birds flew up out of the grass into the trees. All my men declared it was a lion. We did not stop to investigate; as it was getting dusk, we hurried off to get within the protecting circle of the camp-fires.

Swahili porters are very fond of zebra meat. Some travellers have a natural prejudice to eating an animal belonging to the equine species; but the first zebra-steak I tasted I thought rather nice; perhaps the animal I had shot was not a particularly old one. A tough old stallion is certainly not a very inviting dish.

I once saw on the Athi plains a herd of zebras, which must have numbered over a hundred thousand; for, as far as the eye could reach, they presented a dense unbroken phalanx, with young ones by the hundred amongst them. I have never come across any other species but the one known as Burchell's zebra. There is no greater risk of exterminating the zebra by shooting one now and again for caravan or personal need, than there is of wiping off the hartebeest antelope by occasionally bagging one. But I once came across a Eurasian on his way to the coast, who shot a zebra apparently for no other purpose but to brag that he had shot one. I asked him whether he required the meat for food for himself or his caravan. He answered, "No"; and when I said, "Perhaps you wanted it for its hide?" he again replied, "No." Such men must have a very callous conscience. The zebra has a peculiar cry which sounds like "Yap, yap, yap"; it has neither the horse's neigh nor the donkey's bray. The hide makes a handsome mat; but I found in London that, next to the giraffe hide, it is the most expensive to dress and mount. One moonlight night at Campi-ya-Simba it was almost impossible to get any sleep, owing to the incessant call of the zebras, broken every now and then by the muffled growl of some lion; the lions were evidently chasing them. Once on the Athi plains I came upon a dead zebra with two hyænas devouring it.

The "hoo-yee-yooh" of the hyæna every traveller is sure to hear along the greater part of

BURCHELL'S ZEBRA.

the caravan route. I heard it already on Mombasa island close to the hospital. Swahili porters hate the brute, and not infrequently they dread it quite as much as a lion. The hyæna has very powerful jaws and can inflict a most severe wound. Occasionally it is bold enough to venture within the caravan lines and to seize one of the sleeping porters. More than one of my men has thus been dragged along, but owing to his screams and the general hubbub, has been relinquished by the brute. It seems more than a coincidence, that the men thus seized have invariably been the most infirm and emaciated in the caravan. I have a personal grievance against hyænas, besides the one of wounding some of my porters. Three and a half years ago I shot at Gilgil a magnificent bustard, quite different to the common great bustard so constantly met with between Machakos and Muani. I might mention here that the great bustard as a culinary delicacy has been greatly overrated, nor is it such a very difficult bird to shoot. Of course a rifle has to be used. The lesser bustard or pao is a somewhat better bird to eat; it is much smaller, and a shot-gun is preferably used for it. The huge bustard I shot at Gilgil must have been a rare bird, as I have never met with another specimen like it. It had an enormous reddish ruff round the neck, and, next to the ostrich, it was the largest bird I have seen. I got it with a Martini bullet by a lucky shot through the neck, at 200 yards. The skin from tip of beak to tip of toe was nearly twice the length of any chop-box in my possession. It was left, therefore, for the night on the top of the boxes under the awning of my tent. I woke up in the night, hearing a scrambling noise close to me, but too late; some hyæna had carried off my bird, although a night-watchman was on duty a few yards off. It was no comfort to know that the hyæna must have made its last meal, as I had freely used arsenical soap in preparing the skin.

Since then I have never left anything within reach of a hungry hyæna; and care has to be taken not to expose either saddle or harness to tempt these voracious brutes. I have seen but two species of hyæna, the spotted and the brown. The one shown in the illustration I got by setting a trap-gun. The trap is easily set. Tie the bait over the muzzle of the rifle. Use in preference a piece of offal, for instance a bit of highly odoriferous goatskin. Suspend or fasten the rifle horizontally at such a height from the ground, that the hyæna can conveniently grab the bait. Attention must be paid to expose the bait in such a way, that the hyæna cannot seize it from the side, but has to approach the front of the muzzle. Place the trigger at full cock and tie it by a bit of string to the tree or bush behind it; now pull the muzzle forward, and, if the trap is in good working-order, the trigger will at once respond and strike. If the trap works satisfactorily, the rifle may now be loaded and left *in situ*. Any prowling hyæna is sure to be attracted and to immolate itself; the bullet is almost certain to blow its brains out. In a wilderness the only precaution necessary is to warn every one in the caravan, and to see that the gun points away from the camp. Hyænas seem to be attacked by the same sort of tick which is a parasite of rhinos.

At Sakwa's village in Kavirondo a donkey was so badly mauled by a hyæna that it died. Most travellers take some goats or sheep along with their caravan in the event of failing to shoot game or to buy meat from the natives. The animals should be carefully penned up at night and surrounded with a strong protecting thorn-fence, called "boma" by the Swahilies. On my second journey, we had bought some sheep and goats at Kikuyu, in anticipation of continuing our march next morning.

The animals were placed for the night in the customary penfold, outside the fort. Next morning we found that hyænas had carried off two of the sheep, badly lacerated a third which we had to kill on the spot, and wounded a fourth. One such lesson serves a lifetime not to trust to any enclosure offering a single weak point to a possible nocturnal visit from these marauders.

One of the pleasures held out by caravan life consists in culling rare flowers and collecting plants new to science. Some men, as the explorer Teleki expressed it to me, have a

A SPOTTED HYÆNA.

lucky hand. He gathered, more or less accidentally, one day on the march a handful of plants most of which were unknown. But it is not necessary to be a botanist to admire the trees and flowers of Tropical Africa.

Take, for instance, the euphorbia-tree, sure to be met with pretty often along the caravan route. The specimen shown in the illustration grew by the roadside between Kitanwa and Kibero. Its majestic dimensions can be estimated by a glance at the group sheltering underneath it. The whole of my caravan were gathered under it, though they are hidden by the patch of grass which was six to eight feet high. In some parts of the Protectorate the euphorbia furnishes the only firewood procurable, as every traveller through the western parts of Kavirondo soon finds out. It is a poor sort of fuel, and where it is offered for sale, owing to the scarcity of any other firewood, it is not very cheap.

On the whole there is a good supply of firewood along the caravan route, except at the Government stations, where it has to be bought from the natives who bring it to the camp or to the appointed market. Everywhere else the traveller, on pitching camp, sends a certain number of his porters to bring in firewood. The men naturally gather only dry wood, fallen or dead branches, and thus no harm is done to the bush or forest which provides the caravan. The protecting fence for the cattle is supplied by the thorn-bushes. Sometimes, as for instance near the Kedong escarpment, one comes upon a dead forest. The gaunt dead trees on the wind-swept height might form a fitting background for one of Doré's illustrations of Dante's Inferno. No doubt the constant grass-fires must do considerable injury to bush and forest-belt, besides destroying all the young trees endeavouring to struggle for their existence on the grass plains. Grass-fires are not necessarily unmitigated evils, a good many poisonous snakes and other vermin probably perish in the flames.

The general absence of palms, or somewhat rare occurrence of them, along the caravan route is rather noticeable. The cocoa-nut palms of Zanzibar and Mombasa, and along the coast-line at Dar-es-Salaam, Kilwa, and Mozambique, form a picturesque feature of the tropical landscape.

When the traveller has left Mombasa and the coast, he will not see another cocoa-nut palm for the next thousand miles up-country; but there are certain other kinds he is sure to meet with. Some beautiful fan-palms can be seen at Fovira in Unyoro.

This stately tree grows to a considerable height. In some parts of the world cheap fans are manufactured from its plaited leaves; but here, perhaps because of its rarity, it is not put to any use. Every European with a love for the beauties of Nature endeavours to protect such handsome trees from wanton destruction at the hands of savages. The group depicted is near the fort, and on the road from Fovira to Fajao. There is a sinister tragedy connected with it. I was told, one of the Soudanese soldiers was censured by his superior officer and took it so much to heart, that he shot himself at the foot of these palms.

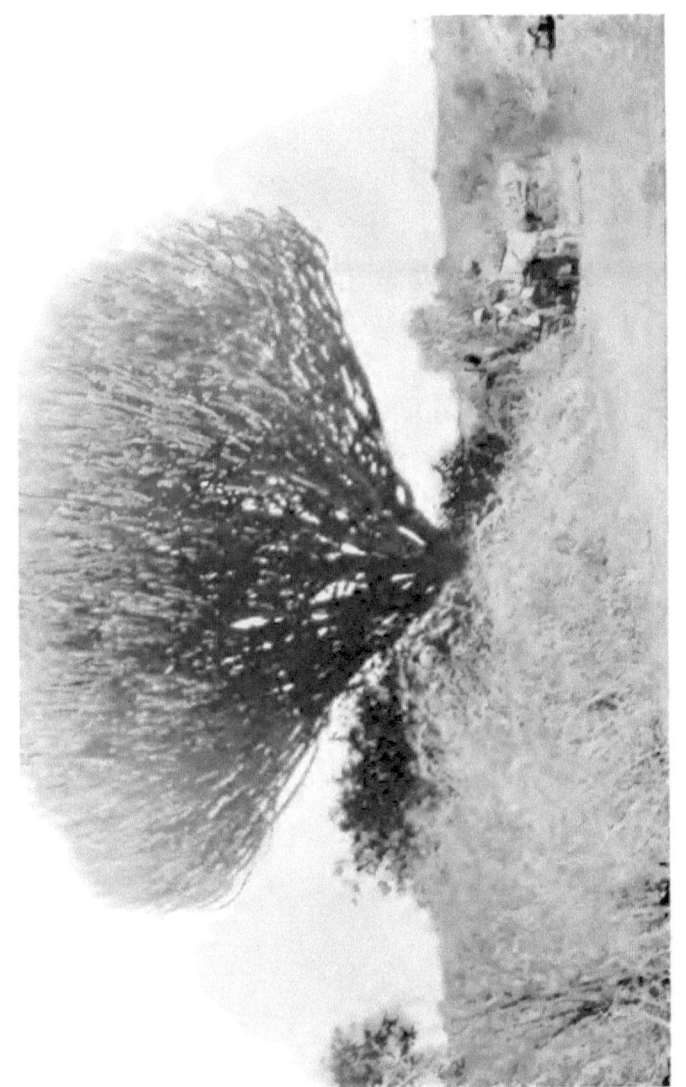

THE EUPHORBIA TREE.

Some travellers have described the danger of being attacked by bees, when the caravan route happens to pass near a tree sheltering a swarm. I have never experienced such a misfortune, though I have had a sting or two trying to hive a young swarm at a station. But I doubt if there is a traveller who has been to Uganda without having been annoyed some time or other by ants. There are tiny yellowish ants of almost microscopic size, veritable dwarfs in the ant world. There are huge black ones, an

FAN-PALMS IN UNYORO.

inch long, real giants compared to the general size of ants. There is the friendly variety which runs over one's hand or face and does not attempt to bite or hurt, and is only in search of scavengering dead insects and refuse. There is the bellicose kind which attacks if one inadvertently invades its domain; and there is the murderous, bloodthirsty species, bent on hurting as long as a spark of life remains in its body. There is also the white-ant, so destructive to a traveller's kit.

The tiniest ants usually commit suicide by the hundred in the traveller's food. The bellicose variety is of a light red colour, and is called "maji-moto" by the Swahilies, which means "boiling-water." Their nests consist of a lot of leaves fastened together with a sort of spider's web. These nests festoon shrubs overhanging some shallow streamlet or marshy spot. The incautious may shake such a branch as he passes under it. Immediately he receives a shower of these warlike insects. Their bite feels like a sharp burn, and whoever is attacked beats a hasty retreat. As a rule, these ants leave the enemy as soon as the enemy retreats and leaves them. But the one called "siafu" by the Swahilies is not to be shaken off; it never lets go until it is killed. The "siafu" march along in their millions. Fire alone will deter their army from proceeding in the appointed direction; and I know of more than one case, where a man has burnt down his hut by accident whilst attempting to repel an attack of "siafu." I have had to run away from this tiny pest. One particular night on my first journey is impressed on my memory. I had stepped beyond the camp-fires, when I thought, for the first moment, that mosquitoes were bothering me; but the next second I rushed in a hurry back to my tent, stripped myself in a twinkling, and called lustily for my servants to help me to pick off these ants from all over my body. Their jaws still clung with a death-grip, even when the bodies had been wrenched off.

The giant ants are usually seen in small colonies, diving in and out of their subterranean tunnels. They never attempt to molest the passer-by.

The well known white-ant raises huge hillocks. The Egyptian pyramids, compared with a man's stature, dwindle into insignificance, if we compare the size of this insect with the structure which it laboriously builds for itself; the proportion is simply stupendous. The white-ant hillock is a common feature in an African landscape. The one represented lay along the caravan route through Singo.

Like bees, the termites have a queen, on whose welfare the prosperity of the community depends. Hence it is a good plan, when clearing off white-ants near a wooden building, to endeavour if possible to find the queen and to destroy her. She is quite helpless, with her fat body nearly two inches long. Her attentive subjects usually keep her boxed up in a sort of dome-shaped chamber, the entrance to which they block up and hide at any approach of danger. The really destructive creature is the tiny little "worker." Among the "workers" may be seen a somewhat larger variety armed with a pair of pincers. These are the "warriors," which come rushing to a breach and will fiercely attack any piece of wood held out for them to bite at. But a curious member of this strange community is the large, black-bodied, and winged white-ant, about an inch long, which issues at certain seasons from vent-holes of the white-ant hillock by the million. The winged termite forms part of the native

A WHITE-ANT HILLOCK.

food. In Kavirondo I have seen natives cluster round such an issuing swarm, catch them by the handful and eat them up alive. In Uganda the natives place a sort of reed frame over the hillock and cover it up with bark-cloth, leaving the vent-hole open, and digging near it a pit into which the ants tumble by the hundred. It is curious to see how these winged ants tear off their own wings as soon as they touch the ground. White-ants are dried by the bushel, and form an article of commerce. On the march through Bulamwezi I had a chance of trying a dish of them fried. They are not at all bad, and supply nitrogenous food where the meat-supply falls short. The chief objection to these fried ants is their greasy taste, though this is the very thing which causes them to be appreciated as a delicacy by the native palate. The crisp bodies have a remote resemblance to shrimps.

The colour of the ant-hill depends on the soil of the locality. I have seen greyish-white hillocks where white clay was in the soil, but more commonly the hill is formed of red earth. The portion most recently built up is usually of a darker colour, and is moist and soft; but it hardens very quickly, and then a heavy hartebeest antelope can stand on it without doing more damage than if standing on an ordinary mound of earth. Old or perished ant-hills are soon overgrown with grass, and very frequently a tree or bush grows on the summit. The curious shape of these hillocks shows that they are built very irregularly, and not with the mathematical precision which is so characteristic of bees. The white-ants met with in Uganda are very different to those I saw in Mauritius. The Mauritian species did not build lofty ant-hills, but usually a black ball-shaped mass round some tree. The winged Mauritian insect which swarmed at certain seasons was small, white, and soft-bodied, instead of being large, black, and crisp-shelled, like the African. Birds used to gobble up the small Mauritian winged insect just as greedily, as the natives do the black African variety. Snakes and other creatures find at times a shelter in the air-passages which traverse the ant-hill; a squirrel I was chasing near Kinani escaped me by diving into one of these tunnels.

It is absolutely necessary for the traveller to have good servants. In the most quiet home-life in England the servant question crops up. But the traveller's welfare depends still more on the sort of servants he engages; they must be honest, willing, sober, and healthy. If, some 800 or 1000 miles from the coast, a servant is dismissed, it is next to impossible to replace him.

The illustration shows my last batch of servants or "boys," as they are generally called; and though, on the whole, I have been unusually fortunate with my "boys," these four were the best I ever had.

They belonged to four different nationalities: Mnyamwezi, Arab, Wahima, and Swahili. As I had two rifles and two guns, each boy had to carry one on the march. The Arab head-boy had charge of my field-glasses, revolver, and a handbag which held a number of small miscellaneous articles, such as cartridge-extractor, matches, cigarettes, tin-opener, twine, scissors, knife, &c. The Mnyamwezi usually carried my waterproof on his head and the tin helmet-box slung from the rifle. The pith-helmet which I ordinarily wear, becomes as heavy as a lump of lead if exposed to a good shower; it is, therefore, placed inside the shelter of the helmet-box at the first warning of a downpour, and exchanged for an oil-skin sou'wester. With servants on the march, it becomes necessary to treat certain duties, such as the carrying of the waterproof, field-glasses, camera, &c., as

MY FOUR "BOYS" ON THE MARCH.

matters of routine, or else, when the occasion for their use presents itself, the traveller finds that they have been packed away into some load or other, and that they cannot be got at! Unless the traveller is very strong and robust, he cannot possibly march with all he may want at a moment's notice slung on to his own person.

The short Wahima boy had charge of my butterfly-net and specimen-box; he and the Mnyamwezi carried also an aluminium water-bottle each. It was the head-boy's routine-duty to see that one of these bottles was filled with fresh-made tea before the march began. I became quite a Chinaman in my appreciation of cold tea, without milk or sugar, as a beverage on the march. If I am fortunate enough to get some milk, I take it with me in the other bottle. The great drawback to carrying milk is, that unless the boys have been well-trained to keep the bottle perfectly clean and sweet, the milk at once turns sour and is spoiled; and unless the quantity of milk fills the bottle completely, the shaking for some hours along the march churns the milk into butter. Only a confirmed drunkard would be so rash as to keep pegging at whisky when marching along.

Caravans follow in single file the "kiangozi" or "guide." Now that there is an open road from Mombasa to Kampala, the guide is no longer required; but on my first and second journeys the "kiangozi" was an important personage. Everything, however, depends on the caravan-leader. While there is danger ahead, he should be the foremost, and where a treacherous foe lies in ambush to cut off stragglers, he should be the last man in the caravan and prevent loiterers from separating from the main body.

On my fourth journey we had a narrow escape from falling into the hands of Mbaruk, the rebel Arab, who for a time rendered the road between Ndi and Mazera's unsafe. An armed escort was sent by Government at stated times to meet caravans, and we had just missed by a day such escort. We marched day and night till the porters were walking along half-asleep, and at last I had to let them lie down for a while. They dropped instantly asleep in the middle of the road by the side of their loads. But being the caravan-leader, the responsibility for the general safety enabled me to remain awake, with loaded rifle and finger on trigger, taking upon myself the anxious watch, as I could not have trusted any of my men to keep awake. It was only for a couple of hours, but each minute seemed to drag into an eternity. Then I roused the men, and we hurried on. Half-an-hour later Mbaruk's bands crossed the very spot, where I had been compelled to let the caravan rest and snatch their short sleep.

The caravan-porter is a careless being, and even the knowledge that a treacherous enemy may be hiding in the bush close by does not keep him awake. One of the mission-caravans thus exposed itself to massacre. It was in 1895, and I was then at Mumia's in Kavirondo. The men who had been told off as night-watchmen fell asleep. The hostile savages suddenly rushed with their spears upon the sleepers and killed most of them on the spot. A few survivors escaped and reached Mumia's. I had to dress their wounds. One man had his scalp slashed open and a flap of it hanging down, he had also a deep punctured wound in the nape of the neck, his thigh was pierced through, and his arm was gashed in several places. Others had spear-thrusts and cuts on their bodies. I believe some twenty porters lost their lives, owing to their recklessness in not keeping some trustworthy men to watch over the common safety.

Camp-cookery is primitive in the extreme, and takes place in the open air; in rainy weather a rough grass-hut is run up to serve as a kitchen. It is very difficult to upset what is called "dusturi," or caravan custom, according to which the cook is exempted from carrying anything but the camp-kettle. The porter who has to carry the pots and pans is styled "cook's mate," acts as scullery drudge, and acquires a sort of prescriptive right of succession to the cook's position. The cook sits by and directs. However little he may have to do, he always expects to be supplied with one or more assistants.

CAMP-COOKERY.

The photo shows the cook comfortably settled in the shadiest spot, and leisurely awaiting the boiling up of something or other in the pot in front of him; the cook's mate is busy peeling green bananas, the only vegetable procurable at the time, and one of the boys is assisting in plucking a bird I had shot for dinner; the big earthen pot behind him shows that it was he too, probably, who had to fetch the water.

If the cook's mate is intelligent, he soon knows as much as the cook, since the latter makes him do all the work; and if he has any aptitude for it, he in time learns something additional from other cooks, when, as now and then happens, travellers meet and share a meal. The judge at Kampala discovered one day that his cook never by any chance prepared a meal; everything was done by the cook's mate, the cook reserving as his part of work the duty of marketing, which led to "perquisites," or, according to Shakespeare, "convey the wise it call." Having done the marketing, the cook not only enjoyed *otium cum dignitate* for the rest of the day, but varied the monotony of his existence by getting drunk. It is needless to say that the usual evolution of cook's mate into cook followed the discovery.

There does not seem to be any *prima facie* reason why cooks should be drunkards, but it is unfortunately the rule and not the exception that they take a little more than is good for them. My cook succeeded his predecessor in office very much in the same way, as had happened in the judge's household; for the expensive one I had brought with me from Mombasa turned out to be a drunkard, and as the Soudanese whisky at Kampala proved too great a temptation to him, it led to his absenting himself without leave for three days on a drinking bout. When "Musa" reappeared, he found "Hamadi Marzuk," the cook's mate, installed permanently as cook.

This brings to my mind a similar episode which happened to two ladies on a visit to the Seychelles Islands. Their cook, a liberated slave, delivered originally from a slave-dhow by a British man-of-war, used to absent himself frequently for a day or so without leave. The kind-hearted ladies, disposed to be doubly kind to one formerly a slave, gently remonstrated, whereupon the man indignantly asked them whether they thought they had to deal with a slave, and promptly took an extra long French leave. When at last he thought fit to reappear, he found some one else installed as cook. A prompt but unsuccessful appeal by him to the magistrate for restoration of what he considered acquired rights failed. The magisterial decision still further embittered his feelings against everything British,—a nation which, according to his view, professes to pity and liberate the poor slaves, and then actually refuses to let them leave off work when and where they like, or take a holiday or two just when the fancy seizes them to enjoy one.

The deeply grafted slave-nature of the negro cannot be straight off eradicated and altered, any more than a cart-horse can be made into a racehorse by simply taking it out of the shafts and putting a light saddle on its back.

Native cooks, unless prohibited to do so, find it most convenient to light their fire at the foot of the finest tree available, as a shelter against the wind. The result is that in course of time a big hole is burnt into the tree itself, and the tree is killed. I have come across some very fine trees destroyed in this way. To the native it is incomprehensible that the European traveller, who may never pass there again, should be solicitous for the welfare of a mere tree, though it be a forest-king some hundreds of years old.

A common incident of caravan life is the friendly chief's visit. He is usually accompanied by a crowd of followers. Conversation is naturally rather limited; but now and then it may prove very interesting, as on the occasion depicted. This

A FRIENDLY CHIEF PAYS A CALL.

chief, dwelling on the west shore of Lake Albert, had met Casati, Emin Pasha, and other distinguished travellers; and he remembered when Emin Pasha's steamers plied on the lake. Unless a native has had some intercourse with Europeans, and has picked up Swahili which serves in Africa very much the same purpose that French does in Europe, as an international means of communication, interpreters are necessary; sometimes several different interpreters are required. I remember, at Hoima, using Swahili which had to be translated into Arabic and re-translated into Wanyoro; how much of the original idea was correctly reproduced I should be afraid to say. On one occasion I told my boy to ask the village headman to sell me two or three eggs. I fortunately happened to overhear how my message was delivered: "You are to bring at once three eggs, two chickens, some ripe bananas, and a lot of native beer, or master will have you tied up to a tree, and order you to receive a flogging of twenty-five lashes with the hippo-thong. Now look sharp." I hastened out of the tent, and I called for some one else to assure the village headman that I had only asked to buy a few good eggs, and that the threat of flogging was an utter untruth. Then I had an explanation with my boy! He seemed surprised that I should find fault with him for the interest he had taken in anticipating my wants by asking for the other items; as for the twenty-five lashes with the hippo-thong, this, the boy declared, was merely a very necessary figure of speech for impressing the "washenzi" (that is, "savages") with becoming respect towards a "white man!"

In Kavirondo the food for the caravan has to be bought; but in Usoga and Uganda the chief or village headman nearest to the camp brings in a supply of provisions gratis, owing to some arrangements made by the Government. Usually it consists of bunches of green bananas, or rather plantains. As a rule, the headman also brings a chicken, some ripe bananas, and a gourd of native brew. The illustration represents a typical scene in Uganda. The headman leading his file of men, women, and children, and hugging in his arms the chicken he intends to offer to the caravan leader. Behind him comes a woman with a gourdful of native beer. Some of the bunches of bananas are carefully wrapped up in banana leaves.

It is only in disturbed districts, either hostile or recently raided by enemies, that the food question may verge on starvation-point. I remember once at Kasokwa in Unyoro, the supply ran so short that we had but three green bananas per man for the day's ration. Another day in Unyoro it was still worse, on the short journey between Masindi and Fovira. My companion had left the selection of camp to one of his Soudanese sergeants, with the result that we had a very long march, and at the end of it no food whatever for our porters. Next day these unfortunate porters had to do another terribly long march of nearly twelve hours to reach Fovira, where sweet-potatoes were distributed to them. We arrived after sunset,

VILLAGE HEADMAN BRINGING A SUPPLY OF FOOD FOR THE CARAVAN

CARAVAN LIFE

when darkness had already set in, and these sweet-potatoes were the first food the porters had received for two days.

The journey to Uganda can be shortened by crossing Lake Victoria Nyanza from Kavirondo to Port Alice. I once crossed in the Church Mission Society's steel-boat. It is a sailing-boat. We took three days from Sio Bay (Kavirondo) to Port Alice (Uganda). We only sailed as long as we had day-

THE CHURCH MISSION SOCIETY'S STEEL-BOAT ON LAKE VICTORIA NYANZA.

light; then we landed, pitched tents, and passed the night on shore. Made entirely of steel, the little cabin on the boat became unbearable with the heat, as there was not a cloud to take off some of the sun's rays. The boat is hired periodically by the Government. My loads, men, donkey, and sheep, all found room aboard. It was on this trip, that I had an accident to my right hand, which produced blood-poisoning and necessitated several operations, two of them under chloroform, performed by the Church Mission Society's temporary doctor; but in the end I lost the use of the metacarpo-phalangeal joint and was left with a stiff joint for the rest of my life.

Caravan life when it rains incessantly day and night becomes decidedly trying, and one longs for a drought; but when one has to suffer from a continued drought, and wearily plods along day after day with the ever-present anxiety whether there will be any water at the next camp, or men and beasts are to die of thirst, then the cry is for rain, rain! I had on my fifth journey a curious experience of a continued drought followed immediately by incessant rain.

News of the drought had reached me at Mombasa; and in anticipation of having to carry water for the caravan, I provided myself with a number of empty kerosin tins. At Maji Chumvi there is a pool of brackish water. It was simply poisonous owing to the drought, to porters of passing caravans washing their ulcers and sores in it, and to an accumulation of filth in general. I had filled my water-bottles at the previous camp. Next day we reached Samburu. Here we found the water-holes absolutely dry. We rested during the heat of the day, parched with thirst, and at 2 P.M., though it was still very hot, we started once more to reach the next camp, Taru. Whilst we were waiting at Samburu, some native women with gourds of water crossed the caravan road; they were returning from fetching some nasty brackish water a long way off, and had a long way to go to their village. It was therefore no easy matter to persuade them to sell us the water at an enormous figure. They knew the value of silver rupees and would take nothing else. I had not enough silver with me, but fortunately my headman was able to lend me some; I bought the precious water and distributed it by tiny cupfuls to my caravan, men and beasts. Some of my men began fighting furiously, accusing each other of having taken more than their share of this foul and nauseating stuff. I had to take a stick and lay about indiscriminately amongst the combatants, some of whom had drawn knives, in order to prevent bloodshed and murder.

Caravans march at the rate of 2½ miles per hour; we did the 10½ miles to Taru in four hours, and arrived at sunset. A large caravan in connection with the new railway was encamped there; and what with their men and sixty donkeys, the famous water-holes of Taru were nearly dry. I had to hurry to fill our kerosin tins with what we could scoop up—fluid-mud it was. I had to drink it too, or die of thirst. My men were too exhausted to do any more marching that night, and the heat was too great to risk a day-march; but about 2 P.M. next day I sent some of the men with the tins of this so-called water on to the next camp, where there was again no water. Three men armed with rifles were left to guard the precious store, upon which the life of the caravan depended. The following night we marched about twenty miles, and found our supply of water safely guarded. Each man and beast got a pint. I could only let them rest from 9 A.M. to 2 P.M. through the heat of the day, and then we went on again. Before we started, I distributed the rest of the water. We reached Maungu, a march of about ten miles, and rested two or three hours. I would not allow the tent

A KIBANDA, OR GRASS-THATCHED REED-HUT.

to be put up, to save the men time and trouble; I threw myself dressed on my camp-bed and slept like a log. One of the men slept so soundly near the fire, that he burnt a big hole into the canvas covering of the rifle he was carrying. Roused by the man on "zam," that is, on night-guard, loads were once more shouldered; and a twenty-miles march took us at last to the river Voi and saved us from further danger from the drought. I feel thankful that we did not lose a single life; but the evil effects of the filthy water were felt by me; my kidneys must have been affected, as I suffered for several days afterwards from severe pain in the kidney-region. The natives and the animals only showed signs of exhaustion, but not of pain. The drought accompanied us without intermission as far as the Tsavo river, but without any further risk to life.

At Tsavo it rained, and from here as far as the Athi river we had day and night incessant rain. The porters got soaked to the skin on the march, and in spite of mackintosh and sou'-wester, I got pretty wet too. Arrived in camp, the tent had to be opened on the muddy ground, and pitched in pelting rain. Everything was damp and sticky and musty. It rained all night. Next morning the tent was folded up, with the rain pouring steadily down. We marched ankle-deep in mud in a continued downpour, as if a second deluge had set in. With cold feet, sopping-wet socks, and squashy boots, we trudged along, bespattered with mud, half-blinded by the rain, and shivering with cold, to reach a sodden camp and repeat the experiences of the preceding days. Fever, diarrhœa, and dysentery broke out in the caravan. At Mto-ya-Mawe I just managed to reach camp, but with a raging attack of fever on me. Next day we got to Muani, and half my caravan being ill, I stopped a full day to rest my men; but the food question was so serious that we had to push on again. We reached the Athi river, where we hailed the cessation of the rain and the reappearance of the sunshine with joyful hearts. From here to the end of the journey we had beautiful weather and only occasionally a rainy day. I was glad, when I handed over my men at headquarters, that I could add that we had not lost a single life on the journey.

In Uganda the traveller sometimes comes across a "kibanda," or grass-thatched reed-hut, which proves a very acceptable shelter to him during the rainy weather, because he can light a fire inside and dry his clothes. The "kibanda" has a door, but no windows; there may or may not be a reed-screen to close the door. The objection to rest-houses of this description is, that they are very short-lived, and soon tumble to wreck and ruin, as there is usually nobody to look after them. The vermin of the neighbourhood take possession of an uninhabited hut. It becomes the haunt of cockroaches, the trysting-place for rats, and the home of bats. It harbours mosquitoes by the thousand, and supplies food for the white-ants. There was a sort of halfway house between Kampala and Port Alice, which provided all these different attractions.

I lived for three months in a "kibanda" at Kampala. The white-ants nearly destroyed the canvas bag of my camp-bed, and I had to keep such goods raised above the ground on sun-dried bricks to prevent the white-ants from getting at them. As for rats, my servant once killed three with one blow from his stick; and the rat-trap I had brought from England I considered one of my most useful investments. After I had killed about a score of rats, I gave up keeping count of them.

The late Major Thruston, when in command in Unyoro, put

THE TRAVELLER'S REST-HOUSE AT FAJAO.

up at Fajao a grass-thatched traveller's rest-house of Soudanese pattern, and he very kindly placed it at the disposal of all who had to visit the station. As he had given orders that the hut should be looked after and kept clean and tidy, it was a welcome boon to every visitor. The hut was surrounded by a reed-fence which secured privacy. A hut for servants, and other sanitary necessaries, had not been neglected. The spot was well chosen, and tall forest trees overshadowed it. On fine days I used to take my meals invariably out of doors, under the pleasant shade of the trees, and watch the green squirrels frolicking among the branches, and listen to the yellow weaver-birds holding their noisy palaver.

Every caravan should be provided with a thoroughly good native headman. Headmen now get as much as 40 to 60 rupees per month, i.e. £2, 10s. to £4. They are allowed at least one and very often two porters to carry their tent and private effects, and they receive double the daily ration measured out to a porter. The headman's duties are important and manifold. He looks after the men, that they do not desert or shirk their work, that they keep together, that they do not plunder or rob friendly natives, that firewood is provided and camp-fires are maintained at night, that night-watchmen are appointed and do their work, that the cattle is protected against wild beasts, that the men get their rations, and that, where necessary, a sufficient supply of food for the caravan is obtained from the natives.

The headman has usually one or more "askaries" to help him. The askari is a sort of assistant-headman, but he has two specially important duties. He has to defend the caravan in case of attack, and for this reason he is supplied with a rifle and twenty rounds of ammunition. He also acts as porter in case of emergency, and, as such, he has to shoulder the load of any one taken suddenly ill. Askaries are paid £1 a month and their rations, but they have to carry their own kit; a porter is not allowed for their special use.

The healthiest style of travelling is on foot. My very first caravan journey, from Lake Nyassa to Kilwa, was on foot from the day of departure to the day of arrival. But on the first journey from Mombasa to Uganda, I rode nearly the whole distance on a donkey. Those who can afford it ride a horse. Some are very lucky in bringing their horses safely through the tsetse region; others are particularly unlucky. One man lost his third and last horse in Kavirondo. The horse requires a good groom, and constant care and protection against chills. The donkey is simply let loose, and has to find its own food. It is a very hardy animal, and wants next to no attention. The white Muscat donkeys at Mombasa are rather expensive; not unfrequently they are dearer than horses. The donkey that has suited my purse and requirements best, has been the ordinary grey Masai donkey. The very first I had, fell one day near Kilungu and sprained its leg which became so swollen that the poor beast could not walk any further. It had to be left behind, and was handed over to some friendly Wakamba. On another journey I lost a very fine donkey in crossing the Nzoia river. It was allowed to swim across, by the side of the native dug-out, its head being supported and held up by some of the men. When near the other bank they cast the poor brute off, and the stupid native struck and pushed it with a long bamboo. The current was very swift, and the bank too steep for landing. The donkey was carried away by the current and sank; we never saw it again. Only once have I lost a donkey from the tsetse-fly.

But my best donkey was "Jack," my last purchase. I bought him at Mombasa for 75 rupees = £5; he accompanied me to Lake Albert, and returned with me to Mombasa, serving me for fully two thousand miles. He never had a day's illness or a sore back; and when I left for England, I sold him for the sum I originally paid for him. He was a young grey donkey and very shy at first, as he had never been ridden. He suspected everybody, and for a long time would not make friends with anybody. The slightest noise behind him or at his side would make him perform sudden gymnastic exercises in which I, on his back, failed to accompany him, with the result that I was landed over his head or thrown sideways. I had one or two rather hard spills. On one occasion I was so badly hurt that, to proceed on the journey, I had to be lifted into the saddle. My Arab head-boy then had the brilliant idea of placing one of my thick bright-coloured blankets under me. I got so accustomed to the soothing influence of a folded blanket between me and the saddle, especially on long journeys, that even when I was well again, I continued the use of the blanket; I can recommend its use, especially for lean individuals like myself. The blanket has certainly proved a great protection to my saddle (which arrived in good condition at Mombasa, notwithstanding exposure on the donkey's back for 2000 miles in all weathers.

"Jack" became extremely tame and docile; he always kept close to the camp, and at once stopped if we called for him. None of my former donkeys would stir a yard without a companion preceding it, thus necessitating my keeping two animals. But "Jack" has always been satisfied to do the journey without donkey-companionship. Only once did he stray from camp. When we left Masindi, we passed through the Swahili settlement, and "Jack" came suddenly upon his lady-love. Both seemed heart-broken at parting from each other, and brayed most lustily together. During the march every now and again his grief found vent in a prolonged and mournful bray. Arrived in camp, he was set free and left to himself. Soon there was a general commotion. "Jack" had disappeared! It turned out, that his love for "the girl he left behind him" overcame a loyalty of two years' duration to his master, and he had trotted back. My boys had the bother of returning to Masindi to fetch him, and for the next two or three days "Jack" marched along in very low spirits.

CHAPTER IV.

THE UGANDA PROTECTORATE.

THE Uganda Protectorate does not mean simply Uganda—the kingdom which the famous autocrat King Mtesa ruled over once upon a time—but it includes also the vast realms around it, territories where no white man has ever passed, lakes only recently discovered by hardy explorers and travellers, and races of men differing from each other in language, in manners, and in customs. Those who read stirring records of explorations and discoveries associated with names like Livingstone, Speke, Grant, and Mungo Park, are very much mistaken, if they imagine that similar achievements are out of their reach because all that can be discovered has been discovered. Within the last few years Count Teleki has added to the map two new lakes, lying close together, and named by him Lake Rudolph and Lake Stephanie. Rebmann, incited by stories, by many believed to be mythical, that a huge mountain, the summit covered with eternal snow, lay in Africa, endeavoured to find it; and the famous snow-clad Kilimanjaro was added to general geographical knowledge, though for some time the discovery was disbelieved in Europe. It seemed impossible to give credence to a story of "eternal snow" under the scorching rays of an African sun.

Kilimanjaro lies comparatively near the coast, and every traveller to Uganda who cares to look out for it can see the white glistening summit; for the caravan route passes within sight of the majestic snow-king. Sitting by the camp-fire, I have listened to Arab and Swahili stories, asserted of course to be absolutely true, though sounding to my sceptical ear even more mythical than Rebmann's story of the snow mountain can ever have sounded in his day. One of the stories asserts as a fact, that far beyond the present limits of the white man in these regions, there lies a land, where gold is plentiful, and where the natives are ignorant of its value or its use, except that the humblest can and does use it as the cheapest ornament wherewith to deck himself. Hardy Arab traders, it is said, have now and again managed to penetrate to these auriferous realms which are difficult to reach owing to enormous foodless tracts which the traveller has first to cross. The knowledge of the road to this land of gold, and everything that might betray its whereabouts, is kept, so they say, a secret by the Arabs. On my last journey I met an Arab caravan proceeding up country, ostensibly to trade for ivory and to shoot elephants if necessary. My Arab servant was an old friend of the Arab in command of the caravan; this led to my having a long chat with them about those gold countries. The Arab told me that if his provisions held out, he had made up his mind to attempt the journey. He was going to buy up provisions in the market at Fort Smith. He professed to know a good deal about the subject, and according to him this gold country lies far beyond Lake Rudolph, a lake which other travellers have visited since Teleki's discovery. The Arab had apparently as firm a faith in the existence of such a gold country as Columbus had in the New World he discovered.

I can quite understand the food difficulty to be an almost impassable barrier. There was a food difficulty on my first journey to Uganda, owing to the caravan route passing for some twenty days through an uninhabited country; but the difficulty is minimised by knowing exactly the number of days it takes a caravan to traverse the distance. A better insight into the risks of travelling through a foodless region, without knowing exactly how long the journey may last, I experienced when I travelled through the Magwangwara country in German East Africa to the coast. The Magwangwara kings had deliberately surrounded their country with an enormous starvation area, by ruthlessly destroying villages and whole races around them. The foodless belt was a greater protection to them than the Great Wall of China has been to the Chinese emperors. This wilderness my nephew and I determined to penetrate. We provided ourselves as best we could for the journey. Before we reached the end of our expedition, we were driven to subsist on starvation allowance, a handful of rice in the morning and in the evening, and one small tin of sardines per day shared with scrupulous fairness. We soon knew by heart how many sardines a small tin usually contains. On this meagre allowance we marched on foot twenty, sometimes thirty, miles per day. From the day we left Lake Nyassa to the day we reached Kilwa took us exactly two months. Sometimes, but very rarely indeed, did an antelope as a windfall find its way to our table.

Count Teleki describes in his book, how he had to shoot game for his caravan; yet more than one of his porters succumbed to want of food, according to what I was told by some of my men who had accompanied Teleki. I have since heard, how other travellers, after crossing such foodless tracts, have found themselves suddenly amongst strange races of men living in comparative affluence, owning flocks and herds, and possessing an abundant store of corn.

The gold-fields that have been found in South Africa make it probable that eastward there are other gold-fields not yet discovered.

We all know how valuable ivory is; in fact, the British Government, to protect the elephant from extermination, has already defined a large area as a sanctuary for it. By recent game laws in British East Africa, the hunter has to pay £25 to start with, and this license permits the holder to shoot not more than two elephants. Yet Count Teleki told me himself of regions he has visited during his explorations, where natives were ignorant of the value of ivory, and where consequently it lay on the ground where the elephant had died. Many a tusk was simply picked up by Teleki. It almost sounds a fable, but I had it from his own mouth, that he returned to the coast with ivory which realised straight off something like £2000. He did not go as a trader, but as an explorer, never expecting to get any pecuniary returns from his journey, still less such a sum.

It is therefore not impossible, that unknown races in some of these unknown regions have a superabundance of gold which, like the ivory just mentioned, is spurned by the foot of the savage who is unconscious of its value.

Hitherto neither gold nor coal, nor any other mineral resources, have been discovered either in Uganda or in the East African Protectorate; some silver was found near the coast, but not worth the expense of working it.

The Uganda Protectorate lies at the Equator; the Equator passes through it. By rights it should be called Equatorial Africa, but this name has already been appropriated by Gordon Pasha, Emin Pasha, Casati, and others to territories lying far north of Uganda and of the Equator. A glance at the map shows that Uganda is nearer to the centre of Africa than the territories, known as the British Central Africa Protectorate, which lie around the Shiré river and Lakes Nyassa and Tanganyika.

The Uganda Protectorate stretches around the Lakes Victoria Nyanza, Albert Nyanza, and Albert Edward Nyanza; it therefore contains the principal sources of the White Nile. The districts into which the Protectorate has been divided are the Eldoma Ravine, Kavirondo, Usoga, Uganda Proper, Unyoro, and Toru. Further subdivision may be expected with every increase in the number of officials.

It is a little misleading to say that the climate of Uganda is a sort of unbroken English summer, because there is a considerable difference between the cold of Mau and the heat of parts of Unyoro. There are areas where white clothing is the most comfortable to wear all the year round, and there are other areas where white clothing is never worn. The heat is never anywhere excessive, nor is the cold. On the whole the climate is suitable for Europeans.

Local labour is cheap, about threepence a day, but the difficulty has been, and still is, to get the native to work for hire; gradually, however, natives are coming forward of their own accord as labourers. The principal export is ivory, on which a duty of 15 per cent. is levied, whether it be elephant-ivory or hippo-ivory. An import tax of 5 per cent. is levied on all imports of whatever nature. Trade in gunpowder and in arms, except under conditions as laid down by the Brussels Act of International Law, is prohibited, and so is the sale to natives of alcoholic beverages. By recent regulations neither are *stills* permitted, except under certain restraints. Smaller taxes, under various names, such as a road-tax of half a rupee per load, and an annual compulsory registration-fee of two rupees and a half on every British subject, are also enforced.

At present the expenditure, not counting the millions spent on the Uganda Railway, is greatly in excess of revenue. The reasons which influenced the British Government to proclaim a

THE UGANDA PROTECTORATE

Protectorate over Uganda, when access to it was difficult and expensive, have naturally become stronger, as regards continued occupation, in presence of the Uganda Railway in construction from south to north, and of the success of the Soudan campaign working from north to south. If England were to withdraw from Uganda, some other European Power would at once step in and take possession, in spite of there being no immediate pecuniary return for the heavy expense incurred by occupation. It follows that an empire like Great Britain, in vigorous growth and expansion, had to take over Uganda.

But to realise Lugard's hope of an East African Empire something further is wanted besides the missionary and the official. European settlers may perhaps be encouraged to join us, by liberal concessions of substantial grants of land with as few restrictions as possible to their earning a livelihood as traders or planters, farmers or stock-breeders, artisans or manufacturers. Coffee, cotton, sugar-cane, and rice, can be grown in some districts, European cereals in others.

No doubt, as soon as a fair start in this direction has been made, European pluck and enterprise will tap other resources not even thought of at present.

CHAPTER V.

THE RAVINE DISTRICT.

MASAI WOMAN WITH GOURD-BOTTLE.

THE Ravine district includes the territory between Kikuyu and Kavirondo. Nearly half-way between the two lies the Eldoma Ravine, where a station has been built, called the Ravine Station, which is now the headquarters of the district. Between Kikuyu and the Eldoma Ravine only wandering nomadic tribes are met with. I have passed along this road more than once without meeting a single human being far or near, and at other times I have found here crowds of natives temporarily settled, scattered kraals, and vast herds.

Before the cart-road was laid down by the late Captain Sclater, the transport of goods from Fort Smith to the Ravine was no easy matter. With perseverance the officer in charge of Kikuyu established a regular service by means of Wakikuyu, more and more of whom offered themselves as porters, till at last caravans several hundred strong were constantly on the move along the road.

Prior to the days of the Protectorate, the Wakikuyu were hostile and treacherous. It is only gradually that they have submitted to the inevitable, and have acknowledged the supremacy of British rule. The Wakamba who fight with bows and arrows, are on one side of them, and on the other are the Masai who use spears and swords. The Wakikuyu have adopted both methods of fighting. A group who visited my camp on my last journey afford a good illustration. The Wakikuyu spear-head

THE RAVINE DISTRICT

is broad and leaf-shaped. The sword is of the Masai pattern, heavier towards the pointed end than at the hilt. The arrows are carried in a leathern quiver which has an ornamental tuft of ostrich feathers and is slung from the back. One of the men wore a short grass-apron, but the majority had adopted the Masai style of wrapping a piece of cotton cloth round the body, passing it over one shoulder, and letting it reach half-way down the thighs. The Wakikuyu are extremely fond of ornaments,

WAKIKUYU MEN.

and deck themselves out with beads, iron-wire, and brass, in the shape of ear-rings, necklaces, bracelets, and anklets. Their huts are hidden away in the woods, as a protection against enemies; and for a similar reason they do not keep poultry, as they are afraid that the crowing of the cocks might betray the whereabouts of their dwellings.

They are always cutting down parts of the forest in order to plant the clearings with various sorts of native corn, sweet-potatoes, yams, and casava; but such constant and ruthless destruction of the forests must bring its own punishment some day. It is not as if there were no other land for them to till, for they abandon the last clearing in order to extract the goodness from the virgin soil of an adjoining area.

On my last journey, I travelled to the coast with a companion who had only been one year up-country; he told me he too had noticed a great destruction of forest even in this short space of time. Forest-laws have been recently passed. They weigh heavy on the white man who is to plant ten young trees for every piece of timber he fells, but are a dead letter as regards the wholesale and wanton felling practised by the natives. A well-organised Forest Department, embracing both Protectorates and placed under an experienced and energetic traveller acquainted with these regions, would certainly add another item to the expenditure, but would as certainly produce incalculable benefits in the future.

The Wakikuyu women carry their burdens slung from a leather strap which passes across the head. They, too, help in the transport service, and carry European loads and boxes, weighing 40 lbs. and more, exactly in the same way. They dress like the Masai and load themselves with ornaments; to see twenty to thirty huge rings of beads stuck through one ear is not at all an uncommon sight. They never go uncovered, and appear to be modest and gentle.

In the latter part of 1895 a large caravan of Wakikuyu and Swahilies was returning from the Ravine to Fort Smith; it reached the Kedong Valley and came across some Masai kraals. How the subsequent bloodshed arose is not exactly known, as only a few survivors managed to escape. According to one story, the Swahilies behaved aggressively towards the Masai and, relying on their superior numbers, tried to levy blackmail. The Masai resented it, and in a moment a fierce carnage was going on. Over 400 of the unfortunate Wakikuyu and Swahilies were slaughtered; for the lust of blood once roused, innocent and guilty were indiscriminately butchered. The news of the disaster was brought to Fort Smith, and was immediately followed by another tragedy; for a trader, Mr. Dick, was on his way up-country. A French scientific mission, also on its way to Uganda, arriving at the Fort, two of their number, military men, volunteered to recall Dick. They found him; but instead of persuading him to return with them to the security of the Fort, he persuaded them to accompany him across the Kedong. What were the motives which prompted the trader, no one will ever know. According to some, he wanted to pay out the Masai for the horrible and wholesale butchery they had just perpetrated; according to others, he thought it a good pretext for capturing their valuable herds. He did seize a lot of cattle; for several hundred head were brought in by the Frenchmen to the Fort. I met these gentlemen a few weeks later in Uganda and, as I knew Dick personally, gathered from them some particulars of the fight. They told me that Dick fought most fearlessly and bravely and, being an excellent shot, dropped one Masai after another. He went to pick up the

WAKIKUYU WOMEN.

shield and spear of a Masai he had just slain, when the enemy made a desperate rush, and at a critical moment Dick's rifle jammed. He turned round to his men to get another, when a Masai rushed forward and speared him through the back, killing him on the spot. The Frenchmen killed Dick's assailant, but fighting against overwhelming odds, they were compelled to retreat to the Fort. In a couple of days they returned to the scene of the fight in order to bury Dick. They found the body stripped naked, and buried it on the Kedong escarpment. They erected a plain wooden cross over the grave, which I saw still standing when I last journeyed that way. The inscription simply states, that the cross was erected by his comrades in arms to the memory of the deceased, slain by the Masai. One of these two Frenchmen has died since; he suffered from fever on his way down the Congo; broken in health he reached Paris, and died.

Poor Dick! I felt sorry for him. He was a most energetic and resolute man, so that the Swahilies had dubbed him "Simba uleia," which means "the lion of Europe." He was too independent a man to get on well with everybody. I was able to render him a slight service, when he was down with fever; and as I declined to accept payment, he sent all his men, two hundred of them, to work for a couple of days at the place which I was then having cleared for the erection of some Government buildings. I little thought, when he said good-bye to me at Kavirondo, that he was about to join the number of those who have found their grave in Africa.

For months the Kedong valley bore witness to the dreadful slaughter. When I passed that way some months later, the roadside for miles was strewn with blood-soaked scraps of clothing and with skeletons. These belonged to mortally wounded men who had tried to escape from the massacre, but had succumbed to their wounds. On reaching the scene of carnage, the skeletons, no longer single as already met with by the wayside, lay in some places by the dozen, where frightened and wounded men had huddled together in the vain hope of finding mercy or safety. Last time I passed I shot a zebra here; and not far from the animal, there lay a human skull, though only a few now remain scattered about.

At Campi Mbaruk I came upon one of the temporary settlements of these nomadic Masai. The huts, seen from a distance, resemble the baker's familiar tinloaf of bread. They are well plastered over with cow-dung, almost touch each other, and are arranged in circular kraals with an inner free space for penning the young calves. The vast herds these humble nomads own are a sight! One is reminded of the possessions of Job, of Abraham, and of Israel. The plain was dotted with black patches indicating densely packed herds of thousands of head of cattle, sheep, and goats, and hundreds and hundreds of donkeys. When the tribe shifts its habitation, the donkeys carry the household goods, especially heavy articles such as long poles and bullock-hides. The women carry the more fragile possessions, such as earthenware cooking-pots. One of the men I saw, was evidently an elder and a man of wealth and authority; he was wrapped in a thick fur-coat made of monkey-skins. His wives were loaded with ornaments of brass, beads, and iron-wire. The Masai women disfigure themselves by hanging heavy chains of iron-wire from the upper portion of the ear, so that it is pulled over the lower. In this way they alter for the worse, what might otherwise have passed as a pleasing oval face.

The Masai have a horrid liking for drinking the warm blood, as it gushes out of a slaughtered animal, and for eating the congealed lumps. If I happened to slaughter a sheep or

AT A MASAI KRAAL.

goat, and any Masai were near, boys and girls would come with bowls to catch the blood and carry it away to their kraal; their blood-smeared mouths and hands were a loathsome sight.

Mohammedans in this respect are the very opposite, and follow the teaching of the Koran, founded on the Jewish law, which ordains that the blood shall be shed on the earth, and shall not be used in any form. It was one of the difficulties I had with my Mohammedan boys to get them to serve me with an underdone steak. Their hidden contempt for it was indicated in their very question whether I wanted "bifstek-ya-dam"—the steak with blood; and most probably they would then serve up the meat practically raw with the blood still oozing out. If I sent it back to the kitchen, it would reappear overdone.

The cultivation of the gourd into every conceivable shape, according to the needs or the fancy of the community, is well known; and, as might be expected, the gourds which find greatest favour with the Masai resemble long-necked bottles. Some of these are curiously shaped like champagne bottles. Gourds are often ornamented with rows of cowrie shells or beads; others have a pattern burnt on them in the style of poker-work.

The Masai woman is an expert milkmaid, but she never uses both hands to milk; she usually holds the gourd-bottle, which is extremely light, in her left hand and milks with the right.

Veterinary surgery, as practised by them, consists in bleeding. I witnessed the operation one day, when a gentleman, afraid that his donkey was ill beyond all recovery, called in a Masai vet., who came provided with a toy bow and what looked like a toy arrow but that it had a very sharp pointed arrow-head. Having felt the animal, the Masai from a distance of about eight or ten inches shot the arrow into its neck, and a stream of dark venous blood at once flowed out. He allowed about three to four ounces to escape, and then, extracting the arrow, the bleeding stopped almost immediately. The operation certainly relieved the donkey at the time; I cannot say if it proved of any lasting benefit, as I had to continue my march next day.

Along the line of the lakes Naivasha, Elmenteita, and Nakuru, the cows which accompany a caravan produce at certain seasons of the year a milk with a most peculiar smell and taste—in fact, "fishy" is the nearest resemblance. Swahilies do not mind this nasty flavour; but I have not yet met the European who likes it. I have been told that it is due to some plant which the cows eat without any injurious effect on their health, though it imparts this very peculiar vile aroma to their milk.

The first Government station the traveller arrives at in the Uganda Protectorate is Naivasha Station. It is built on a plateau which overlooks the lake. The locality provides flat slabs of stone; this made it comparatively easy to build up a stone wall round the fort. Trench and drawbridge afford additional security. Good building timber can also be had, though it is not felled in the very immediate neighbourhood.

THE RAVINE DISTRICT

Most travellers who have been for some years up-country, declare that Lake Naivasha is on the increase; I am of the same opinion. I am under the impression, that a certain copse of thorn-trees which is now standing in the water marks the very spot, where our caravan camped four years ago. This, to geographical science, interesting information could be easily verified by fixing a few poles at the edge of the water, recording the date, and from time to time, say every six months, observing by their position if the lake has increased, decreased, or remained the same. Lake Naivasha has no visible exit, and yet some fairly large rivers, such as the Morendat and the Gilgil, empty themselves into it.

It is a sight to see the waterfowl which frequent the lake. On my first journey, though we arrived here one day and left next morning, I had time to secure an interesting mixed bag of snipe, coot, grebe, wild goose, and a variety of different species of duck. The most delicate for the table were teal and snipe. Flamingo, ibis, and a vast number of other aquatic birds thickly cover the shores. On one journey I saw wild-geese feeding on the adjoining grassy plains by the thousand; but when they are present in such numbers, I found them most difficult to shoot. They were as vigilant as the historic geese which saved the Roman Capitol. They seemed to know exactly how far the shot could carry, and they gauged accurately the distance I might be allowed to draw near, before they flew off with a harsh noisy scream which startled and frightened all the other birds near them.

At the south-east end of Lake Naivasha is the extinct volcano Longonot, with a huge crater on its summit.

Lake Elmenteita and Lake Nakuru are both brackish; and though a good many waterfowl are found on them, the number is insignificant compared to what is seen on Lake Naivasha. At Lake Nakuru I shot a guinea-fowl and an ibis. The guinea-fowl is interesting; for it has been described by the learned ornithologist, Mr. E. Hartert, director of the Tring Museum, as a new species. For a scientific description of the bird *vide* Appendix.

GUINEA-FOWL AND IBIS.

Lake Nakuru is apparently the home of the flamingoes; they seem to be always present in numbers. I was much surprised when I compared some which I shot on my last journey and brought home with me, with others which I had shot on the previous journey. The birds belonged to two totally different species. The one sort is a small, rare bird, with quite a different form of beak to the other which is the large, common flamingo. Amongst my specimens there were some young and some old. In the young the iris is grey, in the old it is bright yellow.

Though the water of Lake Nakuru is brackish, a fair-sized stream flows into it. A number of fresh water springs bubble out of the soil within a few yards of the lake. There are a good many hippos, but they are difficult to shoot. They are shy, and have probably been shot at by passing caravans.

A two-days' march from Lake Nakuru takes the traveller to the Ravine Station. About twelve miles from the station he crosses the Equator. Some facetious individual, signing himself "Snooks," has put up a board calling the attention of the passing caravan to the fact that they are crossing "the line." But though the Ravine Station is practically on the Equator, it is out and out the coldest station in the whole of the Uganda Protectorate.

ANDEROBO WOMAN.

I have met Wanderobo men near Naivasha, but the first Anderobo woman I saw at the Ravine; she was dressed in monkey-skins. The Wanderobo are a race of elephant-hunters. Those I saw resembled the Masai in dress and ornaments. The Eldoma mountain range is inhabited by a race called the Kamasia.

Where caravans used to cross formerly, the Ravine has steep sides, and deep down at the bottom of it there is a mountain stream which, when swollen by heavy rains, may become a fierce torrent but in the dry season is only ankle-deep. Formerly caravans lost a day in crossing the Ravine. By the present caravan route, a few hundred yards higher up the river, caravans can pass without any difficulty whatever. The former Ravine crossing is, however, worth a visit. Pretty ferns, amongst them maiden-hair, grow here in wild profusion.

Mr. James Martin, the officer in charge of the Ravine Station, is a veteran traveller, having done a score of journeys, though not always right up to Kampala. He was the first of the bachelor officials who got married, and his example has been followed by others, from storekeeper to Commissioner. Since English Mission ladies by their presence demonstrated that Uganda suited European ladies, there has been quite a matrimonial epidemic.

From the Ravine the traveller next passes on to the cold and wind-swept Mau escarpment, over 9000 feet above sea-level. Sometimes it is very cold here. I have seen hoar-frost on the ground and a thin coating of ice on the edge of shallow springs. On my fourth journey it was so cold during the night, that my boy in the early morning found, to his astonishment, the water in the pail frozen into a solid lump. He had seen sleet, but never anything like this. When he came to tell me that my matutinal tub was not ready, I was only too glad of a legitimate excuse to snuggle down in the warm blankets for a little longer; so I told him to put the pail near, but not too near the fire, and to call me again when the bath was ready.

It was on the Mau that I captured a new species of butterfly, a green swallow-tail. At the Ravine the orange-yellow swallow-tail of Captain Pringle is quite common in March, and others, equally valuable, are at certain seasons met with here by the dozen.

The caravan-road across Mau was recently littered with dead and dying bullocks belonging to the Government bullock-transport which consequently broke down. The mission doctor at Kibwezi called this form of cattle disease pleuro-pneumonia, but the Government veterinary surgeon, whom I met at Machakos, said there could be no doubt but that it was rinderpest.

Leaving bleak Mau, the traveller descends to the Nandi country, only opened to traffic since the last three years. Formerly the inhabitants were fierce and treacherous. A confirmation of this was the sad tragedy which befell Mr. West, an English trader, at the hands of the Wanandi.

The last time I saw Mr. West alive was at Mumia's. He was then on the point of going to the Nandi country to buy ivory in exchange for cows. I asked him whether he was not afraid to venture with such a small number of men, barely twenty porters, among a race not yet brought under subjection and reported to be hostile. He replied that it might be dangerous for any other white man to try, but not for him, as he had already once visited the country, and although it was only at a frontier village, that he had made blood-brotherhood with a chief. The porters he selected were picked men, some of the best of the porters with whom I had, only a short while previously, arrived from the coast. Little did I reckon, when we shook hands and said good-bye, that it was the last I should see of him, and that he was another about to meet with a violent death.

He was very proud of his little garden at Mumia's. More than once he had generously supplied my table with a dish of green vegetables, and his last words to me were that he had left instructions with his gardener to supply me out of his garden until he returned. He told me that he hoped to be back in a fortnight.

The next news we heard was brought by a few survivors of his caravan, covered with ghastly wounds which I had to treat. According to them, West was received with apparent friendship by his so-called blood-brother. He then sent off some of his men to the surrounding villages to purchase various tusks of ivory said to be for sale. West felt so secure, that he tied up all his rifles inside his tent. Without any provocation on his part, and simply prompted by lust of blood and plunder, the treacherous natives one night fell upon him and his caravan, and massacred all but a very few. Poor West! He was down with illness at the time, and they thrust their spears through the tent and speared him where he lay on his bed. The black woman who had been West's faithful and intelligent helpmate for many a long year was speared by his side. The savages carried off everything, but the naked bodies of the slaughtered were left to be devoured by hyænas.

A curious sequel to this story I heard many months afterwards. It was on my return journey to the coast. I was asked, by one of the officials I met, to take along with me to the coast a man who professed to have belonged to the late Mr. West's caravan and who said he had only now succeeded in making his escape from the hands of the Wanandi.

When I saw the man, I at once recognised him as "Bombom," one of my Wanyamwezi porters who had accompanied West's ill-starred caravan. The man, of course, knew me too, and was delighted to see me again. He accompanied me to the coast, and, as he was in rags, for the sake of auld-lang-syne I rigged him out in a new cotton cloth.

He related to me some curious experiences. West had sent him and two others to a certain village to fetch a tusk of ivory. Arrived at the village, one of the three remained in the hut assigned to them by the natives, whilst the other two were told to accompany two old men to the river. There the two natives looked for an insignificant dry twig washed hither and thither by the current. This twig was a buoy, and by pulling at it they drew two magnificent tusks of ivory, each over five feet in length, out of the river. Bom-bom and his companion were asked to carry the tusks to the village. Encumbered with the heavy load of ivory, they were suddenly set upon by young Wanandi warriors in full war-paint of red earth and grease, who deprived them at once of their rifles and then threatened them with death. Bom-bom tells me that if it had not been for the two old men interceding with the young warriors, he and his Swahili companion would have been massacred on the spot. But one of the old men claimed him as a slave, and the other claimed the Swahili.

They now returned to the village. Here a pool of blood was pointed out, as the spot where the third man they had left at the village was killed during their absence. Near it there were a few other drops of blood, said to be from a chicken their companion was just killing for dinner, when the treacherous murderers stabbed him to death from behind. Bom-bom thought he had a chance of escaping, when no one was watching; but the young warriors were on the look-out, and Bom-bom fled back to the old man's hut, where the murderers were kept with difficulty from following and spearing him.

Bom-bom and the Swahili now resigned themselves to their condition of slavery. They lived separated, as their owners did not belong to the same household. The old man who owned the Swahili decided one day to sell him, and for this purpose took him to another village; but such a wretched sum was offered for the slave, that no sale was effected. The Swahili was a very merry fellow who submitted to his slavery with the greatest equanimity. The old man's daughter happened to be a widow with some children, and the Swahili slave so gained her affections that she married him. He was now regarded no longer as a slave, but as an honoured son-in-law.

Bom-bom was not as lucky as his companion. He was of a different temperament, and submitted with a bad grace to his captivity and slavery. Nor did he at all take kindly to being sent to cultivate the fields in company with women. Nor did any native lady fall in love with him and desire him for a husband. In desperation he determined to escape, and his master apparently helped him off; but not knowing the way out of the country, he nearly died of hunger, and, after wandering for days, he was compelled to return to the village. Here he was at once seized by the natives and tied hand and foot preparatory to being butchered. His Swahili friend arrived opportunely on the scene, and told the Wanandi that he knew an infallible charm for preventing a recaptured slave from ever succeeding in escaping. He professed to be willing to divulge the secret on solemn promise that Bom-bom's life should be spared, in order to test the efficacy of the charm. The natives are very superstitious and equally curious to hear about something supernatural. The promise was therefore readily given, Bom-bom was set free, and a cupful of water was poured over his feet by the Swahili who declared this to be the magic charm. Of course it was only a trick; for if Bom-bom escaped again and was recaptured, his capture would be attributed to the efficacy of the charm. If, however, Bom-bom made a successful escape, he would obviously be out of danger, charm or no charm; and the Swahili was meditating to effect his own escape shortly.

In his heart, the Swahili yearned for freedom, and his wife determined to help him and to accompany him, leaving her children in the meantime in the care of the old grandfather. Owing to her knowledge of the country, this devoted wife got the Swahili safely out of it. Both lived afterwards for a while in a Kavirondo village, and then the wife decided to return to her father's village to fetch her children to the new home and probably to bring her old father as well.

Bom-bom, finding that the Swahili had managed to escape, decided to make another effort. He succeeded; and this is how he came to accompany me to the coast.

Subsequently the Nandi country was reduced to submission

THE RAVINE DISTRICT

by a successful campaign under Major Cunningham, though not till some stubborn fights had been won by the discipline and bravery of the Soudanese troops. In one of these engagements, 200 of the Wanandi were killed. The natives sued for peace, Nandi Station was built, and the caravan route was carried through their country.

When I passed that way, I captured a number of new species of butterflies and moths at Patsho and at Rau.

Nandi is a delightful country, with densely wooded hills and with open valleys suitable for pasturage and tillage. It is not unpleasantly cold, though it is so many thousand feet above the sea-level.

The Wanandi warriors carry bows and arrows, or else a broad-bladed spear, knobkerry, and Masai sword. They usually offered to us, for sale, pots of honey or skins of the black and white Colobus monkey. The monstrous big lump of wood, which they carry as ear-ring through the lower lobe of the ear, shows that the tyranny of fashion exists also amongst savages.

KWAVI.

The Wanandi women resemble the Masai in dress, but they wear different ear-rings. Each ear-ring is a flat spiral, about the size of the palm of the hand, and consists of solid brass wire. It is suspended from the ear by a leather loop. The two heavy ear-rings usually rest on the chest, and are fastened together by a connecting strip of leather. The lower lobe of the ear is dragged down by the weight of brass, till in course of time it nearly touches the shoulder.

KWAVI.

From Kavirondo as far as Nandi Station I was accompanied by Wakwavi, placed in charge of some heads of Government cattle. These Wakwavi belong to a branch of the great Masai race, and resemble them in dress, weapons, and ornaments. They live scattered among the Wakavirondo. We had some heavy showers of rain, and these men came and crouched under the awning of my tent. My boys wanted to drive them off, but

I could not find it in my heart to refuse them shelter, as long as it rained. I was glad, however, to get rid of them as soon as the rain stopped; the natural scent of their own skin, blended with the odour of rancid grease and the fragrance of unwashed clothes, combined to form a bouquet which no European nostril could endure for any length of time.

CHAPTER VI.

KAVIRONDO.

A KAVIRONDO MINSTREL.

SCANTY dress may naturally be expected amongst savages of a low type and living in a tropical climate, but to find oneself among a race absolutely naked is a strange experience; and yet within a few weeks or months the novelty wears off, and one fails to notice anything extraordinary in such a mode of life. The inhabitants of Kavirondo recall the state of mankind in the Garden of Eden before the Fall. Banana-trees and other tropical vegetation around the huts, at least in some parts of their country, would strengthen this impression of being in a garden, were it not for the treeless grass-plains outside the village. Young and old go about in the same primeval garb. Women often wear a curious ornament, in the shape of a tail, which consists of a number of plaited strings manufactured out of some sort of vegetable fibre. A tiny apron of the same material is worn by a few of the women. As it is never worn by the unmarried, I was told that its presence was the equivalent for the European wedding-ring; but I am sure this is incorrect, as I have come across numbers of young mothers and wives without this apron, and have seen widows with and without it. I believe it is simply a fashion, like the tail, without any other object.

The race is well formed and healthy. They are agriculturists; wherever they settle, the jungle around them is soon converted into fruitful fields, yielding sweet-potatoes or various forms of corn. Those who can afford it keep goats and sheep, and the wealthy have herds of cattle. One of the chiefs, I was assured, owned several thousand cows. The native weapon is the spear, a short iron blade on a long wooden staff, usually tipped with iron at the other end to stick into the ground, when at rest. The shields are very curious. The leaf-shaped wicker-shield is evidently old-fashioned. The more common form is the small oval leathern shield of bullock-hide; it has a raised bump or boss punched in the centre.

The women wear a few strings of beads, but the men are inordinately fond of ornaments, especially the young warrior dandies. Iron-wire twisted into a spiral coil round the neck as a sort of collar, or round the leg as an anklet, is the height of fashion. Those who are lucky enough to secure a piece of ivory wear it, if from the tusk of a hippo, as a crescent-shaped ornament fastened to the forehead, but if of elephant ivory, then either as a bracelet or an anklet. In the last few years cowrie shells have come into favour, and are worn strapped round the chest or dangling from the shoulders.

Pink beads are the accepted currency, but even this depends on fashion. With the smaller pink beads we used to be able, on my first journey, to buy food for the caravan. These beads are everywhere refused nowadays, and the traveller would not be able to buy a stick of firewood or a single sweet-potato with them. The beads now in vogue are about four times as large as the former sort.

The Kavirondo hut consists of a circular mud wall of wattle and daub, with a conical grass-thatched roof; and a narrow outer verandah encircles the dwelling. The entrance is very low, and is closed at night by a reed-screen, movable between vertical posts, and securely fastened by a horizontal bar. The interior of the hut is very dark. The hut not only shelters the whole family, but the poultry, goats, and sheep, and occasionally a cow as well. There is no ventilation of any sort. One would imagine a dreadful state of ill-health from these, to Europeans, insanitary conditions; as a fact, the natives are most healthy, except for such diseases as have been imported by passing caravans.

Owing to the destruction caused by annually recurring grass-fires for generations past, the want of wood is becoming yearly more acutely felt by the traveller. The natives can manage to cook their food by using the dried stems of Kaffre-corn or maize or elephant-grass, but the firewood for a camp has to be fetched from a considerable distance, and the traveller has to pay accordingly.

A FAMILY GROUP IN KAVIRONDO

KAVIRONDO

The natives are remarkably stingy and inhospitable, and in this respect contrast unfavourably with other native races. Even though their village food-stores may contain more than the population can possibly require, and their fields may be covered with luxuriant crops, they will refuse food to a starving caravan, and severely punish, and probably kill, any one driven by hunger to help himself to a little from the vast wealth of their fields. They not only insist on payment for everything, but will refuse to sell anything except for the sort of bead that happens to be in fashion with them at the moment. I was stationed at Mumia's, the first Government station in Kavirondo, for some months, and I had an opportunity of witnessing the grasping greed of the natives. It happened that the only beads the Government possessed were white, red, or blue; the pink ones were exhausted. The Soudanese garrison and the Swahili porters were paid their food-ration with these beads; and yet the villagers not only refused to accept the Government currency, but endeavoured to extort famine prices from the unfortunate Government servants. More than once a native would appear at the station and complain, that a Soudanese soldier had snatched a basket of potatoes or flour and had chucked him some strings of white beads, the owner having refused to accept any but pink. As the Kavirondo have not been conquered, but have come peacefully under British sway, they consequently look upon the Government stations as tolerated, and not as the strongholds of the new and powerful masters of their country. Hence difficulties may sometimes cause strained relations. In most cases a judicious treatment of the native chief or chiefs settles the hitch amicably.

The chiefs are generally friendly disposed, will call on the traveller, and bring him a present. The Kavirondo chief Ngira presented me with a black fat-tailed sheep, when I passed through his country on my last journey. Neither he nor his chief attendants were naked, owing to the influence of Europeans having passed frequently with their caravans of clothed porters. In fact, all along the caravan route I noticed, especially among the male population, that a good many were adopting some form of covering, apparently in deference to the clothed strangers that visit them. This covering consists of a piece of goatskin or cotton cloth. Formerly, every man one met carried a spear, but the peaceful British rule has had the visible effect of causing villagers to attend markets without a spear. Very often they are armed simply with a small club which, if long enough, serves also as a walking-stick.

The native bill-hook is quite different in shape to the one used in Uganda. It is used to cut down jungle, rank weeds, and shrubs, as a preliminary clearing of the field; the women afterwards turn over the soil with native hoes of the usual pointed heart-shape. I have seen men working in the fields as diligently as women. Small boys usually serve as goatherds,

THE KAVIRONDO CHIEF NGIRA.

shepherds, and cowherds. Small girls, even from the earliest years, assist their mothers, fetch water, look after the fire, prepare the food, grind corn, and help in the fields.

The Kavirondo natives have no supreme king over them, but are under small independent chiefs. Very often the village elders manage their own affairs without rendering obedience to any one. According to different districts, the natives, though of one race and one language, call themselves by different names, such as Wakitosh and Wakilelowa.

In 1894 a sad reverse attended British influence among the neighbouring Wakitosh. Some Swahilies had deserted to a certain Wakitosh village, and the force sent to demand their surrender proved inadequate. It is difficult to know for certain the details of the disaster, or who were the parties really responsible for the bloodshed, whether the fault lay with our men or with the natives. Most of the men that were sent never returned; they were massacred by the Wakitosh, and the whole of Kitosh became insecure.

A number of new officials just then arrived opportunely from the coast; and one of these, a first-class transport officer, was placed in charge of the district. He had to wait some time before the Government was able to send a sufficiently strong force to assert British authority effectively over the Wakitosh. The expedition was commanded by Mr. W. Grant, and accompanied by a military officer, the civil officer of the district, and myself as the medical officer. It consisted of only a few hundred Soudanese soldiers, but there were several thousand armed native allies, consisting of Waganda, Wasoga, Masai, and friendly Wakavirondo, quite willing, in anticipation of loot, to join in arms against their own kindred.

The Kavirondo live in villages most of which are fortified. The village is circular, and defended by a high wall of earth; a deep trench surrounds the wall. There are at least two entrances, and if the village is large there may be five or six. When the village owns a considerable number of cattle, an open space is left in the centre with sheds for housing it. The huts are arranged close along the wall, with their doors opening towards the central space of the village. Where the population is particularly dense, there are a great many other huts crowding the inner space. These are fenced off from each other in such an intricate manner, that a stranger would not find it easy to pass from one hut to another. Every hut has one or more outdoor corn-stores of the usual pattern, viz., a big basket on trestles with a conical grass-thatched cover.

The massacre by the Wakitosh, followed by the disaster which overtook Mr. West in Nandi, had also rendered the natives of Kabras hostile. A message reached us at Mumias that the natives, having found out that white men were mortal (Mr. West was speared and killed in a treacherous night-attack), had determined to prevent in future any white man from passing through their country. It shows what curious notions some of these savages had hitherto held with regard to white men.

The whole district now became insecure, and the Europeans

up-country were threatened with being cut off from all communication with the coast. This sufficiently explains the absolute necessity of the punitive expedition, unless the Government were prepared to abandon all the Europeans up-country and to surrender the country to the tender mercies of bloodthirsty savages.

The entrance to a fortified village is by means of a narrow bank of earth across the trench, and a low archway in the earth-wall. One has to stoop to pass through such a gate. This entrance can be easily barricaded with heavy logs of wood, and rendered practically impregnable against all native attack. A very common sight on approaching a Kavirondo village is the appearance of a number of inquisitive natives popping their heads above the wall or squatting on it. The rank weeds often hide the trench, and the incautious visitor may fall headlong into a treacherous pit.

When the expedition approached the first hostile village, we saw numbers of armed natives waiting outside their gates as if to give us battle; but as we drew nearer, they retired within their walls and barricaded the gates. The enemy had a few men armed with muzzle-loaders. When the fight began, one of our Waganda friendlies near me had his arm shattered by a bullet. I amputated it there and then on the open field. But when the bullets continued whizzing and singing unpleasantly near me, I removed the wounded behind the shelter of a white-ant hillock and there attended to them. Then I was called in a hurry to see a Swahili shot down a little distance off; on examining him, I found he was dead. A bullet had struck him full in the chest, and must have passed through the heart.

The reason why the Kavirondo have several entrances to their villages, appears to be to enable them to escape by one if overpowered at any of the others. This happened in the present case. Several natives burst out from a gate the existence of which was unsuspected. They escaped, though, of course, there was an immediate rush by our men towards the spot. Strict orders had been given to spare women and children; a few of the women and children however perished. This might happen, and probably does happen, at the siege and capture of every fortified place. There were a great many wounded, and I had a busy time of it. The village

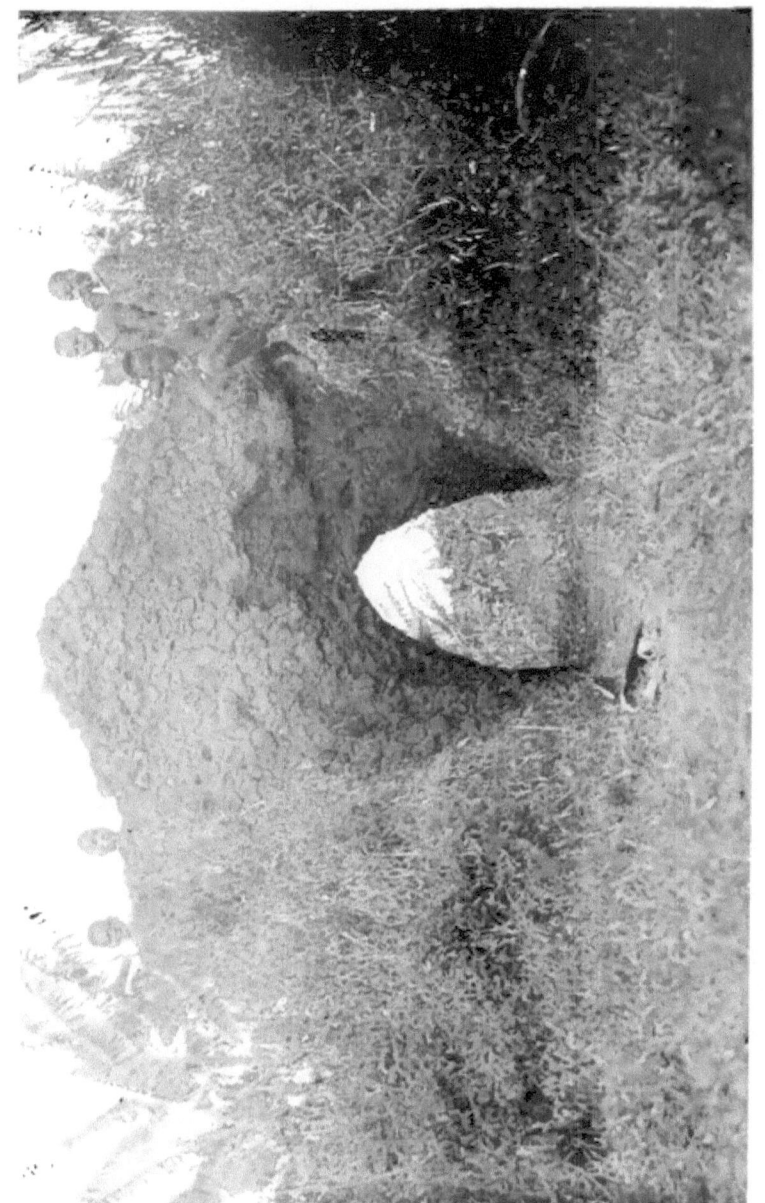

ENTRANCE TO A KAVIRONDO VILLAGE

was plundered and burnt. There was very little for our savage allies to loot—a few shields and spears, and some Kavirondo drums, harps, and stools.

The Kavirondo minstrel with his harp and stool may be met with in almost every village. The stool is carved out of a solid block of wood; it has four legs and a cup-shaped seat. It is very strong, and can stand a deal of hard wear and tear. It is whittled smooth with a knife, and then polished with the rough leaves of a certain plant used instead of sand-paper.

The Kavirondo harp consists of an oblong wooden bowl covered with a piece of leather. Two pieces of wood, slightly diverging from each other, are fixed inside the bowl; a horizontal piece fastens them to each other, and serves as a support for the eight coils of string which converge and meet, where they pass through a hole in the leather covering of the bowl. The sound-aperture is placed somewhat to the right. The minstrel holds the harp to his chest with one hand, and plays with the other. The strings are not made of gut, but of some vegetable fibre.

In the pillaging which followed the capture of a village some accidents happened on our side. One poor boy was brought to me cut all over. The gashes were inflicted with a spear. One of our savage allies had mistaken him for an enemy and had tried to kill him. The boy had one of his thumbs nearly cut off, a spear thrust through the leg, the cheek laid open, gashes on the scalp, and cuts on the arm. He survived these dreadful injuries, but was horribly disfigured and maimed for life.

At the next village stormed, a desperate resistance was offered by the enemy. I wore a conspicuous solar-helmet, and from a loophole in the wall one of the enemy took me as a target for pot-shots. A bullet at last whipped past unpleasantly near my face. It missed; and although a miss is as good as a mile, I raised my rifle in self-defence and gave a return-greeting. Whether I hit or missed I do not know, nor did I care to investigate subsequently, but I was not molested any further from that quarter. Finding the rifles did not inflict any material damage on an enemy crouching behind the protection of the earth-wall, our leader tried the Hotchkiss gun; but the missiles simply passed clean through without shattering the earthen rampart. He then brought the Maxim gun into position. Handling the weapon himself, he cut down the upper half of the wall near one entrance. Then the signal was given to storm the place. I was close to the gate; a number of our men had already entered and scattered to the right and left along the inner wall, when suddenly the enemy made a desperate but vain attempt at a sortie. A Soudanese officer standing by my side was struck by a spear, and fell headlong into the trench.

A BLACKSMITH'S PARAPHERNALIA IN KAVIRONDO.

I saw the blood gushing from his back and staining his tunic. I thought he must be dead, but the wounded man turned over and rested his head on his right hand. He never uttered a groan. With the assistance of two of our men, I had him hoisted out and carried to a place 200 yards off. But as the vertebral column and the intestines were cut through, he died within a few minutes. In the meantime some other wounded were brought to me, and I was kept pretty busy. The village was captured, pillaged, and burnt. The most important booty was cattle, but there were other valuables in the shape of iron-wire ornaments and native hoes.

The most important manufacture in Kavirondo is the smelting of iron ore and the fashioning of hoes. The illustration shows a native blacksmith's extremely simple paraphernalia. In a large basket he has charcoal, and in a smaller basket the red iron ore broken into very tiny pieces. His hammer is simply a heavy stone, the tongs a green twig split half way down. The bellows is double-muzzled and covered with two goatskins which have each a long stick attached. The man who works the bellows stands, and holding these two sticks, he works them up and down. The two hands by thus working alternately produce a continuous draught. The bellows is of wood, and the draught is driven into a roughly fashioned clay pipe, and thus conveyed to the fire. The clay pipe is in sections, roughly held together with wet clay. The construction of the bellows is somewhat peculiar. It is carved out of a solid block of wood, and consists of two separate basin-shaped depressions, each having its own passage tunnelled to the other end of the block. The piece of goatskin which covers each basin must be sufficiently large to be pulled up and pushed down; this movement draws in and expels the air. Wooden shields are old-fashioned and so heavy that the man who carries one has not much chance of using a spear or any other offensive weapon, his whole strength being required to support the shield. Several of the war-helmets I saw, were really wicker-baskets, kept on the head by a leather strap which passes under the chin. They are often ornamented with circles, painted on with red and white clay.

Our leader kept a sharp look-out that the captured women and children were not carried off as slaves, but were handed over to his care. Amongst primitive tribes, war is simply a repetition of what one reads of in the Old Testament—every adult male is put to death, the women and children are captured and become slaves. Native women are often very callous, and readily accept as husband the murderer of their male relatives. Centuries of bloodshed, indiscriminate slaughter, and slave-raiding amongst themselves, have gradually blunted nobler feelings, and reduced these human beings to the level of beasts. The children, having lost their father, and being separated probably also from their mother, soon forget their origin, and grow up as the children of the tribe into which they have been adopted. No doubt a good many of the captured women and children went off with their captors, in spite of the strict watch kept by our leader. I liberated myself not a few, which I happened to see as they were being carried off. It was not always easy to persuade the captive woman to leave her native captor; she naturally imagined that the white man wanted to seize her as his slave. She evidently thought, that under the circumstances the black warrior who had captured her had a better right to possess her.

KAVIRONDO BELLOWS, WOODEN SHIELD, AND WAR-HELMET.

It was at the capture of a village that I witnessed the cruel lust of blood, which is said to exist in every Masai. Two little urchins, four or five years old, attempted to escape from one of the gates; but finding the enemy present everywhere, they ran round the village along by the trench, trying to find a means of re-entry. In the meanwhile, two of our Masai allies had rushed forward from the besieging hordes.

A Masai on the war-path is a horrid object. He is usually naked. Round his waist he wears a broad leather belt carrying a long sword in a leather scabbard. Very often he has also a knobkerry, usually of some hard wood, but I have one in my possession carved out of a rhino-horn. In his left hand he carries a large oval shield, and in his right hand a spear. To one or both of his ankles he ties a peculiar ornament made of feathers, and on his head he wears a similar arrangement of black ostrich feathers fastened to a leathern band which passes round the forehead and occiput. The Masai sword has a straight leather-covered hilt. The blade is narrow, but gradually gets broader towards the end, where it suddenly terminates in a point. The weapon answers its purpose of slashing rather than of piercing an enemy. The shields are made of bullock-hide, and are ornamented with various patterns in white, red, and black. The spear is very handsome, though somewhat peculiar. The long double-edged blade is rather narrow, and tapers to a point. To poise this unwieldy mass of metal, the wooden shaft is almost entirely covered with iron; only a few inches of the wood are left uncovered about the middle, where the hand grasps the spear.

Two of these fierce warriors had darted in pursuit of the two naked urchins who, turning round and finding themselves hard pressed, stopped running and held out entreating hands to their pursuers. The Masai were jerking their spears horizontally, with the peculiar thrusting movement used in striking a victim Friends and foes stopped fighting to watch this sudden side-act, as Trojans and Greeks may have paused to watch Achilles pursuing Hector round the walls of Troy. One of the Masai did not strike his captive, but, passing shield and spear to one hand, he grasped the little boy with the other, hoisted him on to his shoulder, and darted back to our ranks amidst the loud laughter of our savage allies. But the other villain poised his spear and struck the poor trembling child full in the chest. As the boy fell backwards in the grass, the Masai gave one more lunge with his spear and then darted back to where our friendlies stood; and the battle instantly raged with greater fury than before. It all happened within a few seconds, and so quickly, that I had no time to put a bullet through the murderer, though an intense desire to do so now possessed me.

I had already noticed some barbarities perpetrated on dead bodies at the first village we captured, for the human wolves which accompany every army had cut off a hand here and there, in order more quickly to possess themselves of the coveted iron bracelets. It was a barefaced murder this slaying of the little urchin in the sight of friend and foe. Of course it was impossible to discover afterwards the villain among the many thousands who flocked like vultures to the slaughter. In the relentless pursuit of the enemy, these savage allies rendered considerable assistance to the Government. Among the slain in the stronghold were found the principal hostile leaders; and the enemy thereafter no longer made a stand. As we advanced, they evacuated their villages and fled before us.

The Kavirondo are very clever at trapping quails; and as they are also skilful in basket-work, each quail is housed in a tiny basket-cage. A number of these baskets are suspended from a strong pole firmly planted in the ground, and the call of the captured birds lures others to the traps set for them. In some of the more remote villages the natives are quite proud of their captured quails and will not sell even a single one at any price; but nearer the caravan route quails can be bought, though usually rather dear.

In the Wakitosh expedition the Government captured many hundred head of cattle. Half of what our allies laid hands on they were allowed to retain, but the other half they had, according to agreement, to hand over to the Government.

Though the enemy had comparatively few killed, the loss they suffered was a severe punishment to them; villages were burnt to the ground, a serious matter in a district where wood for rebuilding the huts had to be fetched from a considerable distance; standing crops were destroyed; vast stores of corn found in the villages were used up by the invading army; and cattle, their most valuable possession, were captured by the hundred.

I was present when a tusk of ivory was picked up with a bunch of leaves attached to it. It was the equivalent of the white flag amongst European combatants, a signal of submission; and our victorious leader now withdrew the invading forces from the district. Some of the captured women were then liberated, provided with food, and sent back to their homes. They were to convey, on behalf of the Government, assurances to the enemy that all the captives, women and children, would be liberated as soon as peace was established, and that the Government had no intention of keeping slaves. This must

KAVIRONDO

have appeared an astounding generosity to natives accustomed to consider captives as slaves.

Shortly afterwards the hostile chief arrived in person at Mumia's and offered, in sign of submission, to settle with his tribe in the immediate neighbourhood of the Government station. This of course could not be granted, and he returned to his own home, but with all the liberated captives, women

NATIVE BRIDGE OVER THE SIO RIVER IN KAVIRONDO.

and children. Some months later the civil officer in charge of the district made an inspection tour in Kitosh. It was a royal tour, for the conquered natives saw in him the autocrat wielding supreme authority in the country. It will take a long while before they come to know that there is a higher authority in the Protectorate, viz., the Commissioner, who, in his turn, is but the servant of the sovereign authority in the distant land which is the home of the white man.

Pursuit becomes extremely difficult, if the enemy crosses rivers and destroys the native bridges. The difference in depth of some rivers in the dry season and in a state of flood, owing to incessant rains, may be gauged by the huge and heavy scaffolding of the native bridge over the Sio river in Kavirondo. In the dry season it was possible to cross this river by wading through it.

The Wakitosh expedition was followed by one against the Wakilelowa. In discussing the plans with chief Mumia, our friendly Kavirondo ally, Mr. Grant made some allusion to probable difficulties if the recent heavy rains were to continue. Mumia pointed to me and said: "You have got the white medicine-man; why don't you ask him to give you fine weather?" We explained that this sort of thing was beyond the province of all white men, whether medicine-man or not. Whereupon Mumia quietly remarked to him, that if *we* could not do it, his own medicine-man could and would do it at once, provided he were paid. On being asked how much, he said: "one cow." Half in fun he was told that white men do not pay, till they have had proof of such pretensions; but he accepted this as a verbal agreement, and said: "All right! my medicine-man shall see that you have fine weather." Next morning our expedition started, and by an absurd coincidence we did not have a drop of rain, though it had been raining almost daily up till then. We had some lovely days. Of course Mumia was satisfied that his wizard had performed the trifling feat of securing for us fine weather; and our leader had naturally to hand over the cow, as non-payment would have been considered as breaking a white man's word. Where the European villain with his lies and frauds has not yet made his appearance, the white man's simple word is equal to a solemn and binding oath.

It must not be thought, that the native medicine-man has always a pleasant time of it. I inquired of Mumia, how long his medicine-man had been with him, and was told that not many years ago this medicine-man's predecessor was put to death on account of his obstinacy in refusing to provide rain, when the whole nation was suffering from a severe drought. The position of the African medicine-man, though highly honourable and lucrative, is therefore somewhat precarious.

The Wakilelowa were speedily defeated, and the inhabitants of Kabras sued for peace and entered into blood-brotherhood with the civilian in charge of the district. This rite consisted in cutting the throat of a dog, the two contracting parties promising over the immolated dog to be true friends in future, and declaring that they deserved to be treated as the dead dog if false to each other. Such faith these natives had in the efficacy of this rite, that they at once flocked in trustingly from every quarter to our camp, and a brisk market was opened as if such a thing as war had never existed.

Both in the Wakitosh and in the Wakilelowa expedition I saw a good many cases of wounds inflicted by arrows. The bow was a rather poor weapon, the arrows were of every description. I have in my collection some specimens, brought from the scenes of the earlier fights. A few of these arrows are mere pointed pieces of wood without any feathers, others are feathered; some carry a strong sharp thorn, others are tipped with iron. The iron arrow-heads are of every description; some resemble a nail, others have the ordinary triangular shape and sometimes carry one or more barbs. Some of the arrows were poisoned, but the majority were not. The poison used was old and practically harmless; only a slight irritation resulted, which yielded to antiseptic treatment.

Mumia's station takes its name from having been built next to the village of the chief Mumia, but he has since removed his own village somewhat farther off.

One day, close to Mumia's, I came upon a group of grotesquely attired mummers, and was told that it was in honour of a Kavirondo wedding. The young men had smeared themselves all over with red or white clay. They sported a curious head-gear. Two pieces of wood, with long white feathers fastened to them so as to look somewhat like small wings, were attached to a circle of leather which could be passed round the forehead, thus giving the appearance of winged heads. A boy blew a long antelope horn, producing most dismal sounds which were accepted as sweet music by the others. The performers were leaping, jumping, and running races, but stopped to have a look at me as I passed them on the road. Marriage here, as everywhere amongst savages, means purchase. A few native hoes and some goats and sheep will buy almost any girl except a chief's daughter, for he expects to be paid one or more cows. To the native mind this purchase constitutes a legal marriage. The girls pride themselves on the amount which has to be paid for them to their parents, and consider it a public acknowledgment of their worth. They appear to be faithful wives, but the curious fact remains that if their husbands were to part with them to some one else, they would passively accept the change.

Mumia dresses in European fashion, and shrewd traders have got a good deal of valuable ivory out of this vain but stingy chief, by offering him cheap and showy articles of dress. On one of my journeys he paid me a visit in his state robes, his latest brand-new purchase. It was a long bright-coloured dressing-gown! Probably he thought such gorgeous apparel must be something particularly grand and imposing, perhaps the very latest fashion from Europe.

Mumia is a tall lean man; he and many of his subjects have rather long and prominent front teeth. Though he himself wears European clothing, his subjects all go more or less naked. I witnessed a native dance held in his village in honour of twins having been born. Females of every age, from the old grey-haired great-grandmother down to the tiny mite of three years old, joined in this dance which, from a European point of view, was anything but decent. Two tall women, clothed in coloured cotton cloth, on joining in the dance threw off their garments and danced vigorously in the same primitive condition as the other nude dancers. I was told these two were sisters of Mumia.

Among the Kavirondo the women are even greater smokers than the men. The national pipe has a black clumsy clay bowl and a long reed stem. Aged couples seem to require the soothing solace of a quiet smoke more frequently than younger folks.

One day I was called by Mumia to attend his favourite wife. Mumia was then building a new village, consisting of a number of huts surrounding a large inner circular space. I wanted to know in which hut the patient lay, and asked Mumia which was his hut; he replied all of them were his, as all contained his wives and attendants. The village was his dwelling, the wealthy African's many-roomed palace. When he brought me to where the sufferer lay ill, it was so dark inside the hut that I had to light a lantern. The woman lay absolutely nude on the bare mud floor. When I had attended to the patient, Mumia provided me with a gourd-bowl of water, a towel, and some soap. The savage and the civilised were thus strangely combined. What little value Mumia sets on a wife or two, more or less, would appear from what a civilian at the station told me.

Mumia came one day crying and lamenting that lightning had struck one of his huts and had burnt a quantity of his valued European clothing. Some time after, rumour reached the official that a woman had been burnt to death in the same fire. To make sure, he inquired of Mumia. With a gesture expressive of the unimportance he attached to such a question, Mumia answered: "Yes, yes! But think of the clothes I lost—my clothes, my clothes!"

Mumia, though wealthy, belongs to the type of men, met

A KAVIRONDO VILLAGE-FORGE.

with also amongst Europeans, who endeavour to get without payment professional advice and assistance from a medical man; and when they have received it, they are more ungrateful than ever to their benefactor, on the principle, probably, that "the cheaper the article the less its value" applies also to surgical help when rendered without exacting a heavy fee.

On my last journey, in passing through Igaga's country, I had an opportunity of seeing a Kavirondo village-forge in active work. It looked a very tumbledown place, merely screening off the sun from striking direct on the fire. The smith and his three assistants were hard at work; some idlers from the village had dropped in for a chat round the homely "foo-foo-foo-foo-foo" sound of the bellows. I too should have enjoyed to loiter for a while with them; but I had a ten-hours' march to accomplish, past friendly Ngira's district and on to Ndui.

Next day I reached the Nzoia river and crossed it for the first time in the Government ferry. It is a wide and flat-bottomed boat. A strong wire rope spans the river, and by turning a wheel another wire rope is wound up and draws the ferry to the other bank. This is one of the road-improvements introduced by the late Captain Sclater whom the Government had entrusted with the construction of a cart-road to Uganda. He had but just accomplished his task, when he was carried off by an attack of black-water fever and found his grave in Africa.

CHAPTER VII.

USOGA.

USOGA
HUBBLE-BUBBLE.

USOGA
HUBBLE-BUBBLE.

ON the overland journey to Uganda, the traveller on leaving Kavirondo enters Usoga, and he notices a complete and remarkable change in every respect. From the absolutely nude savages in Kavirondo he passes to a race where not even the youngest walk about uncovered; from a stingy and inhospitable tribe he joins one which greets him with a hearty welcome and extends to him a lavish hospitality; from treeless grass-lands he finds himself in a well wooded country and under the refreshing shade of magnificent trees; from circular villages fortified with earth-wall and trench he is among unprotected dwellings, of which a few of the better class have a fragile reed-fence put up for privacy and ornament. The two races differ also in language and in form of government; the Wasoga acknowledge the authority of the king of Uganda, the Wakavirondo do not.

Placed between Uganda and Kavirondo, Usoga, as might be expected, admits the currency of both realms, though naturally the cloth and shells of Uganda are more acceptable than the beads of Kavirondo. The Wasoga prefer red beads, in payment for small purchases. The women wear bark-cloth wrapped round the waist and reaching to the knees; the upper half of their body remains uncovered. The men dress like the Waganda, in bark-cloth or cotton garments.

A family group in Usoga includes a goodly number. The bountiful food supply bestowed by Nature's inexhaustible wealth banishes want and all its attendant miseries, and enables man to provide liberally for his numerous offspring.

They appear to be a happy and contented race, judging from the festive tom-tom and the shrill reed-pipe, which proclaim that a merry-making is taking place in the straggling hamlet. In one of their villages I came upon a huge drum. It reached to the shoulders of a tall woman standing by it with a baby in her arms. It was carved out of a solid block of wood from some gigantic tree. It narrowed towards the base, the diameter of which was less than half that of the upper surface. It was covered with cow-hide, and held together by twisted strips of leather. The Soudanese mutineers had passed this way, and finding the drum too unwieldy to carry off, they had driven their knives through the top leather and had ripped the upper covering open.

The Usoga hut has neither the mud wall nor the verandah of the Kavirondo hut. It is bee-hive in form, and the grass thatch reaches right down to the ground. It is usually very lofty, but the available space inside is considerably diminished by the many props and poles for supporting the roof.

As soon as a caravan has camped, the chief or headman will call on the caravan leader to ascertain how many loads of food are wanted. The food is supplied gratis; a small present in cloth is handed to the chief, not in payment, but in recognition of the courtesy; it is the African mode of showing friendship. The food of the Wasoga consists almost exclusively of green bananas, either roasted in the fire or boiled with the peel left on, or first peeled and then boiled and mashed. The Usoga banana plantations are very extensive, and nestle among the tall trees.

There is scarcely any other fruit to be had in the country except ripe bananas. But for this exception, Usoga is the nearest approach to what the imagination pictures the Garden of Eden to have been. The great tropical heat is mellowed by the leafy shade of the trees into a luxurious comfort. The dead branches supply more firewood than necessary. The banana plantation provides food throughout all the seasons; and thus it is harvest-time all the year round. The banana-tree yields its fruit only once, and then dies; but it provides

A FAMILY GROUP IN USOGA

for the future by sprouting six to ten young trees from the soil in a narrow circle around it. The shade of the bananas helps to keep down the rank weeds. A little labour keeps the plantation clean and sweet; and the soft, juicy stem of the banana-tree can be felled by a single blow from a bill-hook, wherever a superabundance of young trees necessitates their being thinned, or an old tree which has yielded its bunch of fruit requires to be removed.

The well-known grey parrot with the red tail was originally found on the west coast of Africa; but when caravans brought these birds to the east coast, it was discovered that Usoga was also their habitat. They can be seen by the score flying from tree to tree, or screaming overhead as they wing their noisy flight in search of change of scene.

Resting on soft grass-mats under the fitful play of the trembling shadows on the clean-swept ground; catching the soft breeze gently whispering amongst the rustling leaves of the bananas; listening to the distant sough of the mighty forest giants which stretch a hundred leafy arms towards heaven; comfortably and cleanly dressed in simple white clothing; with a mind at rest from worldly cares, owing to the simple wants of this primitive existence being abundantly provided for by Nature; with flowering shrubs perfuming the air, inquisitive monkeys peeping among the foliage, lovely butterflies floating silently from flower to flower, pretty birds skimming past, is like having a passing glimpse of Paradise on earth.

Even under the prosaic verandah of the unromantic station at Luba's, the companion of my first journey was so impressed by the balmy air, the peaceful stillness, the lovely view, that he said to me: "What a place to dream away a year or two of one's existence!" He was a brave major, and had many a sanguinary fight to go through later on, but, like myself, he was enjoying the momentary rest and peace before the busy days of a stirring life hustled us again hither and thither.

Usoga is separated from Uganda by the Victoria Nile. Luba's is situated on the lake, and the traveller here has the first view of Uganda in the distance. The name Luba is familiar to all who have read of Bishop Hannington's murder. It is a pity that the unfortunate bishop made the great mistake of insisting on entering Uganda *via* Usoga, in direct opposition to a popular superstition, according to which the future conquerors

F

of Uganda would endeavour to pass that way. The noble missionary Mackay wisely went to Uganda by the usual southern route, and thus avoided incurring the displeasure of a timid but autocrat ruler. Luba acted under direct orders received from King Mwanga, when he arrested the Bishop and ordered his execution. Luba is a tall elderly man, lean and spare, with a large heavy face. He wields considerable influence over the lake-shore dwellers; but he is a weak character, easily moulded and directed by a stronger mind. He controls scores of boats

USOGA BOATS.

and hundreds of boatmen, and as long as caravans have to cross into Uganda *via* Luba's, he will remain a chief whose influence has to be reckoned with in all transport arrangements across the Nile.

The Usoga boats remind one of New Zealand war-canoes. The boat is long and narrow and has usually a dozen seats; one man sits at the stern and guides the boat with his paddle which is used instead of a rudder; another man sits at the bow and is ready with a long pole to do the necessary punting where the water is shallow; the remaining ten seats are occupied by twenty oarsmen. The boats are formed of long planks, slowly and laboriously chipped from a tree-trunk of suitable size. The planks are stitched together with some vegetable fibre and caulked with water-weeds. The result is that all the boats leak more or less freely; and one man, placed in the middle of the boat, is employed the whole time in baling out the water with a gourd-bowl. From the lower anterior part of the boat protrudes a long pointed nose like a ram, and the stern terminates somewhat similarly. From the anterior part there curves upwards a pole which becomes vertical, is about five or six feet high, and is surmounted by an ornament. The ornament usually consists of a pair of antelope horns, between which a huge bunch of gay feathers is tied. A fluttering festoon of shredded palm-leaves stretches from the base of the antelope horns to the boat. Similar festoons deck both sides of the boat near the stern. In spite of its size the boat can take but five to seven porters with their loads. A large caravan therefore requires quite a fleet of boats to cross Napoleon's Gulf, as this strip of the lake is sometimes called. The bright-coloured bunches of feathers, the picturesque boats, the noisy crowd, make a pleasing and animated scene. The boatmen use paddles made of a remarkably light but tough wood.

The paddles are usually flat and spear-shaped; some have a slightly broader blade than others, but all terminate in a sharp point. The men paddle almost incessantly for the hour and a half it takes to cross the Nile. They sing merrily and keep time with the splashing paddles, and the boat seems literally to shoot through the water. Almost invariably a good-natured but vigorous race takes place, which lightens labour and turns toil into pleasure. The victorious crew then give a shout of triumph and wave their paddles aloft. The men usually strip to the waist whilst rowing, but at once don their bark-cloth on landing.

I had a rather curious experience on my first journey. I was asked to accompany a fleet of about twenty of these boats from Sio Bay (in Kavirondo) to Luba's (in Usoga); my companion was to join me later on. We rowed almost without a break from early dawn to 4 P.M.; then the Wasoga boatmen gave me to understand by signs, for there was not a soul present who could speak to them, that they had done enough work for the day and would like to land; they pointed to a spot where smoke indicated the presence of huts. Believing that they must know their own business best, I nodded assent.

At once the boats placed themselves in a sort of line-of-battle array, and with incredible speed, the boatmen shouting and yelling like mad, we dashed towards one of the numerous inlets.

Instead of the expected peaceful landing, I witnessed with surprise what looked for all the world like a bold attack on an enemy's country. Most of my crews rushed ashore armed with shields and spears. Some terrified inhabitants ran away into the woods, while my lawless mob of boatmen pounced on fowls and chickens, tore up vegetable marrows and pumpkins, seized all the fish they found in the dug-outs, and recklessly cut down banana-trees right and left to get at the fruit. Screams made me hurry unarmed ashore, just in time to save a poor old woman from having three young goats snatched from her. As soon as I had enabled her to retreat to the safe shelter of the woods, I had to save a man whom the boatmen had seized and, for all I knew, were going to spear. The wretches bolted off when they saw me, and the man I had saved ran for his life and escaped.

Then some armed natives deployed out of the banana groves. At the sight of this score of armed men, my 400 cowardly Wasoga robbers fled to the boats. A shower of stones was flung at us and wounded a few. A stone about the size of my fist struck me in the pit of the stomach. Fortunately it was a spent stone, or I should have been doubled up on the spot and would then most probably have been speared. It served as a hint that unarmed I should only be throwing away my life by remaining. Under cover of this shower of stones, some tried to rush us with spears, when "bang! bang!" went off some muzzle-loaders, proving that the natives could also muster a few guns.

When I turned round, I found my men had got into their boats and were vigorously paddling off. I was left quite alone. I reached the lake, threw myself in, and struck out for the boats. I am a very indifferent swimmer, as I get too quickly exhausted. I would not have ventured upon such a performance in time of peace on any inducement. It is astonishing what undreamt-of feats the pressure of circumstances may get the most reluctant of us to attempt! It was my first swim with all my clothes on. I did not relish it, and I have no desire to repeat it. Not one of the boats came to my help. I only wonder I did not get drowned before I reached a boat. The crocodiles had probably been scared off by the awful din. Many of the nearer boats paddled away the quicker when I approached them, in their terror taking me for a desperate enemy wishing to board them. My boy had remained in the boat; but when he drew my rifle out of its canvas covering, my boatmen paused, allowed me to reach them, and drew me into the boat.

With the boat at a pretty safe distance, and with me aboard and now armed with a rifle, my boatmen became quite plucky

THE NEW FORT AT LUBA'S IN USOGA.

again. Pointing to a solitary sentinel posted on a conspicuous rock, they begged me to shoot him. I felt more inclined to shoot them for having been the aggressors. I was told afterwards, that we had landed on one of the Uvuma islands, inhabited by a plucky but treacherous race which hates the Wasoga. The Uvuma islanders fall, for administrative purposes, under the jurisdiction of the official in charge of Usoga.

The Usoga pipe differs from those in use in Uganda and in Kavirondo. The Wasoga use a hubble-bubble; it consists of a small gourd, with a reed mouth-piece at the side and a small red clay bowl stuck on the top. The wooden drinking-cup reminds one of a communion chalice; it is carved out of a solid piece of wood.

It was at Luba's, where the Soudanese mutineers made their first stand and where they murdered three Europeans. Poor Major Thruston had lately succeeded to the highest military post, viz., that of Commandant of the Uganda Rifles, a force composed at that time entirely of Soudanese. He spoke Arabic fluently, and, as I thought, knew the Soudanese thoroughly. But his openly expressed affection for them led him to trust these blacks too much. He was in hopes that his mere unarmed presence would restore confidence, whereas the mutineers immediately placed hands on him and on Mr. N. Wilson, the civilian in charge of Luba's. I can only speak of this from hearsay, as I was stationed at the time in Unyoro.

The mutineers had already placed Major Thruston and Mr. Wilson in irons, when Mr. Scott, in charge of a Government dhow, put in at Luba's. If what I heard is true, Mr. Scott was warned by his own men not to land, but he either could not understand them or refused to be guided. The moment he landed, he was seized by the mutineers and led to the fort. According to one story, he tore himself free and made a rush for his dhow, but, though a burly and strong man, he was caught, overpowered, and placed in irons; and the villains, it is said, threw him on the ground and inflicted a number of lashes with a hippo-thong.

Next day the mutineers made their unsuccessful assault on the small party of Europeans stationed on the adjoining hill. Exasperated by their defeat and in revenge, they, on returning to the fort, murdered the three unfortunate captive Europeans in cold blood. According to some, ghastly suffering was inflicted; according to others, Bilal Effendi, the ringleader, murdered all three by blowing out their brains.

In the subsequent severe fighting around Luba's, hundreds of our Waganda and Swahili allies were killed, but comparatively few of the mutineers who had the advantage of being trained and disciplined soldiers, armed with excellent rifles and with any amount of captured ammunition. Hearing of the approach of Indian troops, the mutineers thought it advisable to move off; they proceeded up the Nile, and finally met with a crushing defeat on their way to Unyoro.

The old fort at Luba's was found to be full of graves of Soudanese mutineers, and it was undermined with holes to shelter those in the fort from the hostile fire. It was therefore destroyed and levelled with the ground, when it came once more into the hands of Government. A new fort was speedily erected. It is close to the old fort, but nearer to the lake. It has been said that the bodies of the murdered Europeans were thrown by the mutineers to the hyænas. A search, however, resulted in the discovery of the remains of one, the skull being recognised by the stopping in some of the teeth. These remains were reverently buried. A wooden cross and a simple railing mark the spot. I was told, that the skull showed a bullet mark through the forehead; this would refute the story of a lingering death having been inflicted.

During these troubles Chief Luba had prudently shifted his quarters to a distance, but he had the good sense not to throw in his lot with the mutineers. Luba's, a quiet haven of rest,

PIGMIES OF THE GREAT AFRICAN FOREST.

and Luba's turned into a pandemonium with the slaughtered lying about unburied and by the score, was indeed a fearful contrast. Suleiman Effendi—I remember him well, for he was sent to me in 1894 to be captain of the Soudanese troops at Kampala when I was in command there—was one of the first mutineers who fell. That he was brave is proved by his being shot close to the British lines. He was buried, but the hyænas dug him out again. Once more he was buried, and again exhumed by the hyænas which, scenting the dead, had suddenly appeared on the scene by the dozen, though previously not at all very common in the neighbourhood.

On my last journey through Luba's I saw two pigmies of the Great African Forest, a man and a woman. In size they seemed children of nine to ten years old. They were originally captured by some other African race and carried off into slavery; in course of time they came into the hands of Mr. W. Grant, the officer in command of Usoga. The male pigmy has a considerable assortment of vices: he is drunken and dissolute to a degree, easily roused to fury, and very vindictive; but he appears to be attached to his master, and accompanies him on every campaign.

From one of my journeys through Usoga I brought a Mozambique monkey and a pair of grey parrots to England. All three did very well in London. "Jim," the monkey, occasionally got loose; but though he could not be caught as he jumped from house to house and tree to tree, he invariably returned at night-time to his cage and slept soundly, thoroughly tired out with his day's romp. To avoid his becoming a nuisance to our neighbours, he was ultimately sent to the Zoo, after having been for over two years the pet of the family. He knew me at once, though he had not seen me for two years. The parrots have stood two London winters already and are flourishing. It is curious that the colour of their eyes, which was originally grey, has changed to bright yellow. They are very good talkers. I bought these birds young. There is a considerable trade carried on in grey parrots, and as there is a good demand for them, they are not cheap even in Usoga. At the coast they fetch as much as £2 to £3 each. I tried at first to get a bird by slightly maiming it with a shot, but the bird I aimed at tumbled down dead: it was a big handsome old bird. I skinned it, and to my surprise I found that the South Kensington Museum was pleased to get the skin. These birds are so very common in Usoga, that no one ever dreams of shooting one for a collection. Museums, however, do not care for cage-birds, but prefer to get a wild specimen; consequently the bird I had unintentionally killed proved an acceptable acquisition to the Museum.

Visiting the ruins of the old fort at Luba's, I came upon a porter playing the "zeze," a Swahili musical instrument. It consists of a flat piece of carved wood, having a gourd-bowl attached to one end. It is three-stringed; one string runs along the flat upper surface, and the other two strings pass along the sides. It is held with both arms hanging down in a most lazy attitude, and it utters a monotonous ting-a-ling sound which is highly appreciated by Swahilies.

The presence of the minstrel twanging his "zeze" was an outward visible sign that peace and tranquillity once more held sway over dreamy, delightful Usoga.

USOGA DRINKING-CUP.

CHAPTER VIII.

THE WAGANDA.

UGANDA SHIELD.

UGANDA (or Buganda) denotes the country, Waganda the race, Luganda their language.

The native constitution acknowledges three estates: the king, the lords, and the commons, known as Kabaka, Siol, and Makope respectively.

Travellers to Uganda, before the British occupation of the country, were astonished to find the inhabitants so highly advanced in civilisation and form of government, when compared with the condition of the savages surrounding them on every side.

The form of government is strikingly analogous to the feudal system. The sovereign is lord paramount; the land belongs to him; he is the fountain of justice and of honour, and his consent is necessary to every decision arrived at by the Great Council of the State.

The lords are subdivided into thirty different degrees of rank. Of the great chiefs there are about ten. They hold certain high offices which carry with them the revenue and administration of some province. For instance, the ruler of the province of Chagwe is called the Sekibobo, and the chief of the province of Singo is known as the Makwenda; the Kangao rules Bulamwezi (written also Bulemezi), and the Pokino has Budu. The great chiefs hold their land direct from the crown, and in return have certain feudal obligations to fulfil; in case of war they have to provide an army; they have to keep the public roads and bridges in repair, and they have to furnish the king with labourers whenever he requires any. The smaller chiefs hold from the greater chiefs on similar terms, and this system is carried down to the smallest and humblest rank of chiefs.

The Makope are the peasant and labouring class. They used to be, to all intents and purposes, the serfs or slaves attached to the land. In return for being allowed to cultivate their fields, they had to work without payment for their chief.

The king, when he wanted money, would claim it from the great chiefs; these, in their turn, would demand it from the sub-chiefs, and so on; the Makope at the bottom of the ladder being ultimately the one who had to bear the burden and who was, not unfrequently, mercilessly squeezed.

The Makope or Waganda peasants dress in bark-cloth in Roman toga fashion. The garment is knotted over one shoulder, leaving the arms bare. The men generally go about barefoot and bare-headed, though some are adopting a head-covering which is either a white cotton skull-cap, a red fez, or a small turban. The system of extorting unpaid labour out of the Makope was formerly universal. It was carried so far that chiefs would even order their men to work without pay for strangers. A chief, for instance, would figure as

WAGANDA PEASANTS.

the generous supporter of some particular missionary by building a house for him as a present, and would reap thanks and praise for his liberality. In plain language, this donation meant that the chief had compelled some unfortunate peasants, under threat of punishment, to provide, without any payment whatever, the necessary material and labour; the work to be done was divided amongst the men, and each one had to do a certain portion. It has happened, therefore, that the missionary has been left for a shorter or longer period with part of some building unfinished, because the man who had been ordered to construct it tried to evade the hateful exaction.

The system of paid labour came only gradually into force, owing to the passive hostility of the chiefs who declined to send labourers; in other words, they prevented their peasants from accepting the paid-labour offered by the Government. In 1894 a few natives applied voluntarily for work, and when they found that it paid them to work for the Government, and that they were allowed to keep what they had earned, more and more came forward; and now, scores waiting for employment may be seen at Kampala every morning.

One of the important duties of a peasant is to keep in order the reed-fences which enclose dwellings and plantations. These reed-fences, when new, look very elegant; but they are most fragile and do not last long. Hence it is a never-ending labour to keep them in order. They are constructed of the stems of the elephant-grass, either in the shape of interlacing trellis-work or as vertical rods bound together by horizontal bundles. A reed-fence consists of a reed-screen suported by poles which are cut from green straight branches, and are driven into the ground at distances of ten feet from each other. The poles frequently strike root and flourish into trees, hence the pleasant leafy appearance of most of these fences.

Calling one day on the Kangao, one of the great Waganda chiefs, I saw a good illustration of the two styles of reed-fences side by side; and in the centre of the enclosure sat a prisoner "in the stocks," shredding with a knife strips of palm leaves into narrower strips preparatory to mat-making.

The punishment of being "in the stocks" consists in passing the foot through a hole bored through some heavy log of wood; a wooden peg is then hammered through, to narrow the aperture and to prevent the foot from being withdrawn. A pad of banana leaves is placed between the log and the ankle to prevent the cruel chafing which would otherwise result; and if the log is very heavy there is a rope attached to one end to enable the prisoner to support some of the weight with his hand.

A peculiarity of Waganda dwellings is the number of outer courts one has to pass through to arrive at the house itself. I once counted twelve of these outer courts. With the wealthier

IN THE STOCKS

classes each court has a hut which serves as a waiting-room for visitors. The number of the courts is more or less indicative of the rank of the individual.

The native hut in Uganda is a cone-shaped building, the grass-thatched roof of which reaches right down to the ground, except at the entrance where it is cut so as to leave a low narrow verandah. Very often the reed-fence of the enclosure meets the hut at the two sides, so that the front half of the

A WAGANDA FAMILY.

hut lies in one court and the second half in another. The heavy roof requires a strong support, and the many poles and pillars used for this object greatly diminish the available space inside the hut which is dark and smoke-stained.

The Waganda style of thatching is the best I have yet seen. The grass seems to lie so perfectly smooth; no rope is required to tie down the thatch which is a good protection against the rain, and only a strong gale could cause perceptible damage. The lower circle of thatch is first attached, then another over it but higher up, and so on to the top. The grass to be used for this purpose is tied first of all into small bundles about 4 or 5 inches thick. The thick end is cut straight; the bundle is held vertically, with the thick end uppermost, and is thumped three or four times against the ground. One would imagine this treatment would smash the thin ends of the grass, but it gives to the bundle the requisite flexibility to lie smoothly. A wisp of the grass in each bundle is twisted, and used as the rope by which the bundle is attached to the framework of the roof. With his stick the thatcher thumps the thatch into a smooth shape and sweeps off the loose grass. Wherever he detects a hollow he lifts the thatch with his stick, and inserts an additional bundle or two, which he does not even take the trouble to tie down, and yet they last perfectly well and do not slip out again.

The women wear the bark-cloth wrapped round the body; they pass it under the armpits, and not over the shoulder. Small children of both sexes go uncovered. Girls wear a curious grass-ring round the waist. If the ring is too loose and likely to slip off, it is upheld behind by a string from the neck.

The native chair or stool is cut out of a solid block of wood. It consists of a basin-shaped seat, a wide base, and a short stem connecting seat and base. In many huts a cradle-shaped trough is seen, cut out of a solid block of wood; this is used for squashing up bananas in the preparation of the native brew.

I have often heard it asserted that formerly a cow, a muzzle-loader, and a woman, were considered equal in value, and could be easily bartered or exchanged the one for the other. This of course has been put a stop to. Polygamy was the rule in Uganda, but when the Waganda became Christians, the men put aside their plurality of wives and retained but one each. The Protestant Prime Minister has only one wife now; I was told he had a couple of hundred before his conversion. I do not know what became of the discarded wives, whether they live as lonely widows, or whether they have in their turn consoled themselves by taking some one else as husband.

One of the useful local industries is mat-making, generally done by women or girls. They use the leaves of the makindo or wild date-palm. The mats are whitish-yellow, soft, clean, and cool. Narrow strips, 1½ to 2 inches broad, are first of all plaited; and the length and breadth of the mat depends on the length and number of the plaited strips sewn together. The illustration shows two girls sitting on a finished mat, busily plaiting long rolls of these strips. How fine and close the work is, can be gathered from the number of separate shreds in their hands in process of being plaited together. Each girl has by her side a bundle of the material wrapped up in a banana leaf.

Neither men nor women in Uganda wear ornaments; in this respect they present a striking contrast to their savage neigh-

WAGANDA MAT-MAKERS.

bours. Their wants are very simple, and the food supply is abundant, consequently they lead a very easy, comfortable, contented life. The food consists almost exclusively of "matoke," the name given to the national dish of green bananas, or rather plantains. These are peeled, placed in a pot with a small quantity of water, and covered over with folded green banana leaves, tightly packed over the mouth of the pot. When boiled through, the bananas are mashed up, wrapped in clean green banana leaves and are ready to be served. The women do the cooking; and as the English missionaries rather pride themselves on living on native food, most of them employ

Waganda women. The true banana is called "memvu," and is eaten ripe, as fruit. There is another sort of banana called "gonjia" by the Swahilies. It is twice the length of the ordinary banana, and is used when ripe. It is somewhat reddish inside, and is rather coarse when eaten raw; it is therefore usually served either plain-boiled, or else roasted in hot ashes; it has a sweet agreeable flavour, and is a favourite dish.

The bark-cloth tree is of national importance, as it supplies the material out of which native cloth is manufactured. More and more of the population are, however, adopting cotton cloth, hence the manufacture of bark-cloth is diminishing every year. The tree grows to a stately height, with a straight stem and a mass of waving branches. The small green leaves give a refreshing shade and are pleasant to the eye. The finest trees I saw in the province of Singo, where a good deal of the bark-cloth is manufactured. The bark is removed by two circular cuts round the stem of the tree and a vertical cut joining these two. The denuded surface is then carefully covered up, by wrapping dry banana-leaves round the stem. Unless this is done, a lot of rootlets grow from the upper circular cut; and whatever bark is ultimately grown is warped and useless. It takes a year or two for the tree to renovate the bark over the exposed surface; it is then stripped off again. The tree is very hardy, and almost any branch, cut off and planted, will spread and grow up into a tree. It is therefore most useful for producing a living stockade or fence.

If the piece of bark does not produce a cloth of the length required for the market, one or more strips are sewn together; and this is sometimes done so skilfully, that it is not easy to detect the portion added, unless the cloth is inspected very closely. In the same way, holes or rents are skilfully patched. The colour is usually a red-brown. Some bark-cloths have a geometrical pattern, but black-patterned bark-cloth went out of fashion before King Mtesa's days. It is now prepared principally to serve as an article of decoration.

The manufacture of bark-cloth is extremely simple. The bark is slightly moistened, placed over a smooth wooden log which serves as anvil, and is then hammered and flattened out by means of a wooden mallet. The head of the mallet resembles a small solid wheel, and is ribbed horizontally along

WAGANDA MU'ENGE-SELLERS

the outer circumference as seen in coins. This allows the hammered portion of the bark to expand laterally along the interstices between the ribbing. As the fibres of the bark intersect in every imaginable direction, it is comparatively easy for the operator to reduce it to a very soft and delicate texture. Skill is required to prevent holes being punched through. A good bark-cloth in 1894 used to cost 250 shells, that is, about 2s., but the value now is over 4s.

BARK-CLOTH MANUFACTURE.

A black-patterned one was recently sold at Kampala for £1. The Waganda ladies rather like the noisy rustle which heralds their approach when the bark-cloth is new and stiff; in this they resemble their European sisters who appreciate the "frou-frou" of silk clothing.

"Muenge" is the native fermented drink, made from the juice of the banana. It is brought to the market in large gourds, suggestive of the public appreciation of it. The gourds rest on the ground on a pad of dry banana-leaves, and often have a wreath of leaves round the neck to keep the fermenting liquor cool. The sellers squat by the side of their gourds, hold up small drinking bowls, and invite the thirsty passer-by to have a "nip" at a ha'penny or farthing per bowl.

Some of these small drinking bowls, made out of a tiny species of gourd, look uncommonly like tumblers or cups. As they are not flat-bottomed, they stand insecurely, and consequently if used for drinking out of, they have to be emptied. On the eve of my departure from Kampala, the Kangao made me a present of a pair of gourd-bowls of exquisitely delicate manufacture, which would rival the finest china. On arrival in

England my wife saw, admired, and annexed them; and now they are enthroned amongst her sacred knick-knacks!

Personally I do not care for "muenge." I dislike its sour taste and smell, though some Europeans rather like it.

"Mbisi" is the fresh unfermented banana juice. My Wahima boy frequently prepared this beverage for me. It resembles water with a flavour of bananas and sweetened, and yet no water has been added. He prepared it very easily. Soft ripe bananas were peeled and placed in an earthen bowl together with a handful of the long, lance-shaped, and sharp-edged leaves

WAGANDA SOAP-SELLERS.

of a very common kind of grass. The mass was crushed and kneaded with the fingers, till the banana pulp was reduced to a sort of water. The grass was then removed, the juice strained off, and the "mbisi" was ready for use. It is a pleasant, refreshing drink. If allowed to stand for a couple of days, it ferments and becomes the intoxicating "muenge." I met some missionaries in Nyassa-land, who made a drink like champagne from the juice of the banana. The trouble was to keep this banana champagne from bursting the bottles. The Waganda often add a handful of "matama" (Kaffre-corn) to their "mbisi" to accelerate the process of fermentation.

Native soap can be bought at Kampala on every market-day. It is very coarse, and in size resembles somewhat a cricket-ball, but it is lumpy. It is not suitable for toilet use, but does very well for laundry-work, though some say that it wears out the clothes more rapidly than English soap. That it can wash beautifully clean, is proved by the spotless white clothes worn by all the higher class of natives. It is fairly cheap, 25 shells per ball, that is, about twopence. The natives are aware of the superiority

WAGANDA POTTERS.

of the imported English soap, and would prefer to buy it, but that it is so very dear. The difficulty in the way of local soap-boiling is the scarcity of obtainable tallow or fat of any description.

Pottery in Uganda is still in its infancy. The three articles most commonly manufactured are the large open-mouthed bowls, used for cooking the native dish "matoke," the bomb-shaped pots for fetching water, and the black pipe-bowls. The vessel used for water is round like an ancient cannon-ball; it has a small aperture and a very short neck. The large semicircular bowl has a thick everted rim. In addition to the common clay which yields the ordinary brick-red pottery, black clay and white clay are found. From these the finest china could be manufactured, if some one who knows the process would start a local china-factory. The Waganda are clever at imitating any cup or saucer, candlestick or flower-vase, which a European chooses to submit to them as a model. These imitations are curious; but it would be a mistake to imagine that they are in common use in Uganda either among natives or among Europeans. There is a potters' settlement about half-an-hour's distance from Fort Kampala. Here I have watched the men at work. They did not use a potter's wheel. The vessel, resting on a soft pad of dry banana-leaves, was turned and shaped by hand. A sharp sherd was used to scrape off any superfluous clay. The rim of the large bowls was added separately in the shape of a long clay sausage. I saw only men employed as potters. They must have a deft hand, a quick eye, and considerable practice to turn out such good results without the assistance of even a potter's wheel. The bomb-shaped water-vessel costs about two or three pence; the large bowls are somewhat dearer. The pots are dried in the shade, and then burnt in a huge fire of elephant-grass and reeds. Very often this burning takes place right in the middle of the wide public road. The Waganda, like other African races, have their own special national variety of pipe. Men and women smoke. The Uganda clay-pipe has a long reed-stem and a short black triangular clay bowl running into a point downwards. It costs about a farthing. Occasionally pipes with coloured geometrical patterns in white and red are brought as curios for sale to Europeans; but I have never seen a native smoke one of these coloured fancy pipes. "Gabunga," the admiral in command of the king's fleet of war-canoes, came to me one day with two of these fancy-pipes which he wished to exchange for a short English pipe. Having effected the exchange, he went on his way rejoicing. The chiefs eagerly copy many of the little differences in habits which they notice between themselves and the English. In their heart, however, not a few of them resent having lost, owing to the presence of the British Government, their former uncontrolled authority.

One of the great chiefs, the Mulondo, told me that he had lost all control over his peasants, because he could no longer inflict punishments on them just as he pleased; and if he tried to insist on their doing a certain work for him, they simply left and migrated in a body to the plantations of some other chief. The Mulondo was not averse to doing a little "business" now and then, and selling to me, with protestations of friendship, some antelope skin at exactly double the price I would have had to pay for it elsewhere. He is dead now—died two years ago. A tall, handsome man he was, cunning, plausible, but in his heart against British rule in Uganda. One day he visited me accompanied by the usual crowd of sub-chiefs and followers. He sat on an English camp-chair, puffing at an English pipe, and he wore an English jacket; and it seemed odd to hear him glorifying those days of King Mtesa, when the European was still an unknown stranger in Uganda. It would certainly have been better for him to have treated Europeans, or at least European inventions, with greater circumspection. One day he wanted to

UPPER-CLASS WAGANDA.

shoot a big elephant. Powder is cheap, ivory dear. He jammed an elephant-gun half full of powder, rammed down a big bullet, and blazed off. I did not hear what fraction exactly of his arm was left. A missionary in Usoga sent an urgent message to Luba's for some one to come and tie up the artery, but in the meantime the Mulondo bled to death.

The king, chiefs, and upper-class Waganda have long ago discarded bark-cloth. They prefer to wear white or coloured cotton-cloth, either wrapped round the body in the same fashion that bark-cloth is worn, or else as a kanzu, the long white garment worn by Swahilies in Zanzibar and at Mombasa. When clean and white the kanzu is most becoming in a native.

Mohammedans like to superadd an unbuttoned waistcoat with crescent-shaped pockets and richly embroidered with silk, silver, or gold. Christians eschew the crescent-emblem of Islam faith, but are keen competitors for any old English waistcoat. Those who can afford it, add to their costume an English jacket, worn unbuttoned; in preference they select one of a plain dark material or of a light neat summer pattern. The Waganda have remarkably good taste, and wear nothing which the most fastidious European could call vulgar, either in colour or design. Another common form of dress is a short-sleeved, open-necked, thin white vest, and a coloured cloth wrapped round the waist and reaching below the knees.

The Waganda have not yet disfigured themselves by putting on European unmentionables, but I am afraid this is merely a matter of time. I have seen on certain grand occasions the Protestant Prime Minister sport a jacket which no doubt was meant to be very effective, swagger, and military, but goodness knows what "blend" of regiments it was supposed to represent. Mohammedans wear a red fez-cap or a strip of cloth twisted round the head like a turban. The higher classes of every creed have adopted this fashion. Some show themselves already in English travelling-caps. Apollo Katikiro, the Protestant Prime Minister, wanting no doubt to "go one better," has appeared in public in a soft felt hat or an imitation straw hat, the latter of native manufacture. He has not yet made the acquaintance of the refined and aristocratic silk hat. But hatters need not despair; there is no saying what may happen in Uganda in the future.

Uganda enjoys the unique blessing of having two Prime Ministers. Formerly there used to be only one; but as he was converted to Protestantism, the opposite faction clamoured to have also a Prime Minister, and have got him now, and he ranks next to the Protestant one. Mugwanya, the Roman Catholic Prime Minister of Uganda, is a fine-looking man, tall and proportionately broad. He usually dresses in white. He and all the great chiefs wear the sandals distinctive of their rank. These sandals are of bullock-hide and somewhat of an oblong saucer-shape. A strip of otter skin passes across the sandal and keeps it to the foot; a further support is gained by a strip of otter skin which forms a loop through which the great toe is passed.

When King Mwanga rebelled against the Government, his

infant son Chua, about two years old, was proclaimed king of Uganda and a council of regency was formed consisting of Apollo Katikiro, Mugwanya, and Zacharias Kangao. For though some of the Roman Catholic chiefs joined King Mwanga, Mugwanya remained loyal to the British rule. All the great chiefs live in houses which have an upper story, because King Mwanga one day issued a royal decree, that they were in

MUGWANYA, THE ROMAN CATHOLIC PRIME MINISTER OF UGANDA.

future to dwell in such houses and forthwith were to build them. Those who did not have the house ready by a certain date were heavily fined, the king of course pocketing the fine.

The "Kimbugwe," or "keeper of the royal umbilical cord," was one of the great chiefs, but the ridiculous title has fortunately been suppressed, in the same way that, instead of acknowledging thirty degrees of nobility, the Government have simplified the matter by acknowledging only the first four degrees as having a right to seats in the Great Council or legislative assembly of the nation. The Kimbugwe became the Kakunguru. He aspired to intermarry with royalty and married the sister of King Mwanga, for which the king made him pay extra heavy. The lady was under a cloud. It appears that some time previously she had taken a great fancy to some one, and that she employed a comely young handmaid to carry her amatory messages. What Shakespeare described hundreds of years ago in "Twelfth Night" as happening when Viola was sent to Olivia, happened in this case. The infuriated Princess wreaked a cruel vengeance on her handmaid.

I was invited to the Kakunguru's wedding. Both he and the Princess are stately figures of noble bearing. There was great feasting and merry-making. Drums and pipes were playing, oxen, sheep, and goats had been slaughtered to provide for the multitude of guests. The expense must have been enormous. Some of the missionaries were present, and in accordance with native courtesy their plates were loaded to an extent that a score of hungry men could not have devoured. Native etiquette makes it obligatory to eat the whole of the enormous helping; but it fortunately provides also for overcoming the difficulty by permitting mouthfuls being distributed to followers. One missionary silently but rapidly emptied his plate by feeding loyal but hungry converts.

WAGANDA MUSICIANS.

The most common musical instruments are the drum and the pipe. The pipe is cut either from a reed or from the slender stem of a bamboo. The upper end is notched, and becomes the mouthpiece. There are four circular holes placed in a row along the lower half of the pipe. The tune is an endless repetition of the same few notes. The drum is carved out of a hollow cylinder of wood; both ends are covered with leather fastened together with twisted strips of hide. It is carried slung from the neck by means of a leather strap. It is most commonly beaten with the fingers, but if the drum is very large, drumsticks are used.

There is another musical instrument, the Uganda harp; but I have only once seen it played in public. It was at the Christmas festivities last year at Masindi in Unyoro, when one of our Waganda allies produced it and played on it. It was a very poor performance, the fault of the player I should say, and not of the instrument. A good many of these harps are sold to the ever eager curio-collector. The wooden bowl is somewhat similar to the Kavirondo harp, but the sound-aperture is nearer the middle. There is only one wooden stick fastened to the bowl, instead of two as in the Kavirondo harp. This stick curves upward, and carries eight pegs, to which the eight strings are fastened. By screwing up the peg, the cord can be tightened as required.

In the punitive expedition against the Wakitosh, the Kakunguru was the general of the Waganda army which numbered over 6000. His wife, the princess, accompanied him to the war, and marched along on foot through fair weather and foul; she was accompanied by a large following of female servants.

There used to be at Kampala a "jinrikshaw," sent up on spec. by some English firm at the Coast. No one wanted to buy it, so it lay for a long time in the Government store. One day the Kakunguru and the Katikiro came to enquire about it. I happened to be in charge of the Fort, and I referred the matter to the Acting Commissioner who sent back word respecting the minimum price that the firm had fixed for the sale of the vehicle. Day after day these two chiefs came and examined the jinrikshaw, pulling it about the courtyard of the Fort. One day the Kakunguru decided finally to buy it and accepted the price mentioned by the Acting Commissioner. He and the Katikiro, both of them heavy men, thereupon got into the jinrikshaw, some scores of men pulled in front and pushed behind, and on throwing the gates of the Fort open for them to pass, they dashed away down Kampala hill full tilt. I said to myself, I wonder how long any vehicle would stand such treatment, but I did not expect the catastrophe to come so soon. Within half-an-hour one man came to the Fort carrying the shafts of the jinrikshaw, another the wheels, and so on, a mass of splintered wood. Then the Kakunguru arrived and solemnly informed me that he had decided not to buy the jinrikshaw. I told him the matter rested with the Commissioner and not with me, but I refused to allow him to leave the broken rubbish at the Fort. At the same time I told him, that as he had examined it day after day, had agreed to buy it, and had taken it away,

UGANDA HARP.

I felt pretty certain he would have to pay for it, especially as it was now smashed to pieces. When I had received instructions to insist on the payment, I found the Kakunguru, although a wealthy man, very slippery to deal with. First he professed he had no ivory, and requested time to send men to shoot an elephant; this being refused, he pleaded for time, two to three months, to send round to all his friends to beg them to lend him some ivory. All this time he had it ready, and was only "trying it on." Finally he paid up, but the trouble he gave me has served me for a lesson. At that time Government courteously permitted chiefs to purchase various articles out of the Government store. All this was, of course, stopped as soon as European firms sent up their representatives to Kampala and opened stores.

On the march through Singo I came upon another form of drum besides the one already described. It consisted of a sort of pedestal, or cylinder of wood, with a piece of lizard-skin stretched over the top of it. A small boy carried it under his left arm, but it was supported by a strap of leather passed over the shoulders.

The Waganda like to do their work to the sound of drums and in company with others. In this way they work ever so much better and quicker. On the march through Singo we had an illustration of it. The courteous sub-chief, where we had camped, sent word over-night to all the villages around, that men were wanted to construct a bridge next morning across a very long and dangerous swamp which we had to pass over. Crowds of villagers came, and I learned something new, when I saw how they proceeded to form a bridge. They cut a wide path right through the papyrus which was standing 6 to 10 feet high above the surface of the water. The stems of the papyrus were cut off close to the water, and thrown in interlacing masses upon the stumps of the papyrus plants. The advantage of selecting the thickest

UGANDA DRUMS.

and densest papyrus growth was obvious, since the papyrus plants had there the strongest hold on the bottom of the swamp and thus offered a firmer support to the superimposed weight. Another reason was that a greater quantity of papyrus stems could be cut for constructing the foot-bridge, and there was less chance of coming upon open patches of water too wide to be spanned. Across this novel form of bridge the whole of my caravan passed, practically dry-foot; and there I came upon the drummers, two little lads, banging away without intermission on their small drums. A man was sitting by and preparing out of split papyrus reeds a tiny fish-basket for capturing the small fish found in these swamps.

Waganda labourers are frequently seen carrying some chopper or axe. The native chopper is a broad-bladed knife, stuck into the thick end of a club-shaped handle. It is an excellent instrument for clearing fields of reeds, shrubs, and bushes. It is not as useful for chopping hard wood as the native axe which is fixed to a similar club-shaped handle, but at right angles to the handle. The blade of the native axe is very small, and yet

WAGANDA LABOURERS.

it can fell the strongest and thickest trees. Another common instrument is a small spear-shaped iron jammed on to a stick; it is used for digging holes for the poles of fences and stockades.

A favourite way with the native labourers of carrying their pipe is to pass it through the shoulder-knot of their bark-cloth garment.

The Uganda shield is cut out of a solid block of wood, though its appearance conveys the impression that it consists of two halves formed by two symmetrical segments of circles, meeting at an angle of 120°, and joined together along their arc. The central conical boss of wood is left uncovered, but the rest of the shield is covered by coloured strips of twisted hide.

These shields appear to be exclusively manufactured for the European curio-hunter, for I have never seen a single one used in warfare, though we had thousands of armed Waganda in the Wakitosh and Wakilelowa expeditions. Such of our allies as did carry shields preferred to use either the Usoga wicker-shield or the Kavirondo one of bullock-hide. There can be little doubt that the Uganda shield, from an artistic point of view, is superior; and when new it makes a handsome wall-ornament.

The kingdom of Uganda had already in King Mtesa's days some form of constitutional government; but as there was no written language in existence to record legislative enactments, it is obvious that an autocratic tyrant could easily over-ride any restrictions placed on his authority. Death and mutilation were punishments the king could inflict at pleasure. Human life was of little account.

When I was in charge of Kampala, Mwanga was king of Uganda. One of the missionaries told me, that before the British occupation of Uganda King Mwanga one day put to death over twenty of his gate-keepers under the following circumstances. A guest, leaving the royal enclosure on Mengo hill, was pushed by one of the gate-keepers, and at once returned and complained of it to the king who thereupon ordered not only the particular gate-keeper, but *all* the gate-keepers to be put to death. Mwanga had learnt his despotic creed from his father, King Mtesa.

Reading the story of Speke in my younger days, where he intercedes with the king for the life of a woman, the picture which represented the scene made a lasting impression on me. King Mtesa gave a sort of picnic to Speke, and when his favourite wife plucked some fruit and presumed to offer it to her lord and master, the king ordered her to be put to death. The king's executioners were a number of small boys who wore a rope twisted round the head. At a sign from the king they used this rope to strangle their victim. The unfortunate woman called out for help, and Speke, horror-struck, pleaded for her life. The king, amused that a white man should care for a black woman's life, gave her on the spot a present to him.

Since then Mtesa has passed away, and all his blood-thirsty brood of sons are gone; but Mtesa's tomb still stands. It is on the top of a hill about twenty minutes from Fort

Kampala. The tomb, a cone-shaped building, is of considerable height. The grass-thatched roof nearly touches the ground, except at the entrance, where a narrow verandah is formed. A large number of props and pillars support the roof. From the entrance a colonnade, about six feet wide, leads to Mtesa's grave at the farther end. The pillars which support the lofty roof are the straight stems of the makindo or wild date-palm. All the pillars near the grave are covered with bark-cloth. The

MTESA'S TOMB.

interior of the hut is strewn with soft grass laid down parallel with almost mathematical precision. It gives one the idea of walking on a thick carpet instead of simply on loose grass. The grass is piled so thick that every footfall is deadened. Gloom and silence guard the grave of the blood-stained tyrant. Brass spears rail it off in front, a chequered cloth with alternate blue and white squares screens it behind, and on each side hangs a brass shield, of which the left-hand one has a lot of tiny brass-bells along the lower edge. In the centre of the row of spears is a curious piece of brass of fantastic native design. A square mound of hard dry clay a foot high is raised over the spot where Mtesa lies buried. In walking up to the railing my foot naturally displaced a few blades of the dry grass. At once

THE WAGANDA

an attendant hurriedly restored them to mathematical order. The tomb is surrounded in a wide semicircle by a number of huts, erected for the use of Mtesa's widows who were constituted keepers of the tomb. Some royal estates were set aside to supply them with the necessaries of life. There cannot be many of them living at the present day. I was introduced to one; she had a pleasant face, and the wool on her head was quite white.

Now and then one is reminded of something analogous in the Uganda of the present day and England in an early stage of its development. The peasants were serfs, practically slaves; Colonel Colville, by the simple declaration that the status of slavery is not acknowledged in Uganda, abolished slavery and all its evils. Of course one knows that every Soudanese household has a number of slaves, and should any of these complain of ill-treatment or express a desire to leave their master or mistress, practical effect is given to the Colonel's, now historic, declaration. On the other hand, there is no uncalled for interference with any man's household.

The royal family of Uganda is of Wahima blood. According to tradition, the Wahima are the aborigines

IN A WAHIMA KRAAL.

of Uganda; but when they were conquered and deprived of their wealth which consisted of vast herds of cattle, they voluntarily offered to serve their new masters as herdsmen. The Wahima are a fine race, what I saw of them; above the average height, with an intelligent oval face and only slightly flattened nose. To see them at their best the traveller should see them at work on their pasture-lands. I came across them in Singo. None of them wore the bark-cloth garment of the Waganda. Some had on a cotton cloth thrown like a mantle over the upper part of the body. It left the arms free and reached as far as the knees. But more often the covering was a cow-hide knotted over one shoulder. The men carried spears, apparently their only weapon. This spear differs from the Uganda spear in having a shorter blade and a shorter shaft. The married women looked ghastly scarecrows, the way they had got themselves up. They wore a good many bead, iron, and brass ornaments. Into their short woolly hair they had plaited all sorts of trinkets, coloured beads, shells, seeds, and bits of wood. The head and body were dripping with rancid butter, and the cloth or skin they wore was one mass of dirt and grease. They were so completely covered up, that only the head was left visible. Most of the girls in the kraal were naked, but not the least bit shy of the white stranger. They seemed a merry, healthy, well-formed lot; but there was not one amongst them that could have been called good-looking. They crowded round me to have a good look at me; perhaps I was the first white man they had ever seen.

As the Wahima are herdsmen, they are nomadic. This probably accounts for the miserable structures they had erected to serve as temporary huts. Out and out it was the humblest attempt at a dwelling I have yet seen, differing as much from a European's conception of a home as the eagle's nest of a few sticks from the weaver-bird's elaborate structure. The hut consisted of a few bent twigs covered over with rubbish, sticks, rank weeds, grass, and perhaps a bullock-hide spread out over the top. The entrance was so low, that even the little girls had to crawl to get in or out; to see a tall man crawling in was a ludicrous sight, reminding one of a long-legged spider. I did not inspect the interior, for though I was travel-stained, there are degrees and limits also to the soiling of one's clothes. The village was more or less circular, but quite unprotected; a proof that the Wahima were not living in fear of either man or wild beast. Outside the kraal there were two huge mounds of cow-dung, dried and caked by the sun; these seemed to be favourite places of meeting of the male population.

The cattle these men were pasturing were magnificent animals, the largest I have seen. Almost every animal might have figured among prize-cattle at an English cattle-show. A peculiarity was the enormous length and width of the horns. Cattle-farming in Uganda, whether for meat extract, horn, bone-ash, or leather, should hold out lucrative prospects to European intelligence and enterprise.

The calves were not allowed to accompany the herds when they went out grazing, but were looked after by the boys and kept near the village. Wherever it was difficult for the herd to get to the water, the streamlet running perhaps in a steep ravine, the herdsmen had erected clay troughs and filled these with water by means of their milking pails. At other spots there were green-wood fires burning feebly and slowly, but emitting dense volumes of smoke. The cattle knew what this was meant for. They hustled each other to get into the stream

WAHIMA HERDSMEN.

of the smoke, where it rolled slowly and heavily over the plain, in order to escape the persecution of the innumerable swarms of flies and stinging insects.

There are several species of these flies; they also attacked the natives. I saw one of the little girls slap her thigh, and, where a fly had just stung her, a big drop of blood oozed out; these troublesome flies can therefore give a very nasty prick, but the child did not seem to mind the pain. I was not stung on this occasion, but some of my caravan were, and they certainly did not bear the infliction with the same equanimity. Sometimes on the march, especially in showery weather, the flies become a great nuisance. I have killed them, almost as soon as they had settled on my neck or hands, and yet the smarting sensation which accompanied the sting would be followed by a blain or a boil. Another sort of fly used to attack my donkey and made it so restless, that I had to stop and search for the tormentor.

The large herds of cattle I saw in Singo belonged originally to King Mwanga, but were seized by the Government, when the king rebelled. They are now being taken care of by Wahima herdsmen for the Government.

In certain parts of Uganda a good deal of sugar-cane is grown, but the natives do not seem to know how to utilise it except for chewing. Some of the Arab traders now and then crush a small amount of cane and boil down the juice to a treacle, but nobody has ever attempted the manufacture of sugar in Uganda. I have lived for many years in the sugar-growing colony of Mauritius; I know, therefore, that mere size does not prove the superiority of one species of cane over another. To judge, however, by the size of the Uganda sugar-cane which was offered for sale to my porters almost in every village in Singo along the caravan route, the production must be very cheap. Canes over ten feet long were sold for a halfpenny, shorter ones for a farthing; and, as far as I could judge, the juice was extremely rich in sugar. I saw thousands of acres of virgin soil, suitable for sugar plantations and lying unclaimed.

When Mtesa died, there was a struggle among his sons for the throne of Uganda. They appear to have had about as much affection for each other as the sons of William the Conqueror. Kiwewa was king of Uganda for a few weeks, when his brother Karema managed to seize him and, tying him to one of the pillars inside one of the Waganda huts of reeds and grass, put fire to the structure. There was not much left of Kiwewa at the end of this brotherly bonfire. But Karema thought he might as well clear off all his brothers whilst he was about it. All fell into his hands except Mwanga, his youngest brother, who escaped from Uganda and found a refuge at the south end of Lake Victoria Nyanza. Karema dug a deep pit, tied his brothers to stakes in it, starved them to death, and then filled up the pit. He did not however reign very long; he was carried off by small-pox on his way to wage war against Unyoro.

King Kiwewa left a son, the young Roman Catholic Prince

Augustine of Uganda. King Karema left two sons, half-brothers to each other; one fell into the hands of the Mohammedans and is the young Mohammedan Prince Ramazan of Uganda, the other was brought up by the French missionaries and is the young Roman Catholic Prince Joseph of Uganda. These two, Princes Augustine and Joseph, are very simply dressed in a long white garment, known as a "kanzu," and a red fez-cap. They wear a small silver cross hanging from a silver chain. When I saw them, Prince Augustine happened to fold his hands, and the silver cross accidentally fell across them. Under this emblem of the Christian faith, in distant Uganda, the young Princes have buried the family blood-feud. Though cousins, they are more like brothers to each other; and no one can foretell what day the one or the other may

THE ROMAN CATHOLIC PRINCES AUGUSTINE AND JOSEPH OF UGANDA.

be called upon to ascend the throne of his ancestors. The royal family of Uganda consists at present of ex-King Mwanga, ex-King Mbogo, the baby-King Chua, and the Princes Ramazan, Augustine, and Joseph. Mbogo has a child, the Princess Fatima, but as Salic law governs the succession, neither she nor various other princesses of the older line have any claim whatever to the throne.

On my third journey to Uganda I was requested by the Government to take ex-King Mbogo with his family and followers along with me from Mombasa. Lugard in his historical book relates how the Mohammedan party in Uganda had proclaimed Mbogo king, and how he managed to end the civil war by getting Mbogo to abdicate in favour of Mwanga. To prevent a fresh outbreak of hostilities, the Government had removed Mbogo to the coast. Here he became homesick, and petitioned to be sent back to Uganda. As there appeared to be no reason to fear any further trouble his request was granted.

To take ex-King Mbogo along with me was easier said than done, and I had a pretty lively time of it from start to finish. He had a dozen wives, and with his followers he numbered sixty souls. The wants of all had to be anticipated and provided for. Then one hitch after another arose and had to be overcome. The Government had fixed the number of porters he was to be allowed; thereupon he informed me that his followers one and all had refused to carry any sort of load on the journey. It was no use to try and reason with him, that Government had fixed the number and was not likely to treble it in order to gratify the laziness of his followers. Mbogo was obstinate; his men were servants, he declared, not slaves. For a while I did not know how to get on, then an inspiration came. I told Mbogo that there was no help for it, but we would have to dismiss all his servants who refused to work, and that not one of them would be allowed to accompany my caravan. I asked for a list of the names, in order that I might stop at once the daily allowance of food issued to them by the Government, and compel them to earn their food where and how they liked. In less than half-an-hour Mbogo professed to have ascertained that every one of his followers was most willing to carry a light load, rather than be left at Mombasa or have his food allowance stopped. Fortunately Mbogo did not know that the Government did not want any of his followers on any account to be left behind at Mombasa.

Other similar trivial matters, and yet sufficient to prevent the caravan from moving, were of constant occurrence, but by good luck I managed to get over them. The following may serve as an illustration. As we were about to start from Mombasa, I saw that a poor little boy had been given a weight of over 70 lbs. to carry, and some of Mbogo's favourites, big strapping fellows, had already passed with trifling bundles of 10 lbs. weight. Every caravan leader knows what it means when porters break down on the march, and here was a boy given by Mbogo to carry 70 lbs. for the next 800 miles. I at once stopped the caravan, and made each of Mbogo's men bring his load to be weighed at the Government store, and I increased or decreased it as experience dictated. I had no further trouble on this score, though it delayed the caravan at the time for a few hours.

Even with trained porters it is not always easy to keep the men from straggling, but the first few days of the march Mbogo's women made precious hard work for me. On some

EX-KING MBOGO, PRINCESS FATIMA, AND PRINCE RAMAZAN OF UGANDA.

excuse or other they would drop out of the ranks; and they never cared how far it might be to the next camp, but would lie down under the first convenient shady tree and fall fast asleep. By the time I had reached camp, I would find some of these ladies missing, and I had the pleasure of going back for them.

The day I camped at Maji Chumvi, I had a curious experience. I passed Count Teleki's camp on the road, and stopped to have a chat, while waiting for stragglers. When I did reach my camp, I found two of Mbogo's wives missing. I went back to look for them, and had to walk some miles beyond Teleki's camp before I found them comfortably asleep under a tree. They declared they were unable to move owing to stomach-ache. Two of my men supported the one, myself and another Askari supported the other woman. On passing Teleki's camp for the third time, I stopped and asked him for some brandy to administer to these women. I then sent some men on to fetch my own riding-donkeys to carry these women to my camp. Teleki, seeing how tired I was, brought his camp bedstead out, and most kindly insisted on my lying down. The moment I did so, I fell sound asleep. The arrival of the donkeys woke me. I tried to help the two ladies to get on the donkeys, when to my surprise I found that both were helplessly drunk.

I naturally attributed the effect to the brandy, though it seemed unaccountable it should have had such an effect. I felt sorry that Teleki witnessed their condition. One of these ladies we tied on to the donkey to prevent her rolling off, and sent her thus to Mbogo, accompanied by some of his men; but the second one was too far gone. Two men had to carry her, whilst I walked by their side. Teleki tried hard to keep me at his camp for the night, and very kindly offered to put me up; but the unfortunate condition of these women made it doubly necessary to see them safe to their husband's tent.

Next day Count Teleki and I camped together at Samburu, and the mystery of the drunken condition of the two women was explained. It appears that whilst I slept, the two went to Teleki and intimated that the brandy had almost stopped their suffering but not quite. He thought he might as well repeat the dose; but every few minutes they applied for another dose, till they were too drunk to come for more. Both of them had a splitting headache next day, but—*mirabile dictu*—they never suffered again from stomach-ache on the journey.

It was on this journey that I found one of the Uganda wooden spears very helpful in marching along, a sort of pilgrim's staff. The Waganda double-edged fighting spear has a rather long blade, longitudinally grooved on each side. The wooden spear is usually over six feet long and terminates in a very sharp point; its other end is tipped with iron, to stick the spear into the ground when not required. The wood made use of for the manufacture of these spears is remarkaby tough and strong, and yet extremely light.

Ex-King Mbogo and I became fast friends, long before the journey had ended; and though some years have passed, he generally honours me with a visit when I go to Kampala, where he is now settled on Nakasero hill. He behaved sensibly and well during the Soudanese mutiny; for the mutineers wrote to him and offered to make him king of Uganda. Mbogo not only promptly declined the offer, but advised them in the strongest terms to return at once to their allegiance to the British Govern-

UGANDA SPEARS.

ment. Had he accepted, the whole of the Mohammedan faction in Uganda would have gone over to the mutineers. His stay at Zanzibar has no doubt considerably enlarged his views regarding the might of the British Empire. He is a strict Mohammedan; and every Friday (the Mohammedan equivalent of the Christian's Sunday) a Mohammedan service is held at his residence, and Swahilies, Arabs, and other Mohammedans flock to it in large numbers. He affects Mohammedan dress. To his native royal bearing he has added some of the Arab polish from Zanzibar. He presents a striking contrast in every respect to the vile and shifty ex-King Mwanga.

CHAPTER IX.

AT KAMPALA.

A NATIVE FISH-CREEL.

THE king of Uganda resides on a hill called "Mengo," and for this reason some call the capital of Uganda Mengo.

Kampala hill was obtained by Lugard as a concession from King Mwanga, and upon it he built his famous fort, thereby laying the foundation-stone of British supremacy in Uganda. The increased and increasing staff of Government officials, the large building in which the legislative native council hold their "baraza" or parliamentary proceedings, the Soudanese market, the busy Swahili settlement, show that Kampala has now acquired a wider sense. In the same way that London has gradually absorbed adjoining districts, Kampala has absorbed Nakasero and other hills.

Kampala, used in the wider sense, is the capital of Uganda and the heart of the Uganda Protectorate, causing its administrative influence to be felt far and near.

In 1894 the officer in command at Kampala had to be invalided to the coast, and Her Majesty's Acting Commissioner selected me as the temporary successor, pending the arrival of some newly-appointed administrative officers. During the four and a half months I held the appointment I was absolutely single-handed, and had to perform all the duties which now are subdivided amongst quite a number of officers and clerks. I had to combine administrative, military, and medical duties; I had to act as magistrate and as commandant; I had charge of the prison and of the police; I was paymaster and postmaster; I was collector and registrar; I was store-keeper and bookkeeper; in fact, I had to carry on by myself the whole of the Government machinery at Kampala, and I had not a single clerk, black or white, to assist me. For a fortnight I was under my predecessor, in order to get an insight into local affairs and "to learn the ropes." The day before I left Port Alice to enter upon my new duties at Kampala, I received my final instructions from Her Majesty's Acting Commissioner. My endeavour whilst temporarily in office, I might sum up: as upholding British prestige and authority, and maintaining friendly relations with King Mwanga and all the great Waganda chiefs, Protestant and Roman Catholic. Lugard and my other predecessors at

KAMPALA SEEN FROM NAKASERO HILL.

Kampala have proved that King Mwanga and his chiefs were a handful to manage, and since I handed over these administrative duties to my successor, King Mwanga and some of the great chiefs have rebelled and caused bloodshed.

The view from Nakasero hill shows Kampala hill in the foreground and beyond it the saddle-shaped hill of Namirembe. The village on Kampala hill is the Swahili settlement, which, with the Acting Commissioner's permission, I laid out. The road, seen in the illustration to lead up to Fort Kampala, I made, superintending its construction in person. It has evidently supplied a want, for it has since been continued over Nakasero hill, and right on to meet the great caravan road from Kampala to the Nile, known as the Usoga Road. Till the

Swahili settlement was laid out, with roads intersecting each other at right angles, it was a horribly filthy place, rendered dangerously insanitary by Swahili caravans camping there temporarily with their Manyema and Wanyamwezi porters who defiled every foot of ground around the camp. The place was a standing menace to the community, and it was with a medical officer's eye that I saw the urgent need of reform.

Her Majesty's Acting Commissioner for Uganda at the time was Colonel Colville, now Sir Henry Colville, K.C.M.G., C.B. Holding the supreme authority in the land, upon his yes or no depended the carrying into effect of every measure. He approved of my plans, allowed me full scope to work them out, and strengthened my hands by the weight of his supreme authority.

With his consent I laid out the village, cutting straight wide roads, pulling down trumpery grass-huts and tumble-down shanties wherever their presence interfered with the road-making, subdividing the land into small holdings, and allotting these to respectable applicants at a nominal rent on condition of observing certain sanitary rules, viz., erecting suitable constructions for the sanitary requirements of their household, and keeping the public road, as far as their particular holding was concerned, clean and free of weeds.

The village community, consisting principally of Arab and Swahili ivory traders, thoroughly approved of these various measures. The last time I arrived at Kampala from the coast, quite a number of these traders came to greet me and to shake hands. It was pleasant to find I was still kindly remembered by them, though some years had elapsed since the Colonel's temporary successor relegated me to my original medical appointment.

The ivory exported from Uganda is either elephant ivory or hippo ivory, but the latter is considerably cheaper because all the tusks are comparatively small, and the finest and heaviest tusks of the hippopotamus lose in value because they are curved into a semicircle. Even elephant ivory to be valuable must be of a size sufficiently large to allow of the manufacture of billiard balls. As might be imagined, America is the best market for ivory. The traders have several names to designate the different qualities; the very best is known as "baboo-uleia," and the next quality is "baboo-ketsh"; anything inferior is scarcely worth exporting, as the expense of transport over 800 to 1000 miles instead of leaving a profit would probably entail a loss.

It requires considerable experience to be a good ivory buyer; I have known what appeared to me a fine and valuable tusk to be pronounced worthless owing to an almost imperceptible notch at the very tip. This, I was told, was a sure sign that a split existed right through the very centre of the tusk. A purchaser expending £100 on such a tusk might not be able to sell it again for 100 shillings.

Kampala is essentially a city built on hills: Kampala hill, with Fort Kampala on its summit, with the various Government offices, and with the Swahili settlement on one side; Mengo hill, with the residences of the king of Uganda and of several of the great chiefs; Namirembe hill, with the Protestant Cathedral and the Church

ARAB AND SWAHILI IVORY TRADERS.

Mission Society's Station; Rubaga hill, with the Roman Catholic Cathedral, and a settlement of the French Algerian Mission; Nakasero hill, with the European traders and the Soudanese village; and on another hill Bishop Hanlon has erected an English Roman Catholic establishment.

Between Namirembe hill and Kampala hill there lies a small plain. It is one of the concessions secured by Lugard. There was no direct road leading from Fort Kampala to Namirembe hill. I decided to construct one. It has proved useful; my road only led across the plain to the foot of the hill, but my successor has continued it right up as far as the shoulder. The open space between the two hills I proposed to utilise as a public recreation ground; one of the four roads which delimit it exists from Lugard's day, the other three I made. When the arrangements for holding on it the first sports were nearly complete, the Acting Commissioner was taken seriously ill and had to be invalided to the coast. I was ordered to accompany him, and my administrative duties at Kampala ended.

The recreation ground, however, still exists; and the last time I arrived at Kampala a vigorous game of football was going on, white men and niggers taking part in it. I have always understood football to be a game for the younger generation. Cricket we know can be played up to mature age, as proved by the present cricket-king in England. It was, therefore, highly interesting and amusing to watch the Namirembe Archdeacon footing it with the youngest. While the Acting Commissioner, the Judge, and myself, were looking on and watching the game with interest, one of the younger officials got a bad kick and sprawled on the ground. Fortunately no bones were broken. He was carried by sympathising friends to his house, and for a while he had to give up football and also Government duty. A few days later, I had to attend another who had ricked his knee at football; he too went off Government duty for some days. But these little mishaps did not deter the Namirembe Venerable!

To the right of the recreation ground, and separated from it by one of the roads which I constructed in 1894, lies the native market with its half-dozen huts.

Another market, known as the Soudanese market, is just at the foot of Kampala hill. The white flour offered for sale in baskets or open grass-platters looks very tempting, but when used for baking produces a dark-brown crumbly bread. This white flour is not wheat-flour, but either mohindi (maize), or matama (Kaffre-corn), or mohogo (casava), or disi (banana). Banana-flour is made by peeling green plantains, cutting them lengthways down the middle, drying them in the sun, and then pounding them into flour. There does not seem to be very much nourishment in it.

The police force at Kampala originated in 1894 during my short tenure of administrative duty. A trivial incident, a Soudanese soldier arresting a Wahima herdsman for causing disturbance in the native market, drew attention to the fact of there being no special department of police. I submitted to

AT KAMPALA

the Acting Commissioner the advisability of establishing such a staff as a distinct and separate body. The scheme was sanctioned, and as a preliminary experiment the Colonel approved of twenty men being appointed. Some simple rules were drawn up, the men selected, and the police force came into existence. At first Soudanese soldiers were chosen; but now Waganda are employed, probably owing to the mutiny and the disarming of the Soudanese at Kampala. The present uniform is white, with dark blue putties, and a red cloth turban, one end of which is allowed to hang down the back. The men are armed with the Government rifle, and wear a light brown leather cartridge-belt. They also act as prison-warders.

KAMPALA POLICE.

The administration of justice in Uganda is based on the treaty with King Mwanga, under which the British Government assumed the responsibility of a Protectorate over the kingdom. The African Order in Council and the Brussels Act of International Law regarding sale of spirits or rifles to natives guide the judicial decision in other matters.

One of the latest improvements in administrative expansion was the appointment of a barrister-at-law, Mr. Collinson, as legal adviser to the Government. All judicial decisions above a certain penalty have to be submitted to the High Court of Bombay; and *a fortiori* no sentence of death can be carried out by the Government without the sanction of the High Court.

The king of Uganda has his own native court of justice; he has no right to try any but his own subjects; consequently matters in connection with aliens of every description, whether European, Swahili, Soudanese, Lendu, Indian, or Armenian, cannot be tried in the king's native court. The king's court may, however, pass a sentence of death upon Waganda, and may order such sentence to be carried out without reference to the court at Bombay. Accordingly, three Waganda murderers were hanged not very long ago. I was not called upon to be present at the execution to pronounce whether life was extinct. One of the young officials was entrusted with seeing that the arrangements at the gallows were in order. He came to me and wanted me to tell him where the knot should be applied,

A CHAIN-GANG AT KAMPALA.

and what distance should be allowed for the drop. As I have never been a hangman, and do not aspire to such an office, I declined to discuss the subject; but when I was urged on the plea of humanity, I reluctantly told my interrogator, to enable him to perform his unenviable work expeditiously, what I had read or heard about this gruesome subject.

One of the forms of punishment made use of by the Government is the "chain-gang," which means hard labour.

The number of convicts in a chain-gang depends on the length of the chain. An iron ring is placed round the neck of each, and the chain is then passed through the two eyelets of the ring. One end of the chain is secured by a large iron ring, the other end by a padlock. The neck-ring consists of two separate halves which move on a fixed pivot at the back and carry each an eyelet in front.

On my first journey to Uganda we had a strange incident at Kabras in connection with a chain-gang. The Swahili in charge of it hit upon the plan of doing wholesale robbery by utilising his own gang of prisoners for the job. Apparently he foraged pretty successfully, judging by a couple of fowls, a lot of sweet-potatoes, some ground-nuts, and other items produced. Our caravan leader heard of it, stretched out the culprit, gave him some lashes, and then added him to the chain-gang. The stolen goods were confiscated, and a new warder was appointed to take charge of the prisoners, now increased in number by the addition of the former warder.

One of the cases I had to try at Kampala in 1894 was a curious repetition of Potiphar's wife *versus* Joseph. The lady in question was a princess, save the mark! of the royal family of Uganda. Joseph was represented by a headman named Musa. The lady in this instance also produced a garment, belonging to Musa, and she very nearly landed her Joseph in prison. Musa gave a straightforward account, and said that a fishmonger was present at the scene, of whom he bought some fish which he gave to the princess. Questioned about the fish, the princess declared she herself had bought it and had handed it to her handmaid, a slave-attendant, who was prepared to swear to anything her mistress had stated. Luckily for Musa the fishmonger was found, brought to the court, identified all the parties concerned, and proved Joseph's—I mean Musa's—story to be true. As this case involved a princess, the Prime Minister and a number of the great Waganda chiefs were present at the trial and concurred in the decision. I heard afterwards that the princess was a woman of extremely shady morals.

A native fishmonger is a singular sight; as a rule, the fish he offers for sale are about the size of small sardines, dried in the sun and strung in rows. One row costs a penny and contains about a dozen fish.

In another case I had to try, one of King Mwanga's wives

was the accused. This good lady coveted some trumpery iron ornaments worn by a Lendu woman, and deeming herself safe in her exalted position, she assaulted and robbed the Lendu woman on the high-road. Two Lendu men hearing the screams came to the assistance of the maltreated woman, but were set upon by a number of Waganda and badly handled. The three Lendu came to the Fort to report the matter and to be treated. One of the men had one of his thumbs split open

A FISHMONGER.

and so injured that I had to amputate a portion. The woman's back was streaming with blood. The charming creature who had thus enforced her royal wishes was summoned to the Fort; naturally she refused to come, and took refuge in King Mwanga's so-called palace. I informed the king that his royal spouse was "wanted" on a serious charge of highway robbery with violence. He replied that he was most anxious to assist the Government, but unfortunately he was unable to find the lady in his enclosure. Thanking him for the assistance he had offered, I intimated, that it within half-an-hour the accused did not arrive at the Fort, I should send a strong body of armed Soudanese to assist his majesty in a thorough search.

The lady was sent immediately, but accompanied by a mighty following of all the great chiefs, from the Protestant Prime Minister downwards. When the charge was thoroughly proved and the great chiefs had concurred that the accused was guilty, I asked the Prime Minister what sentence in his opinion should be passed on the woman. To this he gave the evasive answer, "She is a queen; she is King Mwanga's wife." Those who know what is meant by "shauries" with Waganda, can picture the wearisome discussion which followed for hours, the chiefs admitting that the woman was guilty, but declining to pass a sentence on her because she was a queen and King Mwanga's wife; ultimately a sentence of three months imprisonment was passed, and confirmed by Her Majesty's Acting Commissioner.

The Lendu women at Kampala in 1894 went practically naked but for a covering of leaves in the Makraka fashion. They too are benefitting by the British occupation of the country. This can be seen in the illustration of a Lendu mother with her baby. She and her husband accompanied my caravan from Kampala to Luba's on my last journey. Every Lendu woman in my caravan was respectably attired in a white cotton petticoat reaching from the waist to the ankles. Ear-rings, necklaces, bracelets, further testified that they were comfortably well-off. The baby was carried in a peculiar sort of sling plaited out of strips of palm leaves. It supported the baby pick-a-back fashion with one leg dangling free on each side. Fastened by leather straps to the mother's waist and shoulders, the sling left the arms of the mother free. But a queer covering, shaped like a candle-extinguisher, was shoved over the baby's head to shield it from sun and rain. This cone-shaped cover was also made out of plaited strips of palm leaves. Finding that I had photographed her, the woman was not very pleased, and expressed her doubts whether such magic arts of the white man were likely to be productive of a blessing either on her or her baby; but she promptly changed her mind on the subject, when I gave her a present of a pat of butter which I had watched her haggling for.

The Lendu at Kampala came originally as slaves and followers of the Soudanese. The Lendu country lies beyond Lake

I

Albert, on the other side of the Lur country. It is said that the Soudanese in passing through enslaved a good many, and that other Lendu followed voluntarily owing to famine. Many of the Lendu are now paid Government labourers and are earning a comfortable wage. That they are of a low type is shown by a case I had to try at Kampala. A Soudanese soldier complained that he had paid a large sum to a Lendu to get a Lendu woman; she had remained with him as wife and cook for a few months and had then returned to her Lendu husband. It must be remembered that to obtain a wife by purchase is the

FRONT OF PROTESTANT CATHEDRAL ON NAMIREMBE HILL.

universal rule, and not the exception in these countries; it is not slave-dealing in the accepted sense of the word, though it is open to question whether it does not fall under the same heading. A proof that it is not slave-buying is that the woman knew she was still a free woman and had acted accordingly. The Soudanese soldier was naturally very much disappointed that his payment of purchase-money could not be accepted by me as constituting any right whatever over the woman.

The day of rest the Lendu community spend almost invariably in dancing and jollification. A Lendu dance consists in hopping more or less slowly in single file around the musicians. The dancers frequently daub and smear themselves with white clay. Only small children don the national dress of leaves;

A LENDU MOTHER WITH HER BABY

women often stick a bunch of leaves outside their petticoat in memory of bygone days. The dancers usually carry a stick or leafy branch; a good many have a tiny reed whistle to add to the musical din. One dancer, I noticed, was very proud of a head-dress he had invented for the occasion; it was a small reed-bowl worn as a cap, with a tuft of feathers stuck on top of it. The band consisted of drums, horns, gourd-rattles, and almost anything that would swell the noise, and yet they managed somehow to maintain a monotonous tune, somewhat mournful and wailing, but of assistance to the dancers in keeping time.

The wonderful conversion of the Waganda to Christianity is a striking illustration how easily vast multitudes may be influenced by a few men, just as the Ephesian throng was ready to shout that their Diana was great. That there are a number of sincere and real conversions among the Waganda may be granted, but it is rather difficult to believe that so many thousand men, women, boys, and girls should all have realised at the same moment and suddenly, not only the inestimable superiority of Christianity over Mohammedanism and heathenism, but should have grasped the relative merits between Protestantism and Roman Catholicism, so as to enable them to choose either in preference to the other. It seems sad that a fratricidal war should have broken out between the two factions, as related by Lugard; but intolerance and bigotry are dangerously near to every sudden conversion, and Uganda was not to be the exception.

I happened to be at Kampala when the Protestant cathedral on Namirembe hill was blown down by a violent gust of wind. A new cathedral was speedily erected. The huge grass-thatched roof requires some hundreds of tall palm-stem pillars to support it. The cathedral carries a plain cross. The elegant reed-work of the walls is neatly finished off, but otherwise it is simple in the extreme. It is an impressive sight to see the thousands of worshippers flocking to it on a Sunday morning.

To a certain extent this universal conversion by the thousand is an outcome of the deeply-grafted feudal system. The great chief becomes a Protestant or a Roman Catholic, as the case may be, and at once most of his sub-chiefs adopt the same form of worship; peasants, as a matter of course, follow their sub-chiefs. It becomes a mark of superiority to be able to read and write, and immediately every one tries to attain to this level. A good bell-wether is of inestimable value to a shepherd, and the bell-cow that acts as leader to a herd on giddy mountain heights in Switzerland has been known to fight desperately with others for her distinguished but perilous position. If proverbially dull-brained animals can exercise this influence over a herd, it does not seem improbable that the animal on the top rung of creation's ladder, and known as *homo sapiens*, should on occasion similarly sway a multitude of his own species.

During my stay at Kampala I gathered, that chiefs, great and small, considered it their most important daily duty to attend

RUBAGA HILL SEEN FROM NAMIKEMBE.

from nine to twelve biblical instruction. As they are intelligent pupils, there is nothing surprising in the remark once made to me by a missionary, that he could not find questions hard enough to "stump" the adult scholars who had been attending this course for a number of years.

The French Algerian Mission, known as the "White Fathers," have settled on Rubaga hill. These hardy missionaries devote their life to the cause; as a rule, they die out here, unless some one completely broken down is invalided by a medical man before it is too late. The Church Mission Society grant a full year's leave to their missionaries after every five years of work, but these White Fathers have no restful leave of absence to look forward to. I had the privilege, although myself a Protestant, of enjoying the friendship of more than one of this heroic band. I knew the Venerable Père Guillemin when he was simply Father Superior; he became Bishop, and shortly afterwards he died. Sir Gerald Portal in his book mentions the hospitality of these White Fathers. I, too, have had the honour of being invited to their table. One evening Judge Collinson and I were their guests, and I tasted for the first time a ripe mango in Uganda. Last time I visited them they told me they now formed the "quadruple alliance," because one of their number happened to be a Frenchman, the other a Belgian, Monseigneur the Bishop an Alsatian, and the fourth man, if I remember rightly, an Austrian.

These White Fathers have a rule, which the Church Mission Society has also adopted, of never having a missionary living lonely and solitary by himself. There are always two at least together in every mission station, and if death removes one, another is sent to make up the number. They devote some of their leisure to gardening, and to be able to enjoy a ripe mango from a mango-tree raised by them from seed is sufficient proof that merited success has rewarded their efforts. The courteous greeting extended by their

AN ALBINO-NEGRO.

converts to passing strangers is noticed at once by all accustomed to the surly indifference of Protestant native converts towards any white man they do not happen to know.

A white negro belongs to the same class of curiosities of Nature as a white blackbird. There is at Kampala a boy who is an albino-negro. He is a perfect negro as shown by his features, his woolly hair, and by the formation of his skull; but his skin is white. This white colour is unlike a European's, because all Europeans, men and women, are bound to tan more or less in Africa. This poor albino presents a pitiable object of neglect. As dirt shows more readily on his white skin, he always looks dirty compared to his black playfellows. The glare of the sun hurts his sensitive albino-eyes, and has caused his keeping the right eye habitually closed and his blinking with the left eye. This photophobia has produced the habitual effort of twisting the face, so as to mitigate the pain which the rays of light cause, when they strike his unprotected iris; and in this way his mouth has been pulled awry, and his features have assumed an unpleasant and unhappy expression. When I examined his eyes the last time I was at Kampala, they looked decidedly more grey to what I noticed four years ago.

Kampala has two Christian Prime Ministers (the one a Protestant, the other a Roman Catholic) and three Christian Bishops (the one a Protestant, the two others Roman Catholics). With this storage of power and of evangelising force, one would imagine that Kampala must be a sort of "New Jerusalem," a city of saints. But there is not another place I know, either in Uganda or in the East African Protectorate, where "so many thieves break through and steal." On my very first arrival at Kampala I had an illustration of this fact. The captain, then in command of the fort, on ushering us into the mess-room, wanted to refer to the clock. "Well, I'm blest," he exclaimed, "they've stolen the clock!" The clock, it appears, usually stood on the sideboard. As he went on chatting with the greatest equanimity about other matters, and took the theft with such perfect composure, I thought it was simply a joke, especially as my companion, the major, laughed very heartily. When our host had left the room, I found that it was not a joke, but real earnest. I thereupon expressed to my companion my admiration for a man who could take loss and annoyance with such gentlemanly fortitude, as it was impossible to replace the clock without writing to England for another to be sent out, and this could not possibly reach Kampala under eight months. My companion explained how it was, that the captain took it so coolly. "One usually takes another man's misfortunes with heroic indifference," he said; "the clock does not belong to the captain at all, but to the

AT KAMPALA

other man who is away, and who will probably not take it quite so calmly when he hears of the theft." This happened in June 1894. Since then there has been further phenomenal missionary activity at Kampala and in Uganda. The number of missionaries, white and black, I mean European and native, at the same rate of increase, must become legion in the future. They are composed of priests and laymen, males and females, Protestants and Roman Catholics, married and single. I should not venture to compute the thousands of natives that have been baptized and the number of benighted souls that have been saved. But the devil seems to have become aware, that he must bestir himself, hurry up and strengthen his forces, if he does not want to see the Millennium arriving at Kampala earlier than elsewhere. This may account, why the thieves have grown infinitely bolder at Kampala at the present day, and they do not spare missionaries either. One day one of the Mission ladies was terrified by a thief in her room. This emissary of Satan snatched up some of her property and escaped.

The last time I was at Kampala, I saw a mixture of troops drawn together from various sources, owing to the Soudanese mutiny. Amongst these were a number of East African Rifles hurriedly sent up from Mombasa. Dressed in brown kaké, with red fez and dark blue putties, and wearing boots, the soldiers looked very smart. Those I saw were all rather short; this fact

THE EAST AFRICAN RIFLES.

and their smooth African faces gave one the impression of their belonging to a corps of boys.

When I passed through Mombasa, men were being recruited for the Uganda Rifles. The scarcity of men available to enlist became apparent, when one gentleman recognised his former cook, and another his former boy, amongst these new levies who have been dubbed by some facetious joker the "Knick-knacks," under which sobriquet I heard of them already some hundreds of miles up-country. In future, Indian troops will also be stationed in Uganda.

When the British Protectorate was declared over Uganda, I

FORT KAMPALA SEEN FROM THE NATIVE MARKET.

happened to be in charge of Fort Kampala, where the historic document ratifying the treaty was signed by Colonel Colville and King Mwanga who, instead of writing his name, always used as his signature the word "Kabaka," which means king, for every official document. The signatures of these august personages had to be witnessed, and for this the two Prime Ministers and myself were selected. On this occasion one of the great chiefs was so impressed by the splendour of an English colonel's full ceremonial uniform, that he lost no time in approaching on the subject the representative of an English firm, and offered a great quantity of ivory for "a suit exactly like the Colonel's," cocked hat and spurs included.

Another minor episode which happened about that time and which now appears almost comic, looking back at it through the vista of several years, was far from comic to me then. A seething unrest seemed to pervade the Waganda. It led to sanguinary fights under Lugard, and taxed his skill and patience to the utmost. It burst out in fresh vigour in the last rebellion of Waganda, when King Mwanga and some of his great chiefs took up arms against the British Government. Though hundreds have been slaughtered, and the king has been declared deposed, he still defies the Government, and holds his own in some parts of the Protectorate; it is said he has some hundreds, according to others some thousands, of adherents armed with guns. I became aware of this turbulent native spirit during my period of authority at Kampala. I had reliable information that plots against the Government were brewing. There were at least half a dozen different plots. King Mwanga wanted to get rid of Apollo Katikiro, some of the ambitious chiefs wished to turn out Mwanga, others longed to oust the British Government. One of the leading chiefs concerned in these matters was Mwanika. It was an anxious time for me, a civilian temporarily in command of a fort and of Soudanese troops, and responsible for the maintenance of peace. I kept myself thoroughly informed of every movement of the conspirators and, drawing my lines closer and closer, waited for one to commit himself sufficiently to seize him. The disturbing news reached also the late Captain Dunning in distant Unyoro, and he wrote to me about it, as he was unaware that I was alive to the danger menacing the Government. Under pretext of collecting men to rebuild the Protestant cathedral, noisy demagogues were beating drums and parading the outskirts of Kampala with armed men. Mwanika, I heard, was laying in arms and ammunition.

In the night I received an urgent message to see the Acting Commissioner who lay ill at Port Alice. Port Alice is some twenty miles off. I took every precaution with my Soudanese officers, in case an outbreak should happen whilst I was away, and then I hurried off to Port Alice in the darkness of the night. I found the Colonel asleep, and not wishing to wake him, I went round to the tent of the gentleman who subsequently became temporarily the Acting Commissioner. Here I was given a blanket, and invited to make myself comfortable on the floor until daybreak, when I should be able to see my patient.

Those who have been to Port Alice know something about the mosquitoes there. The late Captain Raymond Portal describes them humorously as of the size of elephants. I have met with a good many varieties of mosquitoes, the grey, the zebra-striped, and so on; but Port Alice has its own special breed of a reddish-brown colour, twice the usual size, and armed with weapons twice as powerful. It is a well-known fact, that the male mosquito is not bloodthirsty; it lives a vegetarian life, and, though "bearded like a pard," is harmless. It is the female mosquito which is the hateful blood-sucker. When I lived at Port Alice, on the top of the hill, in one of the primitive structures called officers' residences which we pioneers of the Government had to put up with in those bygone days, I used to light a fire of green-wood every night to smoke these pests out.

The few hours I spent that night on the floor of the tent, after a ride of twenty miles, I am not likely to forget, eaten up alive in the meanwhile by the mosquitoes. The tent was pitched in a grassy opening surrounded by a mass of shrubs and forest trees. With early dawn I attended on my patient, prescribed for him, had a hurried breakfast, and then started on my twenty miles' ride back to Kampala. I reached Kampala very late in the afternoon, as the forty miles in less than twelve hours began to tell also on the horse.

WAGANDA SPEARMEN.

On the outskirts of Kampala I came suddenly upon a noisy crowd of natives beating a war-drum. Inquiring who they were, I heard they belonged to Mwanika, and that it was his drum. They fled in every direction, but after a smart chase we captured the drum and drummer. Not far from the king's palace we came upon a second huge crowd; a large number of the men were armed with spears and some with guns. A man dressed in spotless white was haranguing the crowd, and whenever the speaker paused, the crowd shouted, and a drummer standing by hammered away lustily on a drum. I had pre-arranged with two of my Soudanese that, if we should by any chance meet a similar turbulent crowd, one should approach the drummer without attracting attention if possible, and the other should similarly make sure of capturing the ringleader, while the attention of the crowd would probably be fixed on me.

We came round the corner so suddenly upon the orator who had his back to us, that I was at once at his side. He became aware of my presence by the consternation of his audience. I inquired who he was and to whom the drum belonged. I was told he was Mwanika's headman, and that this drum too belonged to the same chief. The crowd fled in a moment, but drum, drummer, and orator were secured.

We arrived at the Fort; and, in presence of these alarming events, I decided to capture Mwanika himself that night. Not to rouse the suspicion of any Waganda watching us, we collected Soudanese soldiers at intervals by twos and threes from their settlement. Having armed about forty of them, and also some of our reliable Swahilies, I told them my plan: to go to Mwanika's house, surround it, demand entrance, and arrest Mwanika. I pressed upon my men that I wished to avoid bloodshed, and that if any one fired his rifle without permission, I should punish him most severely. I told them that I myself should knock at the door of Mwanika's house: if I was fired at and fell, then, and then only, should they have the right to use their rifles and capture Mwanika at all costs. I fully expected armed resistance, and I did not relish the prospect of being shot down ; but having accepted the command of the Fort, I felt I must bear the risks as well as the honours of the position. To find the house, I used Mwanika's captured headman as a guide, and to prevent treachery, I handcuffed his right wrist to the left wrist of one of my most trustworthy men ; an armed Soudanese soldier was told off in addition, in case the headman should attempt to betray us. We found the house, surrounded it, and I demanded to see Mwanika. Whilst I stood at one door, a naked man, brandishing a long knife, dashed out by another. One of my men attempted to seize the fugitive, but failed. It was Mwanika who thus escaped and took refuge with the Protestant Prime Minister. I searched the house, and carried war-drums, rifles, gunpowder, and cartridges to the Fort. It was a hard day's work, and I was dead tired when I went to bed.

Next day all the great chiefs, with the exception of Mwanika, assembled at the Fort. I demanded the surrender of Mwanika to stand his trial on a charge of trying to foment and raise a rebellion against the British Government. I hinted that all present would have to remain and wait till Mwanika appeared. Thereupon urgent messengers were despatched by the chiefs ordering Mwanika to appear at once. He came, and was

MAIN-ENTRANCE OF FORT KAMPALA.

allowed to depart again, as both the Protestant Prime Minister and the Sekibobo went surety for Mwanika's future behaviour. The Sekibobo was a man I greatly esteemed. He was a loyal supporter of English rule in Uganda. His word could be safely relied on; and his word being pledged that Mwanika's future behaviour should be above suspicion, was, in my opinion, the best security that Mwanika would now be rendered absolutely harmless. The Sekibobo has died since, and the Government has lost in him a strong support. The assembled chiefs then agreed that Mwanika's confiscated war material should remain in the Fort for four months, and should then be restored, if not another rumour as to his disloyalty was heard; but that it should be permanently seized by the Government, if directly or indirectly he caused the spread of disloyal sentiments.

In this way all smouldering disloyalty was extinguished, and the rebellion was nipped in the bud without bloodshed. In fact, such absolute security now followed, that when I handed over Kampala to my successor, he subsequently decided to pull down the stockade which protected the Fort and to fill up the trench around it.

Since then three years have passed, and a Waganda rebellion and a Soudanese mutiny have occurred, and it has been found necessary to build up a new Fort as speedily as possible. This new Fort is larger in area than the old one which was still the one originally built by Lugard; but instead of a wooden stockade there are now high strong ramparts of earthwork surmounted by some brickwork. The new trench is also deeper and wider than the old one.

The main-entrance of Fort Kampala is a massive structure, with a field-gun mounted on the top of it. A draw-bridge gives admission to the Fort during the day and, by revolving round an axis, acts as a barred gate at night. This ingenious piece of mechanism is the work of Mr. Pordage, whose engineering skill was requisitioned in constructing the new Fort.

When last I saw Fort Kampala, the mutiny scare had not yet subsided, though no mutineer has approached its walls. The outcome of the mutiny is, that a more liberal allowance has been granted to meet Government expenditure, and that the British nation has a firmer hold than ever of the Uganda Protectorate.

CHAPTER X.

THE SOUDANESE.

THE British Empire is too vast, for every ratepayer to know exactly what is happening in every one of its distant outposts, or how the money is spent which his representative in Parliament has voted. He is satisfied, and rightly, that "no news generally means good news," and that the wisest policy is to "leave well alone." He is confident, and with justice, that anything wrong or unusual, should it happen, would soon be brought to his notice by the Press, the trusted and trustworthy guardians of public interests. Thus it came about that attention was directed in 1897 to the Soudanese in Uganda, and then only because they had mutinied. The mutiny, though absolutely insignificant when compared with the momentous Indian Mutiny with its gigantic interests at stake, had some resemblance to its prototype: in arising from general discontent due to some apparently trivial causes; in black troops, armed and drilled by Europeans, turning their weapons and their knowledge against their benefactors; in brutal murders perpetrated with relentless and undiscriminating ferocity against defenceless white men who had fallen into the power of the mutineers; finally, by the prompt assistance rendered by the Home Government to suppress the mutiny and to remove its alleged causes.

The Soudanese have proved that they are made of the right fighting stuff, that they possess the two indispensable qualities of obedience and courage, and that they are eminently suited for the purpose for which Lugard selected them. No German military officer can hold a more exalted opinion than a Soudanese, as to the immeasurable superiority of the military career as a profession. His one ambition is to be a soldier.

A Government Medical Officer in Uganda sees a good deal

of the Soudanese. He not only attends the European officials, Goanese and Armenian clerks, Indian artisans, Swahili porters, local labourers and prisoners, but also the Soudanese soldiers, and accompanies the troops on military campaigns and punitive expeditions.

It is already a matter of history how the Soudanese came to Uganda, where they are aliens quite as much as any European. The Dervish success in the Soudan, culminating in the fall of Khartoum, when Gordon Pasha lost his life, drove out of the country what remained of the troops wearing the Egyptian uniform. These fugitives carried their arms and ammunition with them. Having knowledge of the advantage of military discipline, they followed with implicit obedience their leaders, and, owing to the superiority of their arms, they found themselves masters of the territories which they had been compelled to invade. Left to forage for themselves, they became raiding bands; but they knew that unity meant strength, and they held together to resist the common enemy.

According to Mohammedan notions, slaves are lawful spoil; and captives, boys as well as girls, would thus be added to the household. These children of different races, speaking different languages, unknown to each other and to their captors, soon forgot their own language and learnt to speak the tongue of the Soudanese. Many—I believe I may venture to say most—of our so-called Soudanese soldiers are not true Soudanese, nor even their descendants, but purely and simply their slave children grown up. Some soldiers could tell me that they were Bari, Makraka, Lendu, or Lur, words familiar to my ear; others again would mention some unfamiliar name, or not know themselves what country they came from.

Lugard, hearing of these dangerous hordes on the borders of Uganda, by a master-stroke converted them into useful allies. Others who succeeded him in authority followed his example, for shortly after my arrival in Uganda another company of these wanderers was enlisted. I remember the curious spectacle they presented at Port Alice, when they were told to fall in for the preliminary inspection-parade. Some still wore portions of a former uniform, others had practically nothing on but a loin-cloth. Their weapons were equally incongruous. Many of the men were sound and healthy, others were feeble and infirm; some were greybeards, others mere boys. Yet amongst the worthless husks was found good and valuable grain, well worth the sifting and looking for.

The Soudanese having found themselves superior to the different races they met with in their southward progress, acquired a very considerable amount of self-confidence, and, as a matter of course, they looked down on the Waganda. They now formed the standing army in Uganda, and were bound to support the white man, from whom they were receiving pay, rations, and clothing. Frugal and thrifty, and

THE MILITARY WATCH-TOWER AT KIBERO.

accustomed to manage on very little, they gladly accepted to be provided with daily rations and clothing, and four rupees, that is five shillings, per month as pay. The presence of this standing army strengthened British influence and authority in Uganda itself, and their successful punitive expeditions against the Wakitosh, Wakilelowa, and Wanandi extended British supremacy over adjacent regions.

The Soudanese have also rendered excellent service in guarding the frontiers of the Protectorate. The military watch-tower at Kibero, on the east shore of Lake Albert, is simply a mud-structure, but will serve as an illustration of the rough and ready, though useful, methods employed in the country.

THE SOUDANESE

Polygamy is the rule with the Soudanese. Imam Abdulla Effendi, the Soudanese officer in command at Kibero, had seven wives and five children. On my first visit to Kibero I was the bearer of a judicial decision against him. He had just divorced a wife, and she had appealed at headquarters. I had been instructed to see that the sentence of the court, ordering Imam Effendi to refund her dowry to the wife he had just divorced, was carried out in my presence. Thereupon he regaled me with the whole story; how his undutiful wife, instead of serving him with his dinner, chose to throw it at his head; how he had then ordered one of his subordinates to seize and imprison the woman for the night; and how next morning he had divorced her. I assured Imam Effendi that the case had not been heard by me, and that I was merely instructed to see that the wife, having been divorced, received back her dowry in accordance with established local Mohammedan custom. As a specimen of what one has to put up with, in dealing with natives, I give a few sentences of what took place.

I. "You are to refund to this woman her dowry."

He. "God knows, I have already refunded it."

She. "It's a lie; he has only given me eight yards of cloth."

I had now to examine numerous witnesses, some swearing that only four yards of cloth were paid, others swearing equally hard that eight yards were paid. Finally I ascertained that forty rupees, about £2, 10s., was still due to the woman. This I ordered Imam Effendi to refund.

I. "You are now to refund to the woman forty rupees. Have you got the money?"

He. "God is witness, I have nothing."

She. "It's a lie; he has cows, and goats, and sheep."

And so it went on. Having ascertained that he had some cows, goats, and sheep, and the respective local value of each, I knew that he would rather part with goats and sheep than a cow. As the value of a cow had been stated to be equal to forty rupees, I pointed out to Imam the simplicity of his settling the whole matter by handing over one cow to the woman.

Imam trembled for his cow, and urged me to let him pay up in goats and sheep. As the woman agreed to accept three sheep and two goats as the equivalent of forty rupees, I consented to the arrangement. The goats and sheep were sent for. I had

K

threatened, that if he picked out the worst in his flock, I should certainly decide on the simpler settlement of payment by one cow which his divorced lady should have the right to select. Imam brought five beautiful animals; and wiping the perspiration off his face, he eagerly entreated the woman to accept them and to depart. With natives, when once the parties to a purchase or contract have accepted and separated, the transaction is supposed to be binding and it cannot be annulled.

SOUDANESE.

Hence his hurry to get her to accept and go. On my second visit to Kibero, Imam had already filled the vacancy in his household by marrying another. In the meantime his divorced lady, the wealthy possessor of three sheep and two goats, notwithstanding her having flung the dinner at her previous husband's head, had also had offers, and having decided which to accept, she too felt consoled.

The humbler class of Soudanese women and girls still wear the "raha," or petticoat of plaited strings. It is really their national costume. This "raha" consists of a number of plaited strings falling in a double or treble row from the encircling waist-belt. At first sight this dress would scarcely seem as good a clothing as leaves, but in reality it is one of the most effectual coverings I have yet met with amongst African races. For whether they stand, walk, run, sit, kneel, or stoop, the strings will always fall around them gracefully.

All the hard work in connection with the food question is performed by women. They clear the patch of jungle which is to be the field, they till the soil, they plant, they weed, and they gather in the harvest. They prepare the native brew, they distil the native whisky, they look after the poultry, and they fetch the firewood. In addition to this, if they can possibly manage it, they will try a little retail business, and endeavour to sell something or other to the passer-by at double the price they paid themselves. Of course, the more women there are in a family, the easier it is for them to get through this amount of work; hence the females of the household thoroughly approve, if the head of the family adds extra assistance in the shape of additional wives. Marriage of course means purchase. The father expects to receive for his daughter a certain sum which varies according to his own position. Some of these sums are enormous, and remind one of Jacob forfeiting seven years' wages as a payment for Rachel.

A Soudanese wedding is an expensive affair for the bridegroom, notwithstanding the pecuniary contributions of the wedding-guests. The style of the entertainment depends on the rank of the bride. If she is simply a slave girl added to the harem, her arrival does not cause any greater excitement than the purchase of an additional sheep or goat. The girl is in reality a servant, but she is a wife at the same time and her children rank equally with the legitimate offspring, in accordance with a deeply rooted custom of great antiquity. It has its advantages and disadvantages. The childless wife is not likely to look with favour on the child of the handmaid, and the Soudanese Abraham may be driven by his Sarah to expel the Hagar and Ishmael of his household. On the other hand, even a Khedive of Egypt, though the son of his father's slave, has succeeded to his father's rank and wealth by natural right, indisputable according to Eastern customs and Mohammedan teaching. When the bride is a girl of rank, the bridegroom has sometimes to provide her with handmaids for her own private use, in the shape of a slave girl or two; to buy her silver or even gold ornaments; to equip her with suitable clothing and the necessary household-kit, besides the heavy sum which he has to pay, cash down, to the father.

Then comes the wedding-feast. Booths are constructed of palm-leaves and branches; fowls, sheep, and goats are slaughtered; and if the bridegroom is of high rank and position, he is expected to kill also a bullock or two for the feast; native beer is provided in huge gourds by the score; drums are beaten without intermission day and night, unless the long-suffering European official is driven to insist that from

10 P.M. to 6 A.M. there shall be a cessation of drum-beating and turmoil, in order to enable the non-participators in the revelry to sleep; other musical attractions are provided, such as horns, gourds, rattles, castanets, and triangles, and girls and women singing. Then there are the open-air dances, circling around the musicians, until the clouds of dust cause the choking and perspiring dancers to rest for a while and to refresh themselves at the gourds of native beer. Custom has fixed what the wedding-guest, according to his rank, has to contribute in cash towards the expenses of the wedding entertainment; the private soldier pays about a tenth or a twentieth of what the officer has to pay.

The Soudanese ladies plait their woolly curls into short, close-lying tresses reaching to the nape of the neck. They wear very few ornaments; this one a bracelet, that one a necklace. Some wear ear-rings, others a sort of button in the outer cartilage of one of the nostrils. Their dress is very simple, consisting of a single piece of cotton cloth of sufficient length, deftly thrown around the body. Some, in accordance with Mohammedan precepts, will cover also head and face. A graceful and common squatting posture is to drop on the knees and sit on the heels.

The Soudanese hut consists of a circular low wall of reeds and grass, with a conical grass-thatched roof. The same opening serves as door, window, and exit for the smoke. The whole family lives in one and the same hut with all its possessions, including poultry, sheep, and goats. The opening into the hut is so low that one has to stoop to enter, and the hut itself is so dark, that even in day-time I have had to strike a light to see the patient I was called to visit. Sometimes the smoke from the wood-fire which is usually in the centre of the hut, has been so unbearable, that I have had from time to time to get into the outer air to rest my aching eyes and throat. The household effects are but few: a light wooden couch, a low wooden settle, a small wooden mortar, a long pole serving as a pestle to pound dried casava-root into mohogo flour, grindstones to grind Kafire-corn into matama flour, some earthen vessels, a gourd or two as water-jugs, and a few grass-mats and grass-platters.

In a typical scene in a Soudanese village, the lady will be seen sitting on a low settle at the door of her hut and superintending the domestic work; there will be the boy sent to fetch water; there will be women either pounding or grinding corn, and there will be poultry about. Castor-oil plants are usually found in the village, stretching out their broad green leaves.

One day at Hoima I came upon a group of Soudanese children gambling for locusts. The gambling instinct seems to be widely disseminated. The stakes were not "high"; the locusts were fresh caught. Countless millions of locusts had passed over Hoima for the last few days. October seems to be their breeding season in this part of Africa. The male insect has a yellow head; the female is generally somewhat larger in size, and her head is more of an orange-red. All native races eat locusts; with many it takes, and has to take, the place of the British workman's beef and mutton. In a good many villages sun-dried locusts are an article of commerce. The Soudanese are particularly fond of them. As soon as a swarm of locusts has settled, every woman and child in the village turns out to catch them.

IN A SOUDANESE VILLAGE.

My men were all very busy catching locusts by the handful, toasting them on the fire, and eating them with evident relish. My Arab servant was munching some when I drew near. With true Arab politeness he at once invited me to share in the feast. I always like to try a native dish, and I accepted. Wings and legs are apparently removed before the toasting begins; the long soft body and the crisp head form the delicacy. I determined not to let my European prejudices influence me, but to give the dish of grilled locusts a fair trial. I thought how, nearly 1900 years ago, John the Baptist had enjoyed them plus wild honey. The one I was eating was rather nice. I agreed with my Arab servant that, should the meat supply fall short, a dish of locusts would be a very enjoyable substitute. By the time I was eating the second locust, it seemed to me absurd why one should have a sort of lurking pity for John the Baptist's daily menu, unless it be for its monotony; and I felt convinced that I should get tired of honey sooner than I should of locusts. I could think of no other objection against a daily dish of locusts but the one which caused the Scotchman to resent the daily serving out to him of fresh salmon as rations. I was getting on splendidly, and enjoying myself, philosophising the while, when my Arab boy, smacking his lips, said, "Delicious! Full of eggs!" Now, a shrimp or bloater "full of eggs" is not half bad, but a locust full of eggs! Phew! My appetite was gone, and I did not feel inclined for more locusts, at any rate that day.

At Kitanwa, in Unyoro, the locusts arrived in their countless millions, and I noticed that the Soudanese soldiers worked hard to scare these devourers off their potato-patches and corn-fields, by waving branches and by moving about among their crops. They showed in this respect a superior intelligence to the apathetic Lur and Wanyoro, who remain sitting and looking on indolently, whilst their crops are being ruined before their very eyes—not an effort being made by them to scare off even a small swarm of locusts. The Soudanese could only make the locusts "move on," so to speak; when a large swarm has once settled, it will scarcely stir, and all that can be done is to drive it on to the adjoining jungle. One has to witness the destruction caused by a large swarm in order to get even a faint conception of the appearance of the ruined fields and plantations. A field of green tender corn is left bleak and bare, the corn being eaten up to the very roots. A flourishing banana plantation looks as if a sudden blight had struck it; the gaunt stems remain, with the bare mid-ribs of the leaves sticking out.

More than once have I had to act as paymaster to the troops; and at Kitanwa I had the duty of dealing out a treble payment to the garrison: first, to serve out the monthly rations: then, to issue the monthly pay; lastly, to measure out the half-yearly allowance of clothing, which consisted of five yards of "americani" and four yards of "bombay" to the non-commissioned officers and men, and six yards of American drill to the officers. For measuring out, the "yard-stick" was used; but for the first two payments I had to use the "rupee-stick," so called because it measured off a quantity of cloth representing one rupee in value.

The men have to be their own tailors, and it is astonishing what neat white uniforms they can produce. The thread they obtain by unravelling a long narrow strip of "americani" cotton-cloth, or, more economically, by spinning it for themselves out of cotton from the nearest cotton-plant.

At Fajao I came upon a Soudanese corporal solemnly spinning cotton-thread for his tailoring work. He was much too engrossed to notice anybody or anything. Remembering the unflinching bravery with which these Soudanese meet death on the battle-field, this scene recalls the veteran greybeards of Napoleon I.'s army, knitting stockings with the musket by their side. The corporal was holding in his left hand a small amount of raw cotton-

SOUDANESE CORPORAL SPINNING COTTON-THREAD.

wool. The spinner, shaped like a top, has a slender quill-like prolongation which points downwards, and which has to be twirled from time to time. What looks like the body of the top is really a certain quantity of white cotton-thread already spun and wound up. The last bit of the spun-thread is hitched into a tiny notch on the upper rim of the spinner; and the terminal end, thus secured, passes upwards on to the loose cotton-fibres which are yet to be spun. When about a foot of thread has been spun, it is liberated from the notch and wound up on the body of the spinner. The terminal end of the thread is then replaced in the notch. The spinning may thus be discontinued at a moment's notice, or it may be continued as long as the supply of cotton-wool holds out.

Wherever a Soudanese settlement is formed, within a short time cotton-plants will be found growing wild in the fields or in the neighbourhood, owing to scattered seeds. Cotton thrives in the Uganda Protectorate. When the Uganda railway is completed, provided the transport rates on raw cotton from Uganda to the coast are made so as to encourage enterprise in the direction of cotton production, the cotton-planter may probably find it worth his while to direct his attention to the capabilities of Uganda.

Until I saw lofty cotton-trees, with tall straight stems, at Parumbira, a place on the north-east end of Lake Nyassa, I was unaware that cotton-trees and cotton-plants are two different things. The cotton-tree has no value whatever, whereas without the cotton-plant the human race would suffer. The reason is obvious: the tree requires years to become a fruit-bearing tree; the cotton-plant is a shrub, which in favourable localities grows up in a few months and then flourishes like a weed. I collected from the fallen pods at the foot of the cotton-trees at Parumbira, with the assistance of a few natives and on payment of a few strings of beads, sufficient cotton-wool to make myself a mattrass and two pillows. The pillows served me through the whole of my overland journey from Lake Nyassa to Kilwa.

A large cotton-shrub covered with ripe cotton gleams as if covered with snow-flakes. As the green pods ripen, they split into three and gape. As the peel dries up, three fluffy snow-white masses of cotton-wool like silk-cocoons protrude and invite the passer-by to gather them. A number of seeds are wrapped up inside each cocoon.

Soudanese settlements are everywhere laid out on the same general lines, and the one at Kibero may serve as an illustration. From a distance the settlement looks like a square enclosure. On drawing nearer to it, one sees that this enclosure is cut up into a number of smaller squares by straight narrow roads which intersect each other at right angles. If one of these smaller squares is still too large for one family, further subdivision takes place by means of reed-fences. Thus every household has its own enclosure, in which to erect the hut or huts necessary for its comfort, and it has also its own private open-air sanitary convenience dug and fenced off. The enclosure is kept clean, ashes and rubbish being swept up and carried outside the settlement, where in course of time they form

THE SOUDANESE SETTLEMENT AT KIBERO.

rubbish-heaps of considerable size. Reed-fences are usually constructed of the stems of elephant-grass; but they require constant renewing, unless the stems are planted for a few inches into the ground, when very often they strike root and sprout up into a living fence. The roads which intersect the settlement are sometimes rather narrow, but on the whole are kept fairly clean.

The Soudanese do not seem to care to become domestic servants; when they are young their parents have need of their services, and when they are adults they prefer to be independent. Two young lads accompanied my caravan to the coast in 1895. One of these lads I recognised in my caravan in 1898. I enquired what had become of his companion "Haggenas," and I was told, that Haggenas deserted to join the mutineers. The desertion cost his life; for the mutineers mistook his intention, and shot him dead, before he had time to explain. I have only once had a Soudanese as a "boy"; he was taken on as an extra hand, as I had four servants already. A native officer at Masindi brought him to me with the words, that this was the best lad in the settlement. I know I am rather liable to be influenced by first impressions, and this lad's appearance was certainly not prepossessing. He appeared before me naked, with the exception of the tiniest imaginable loin-cloth, he also habitually screwed up his eyes, imparting to his face a most sinister expression.

Mentally I put him down as a first-rate rogue; but in presence of the native officer's eulogies, and unwilling to condemn a lad in destitute circumstances merely upon personal prejudice at first sight, I admitted, though with considerable hesitation, this treasure to my household. Of course I had to issue to him at once a sufficient amount of cloth to dress himself properly. Scarcely had he entered my service, when I missed my penknife, and as I had never lost anything with the other servants, I could not help suspecting the new-comer. Living in bachelor style, one is necessarily entirely at the mercy of one's servants in these distant regions. I may have been hitherto particularly fortunate; but I have scarcely ever lost anything through the dishonesty of a "boy," though I have lost more than one load owing to a dishonest porter absconding with it on the journey.

My companion at Masindi had a Soudanese servant whom he had to send to prison for selling his socks. Stolen socks are difficult to dispose of, because natives go barefoot; but knives of every description are in great demand. What more I might have lost I do not know, if just then I had not had to go to Fovira, where my new acquisition was recognised by some Swahili traders. I now found out, that this broth of a boy had just completed a term of imprisonment for malicious arson, by which these very traders had lost heavily. Whether it was this discovery, or the strict watch I kept upon his movements, but my Soudanese lad suddenly requested to join his father who, it appears, was one of the Fovira garrison. I promptly gratified the filial request by parting with the boy on the spot, although he had got a new suit of clothing out of me but a couple of days ago. A month or so later, he turned up again at Masindi in his former naked condition, with a story of cruelty against his father whom he accused of stripping him of his new suit of clothes. He begged me to take him on again as a servant. This being refused, he tried unsuccessfully to get my Arab servant to take him on for daily rations without wages. Since then I have not been very keen to try another Soudanese lad as a domestic servant.

We were at Ufumb in Unyoro when my companion, the military officer in command of the district, received news that

THE SOUDANESE CAPTAIN, SURUR EFFENDI, AND HIS FAMILY.

ex-king Mwanga of Uganda had escaped from German control, had re-entered British territory, and was supposed to be working his way towards Unyoro. Consequently, on reaching Fovira, my companion remained but one day to pay the troops, and then left for Mruli, the frontier station of Unyoro.

That same night some alarming symptoms showed themselves, of the effect the mutiny in Uganda was having on our Soudanese soldiers in Unyoro. My companion, before he left me, had mentioned to me that Surur Effendi, the Soudanese captain, had reported Farijalla Dongolawi Effendi, his first lieutenant, as being disloyal. My companion had thereupon requested that witnesses should be brought forward to substantiate the charge; but Surur Effendi would not venture on such a step in presence of the mutinous spirit which he knew pervaded his troop.

Scarcely had my companion left, when the Soudanese called a mass-meeting for the night, being summoned together with the call, "Number one fall in." I remember I was roused out of my sleep and heard the words; but I thought I must be dreaming, and I fell asleep again. When my Arab boy repeated the words to me next morning, I at once remembered that I too had heard the call in the night. At this mass-meeting they publicly discussed putting my companion to death and seizing me. I was not to be put to death, either because they did not hate me, or because they wished to secure my medical services. At any rate, my lot was to have been captivity in their midst. My captivity would no doubt sooner or later have ended in my being murdered; for Major Thruston and his two unfortunate companions at Luba's were not massacred straight off, but were first made prisoners and subsequently murdered.

The Unyoro Soudanese were fully aware of all that was happening in Uganda. They had just heard that the mutineers, originally hemmed in at Luba's, had broken through, had crossed the Nile, had landed in Uganda Proper, and were making their way towards Unyoro, where the great bulk of the Soudanese happened to be stationed. The Fovira garrison apparently felt inclined to throw in their lot with the mutineers, their own kindred and relatives. The disloyal officer was said to be the first lieutenant, Farijalla Dongolawi Effendi. But Surur Effendi, the captain, refused to give his consent to the soldiers making me a prisoner there and then. He warned them, that if they attempted to lay their hands on me, he would get me into a boat and accompany me down the Nile, leaving his wives and children to follow overland or in other boats as best they could. This determined attitude of the captain saved my companion from death, me from captivity, and in all probability saved the various Soudanese garrisons in Unyoro from irretrievably linking their fate with the mutineers.

How serious and critical the situation was on this night, may be gathered from the fact, that all my porters, Lendus and Swahilies, fled for safety to the woods and passed the night in the trees. They cautiously returned next morning on finding that I was still alive and at liberty. Some of my Lendu porters had overheard the talk of putting the white men to death; their terror had communicated itself to my Swahili porters, and so they all had fled. None of them could have assisted me, or even warned me; for I slept inside the fort which was guarded, as usual, by Soudanese sentinels on duty at the gates. Neither had I a single one of my servants with me; they, too, retired at night to a hut which was outside the fort.

Next morning I saw these two officers walking together down the broad avenue which leads to the fort, and I had my chance of taking a snap-shot photo. Surur Effendi, however, did not like having been photographed in every-day working costume. I had to promise to take him in his best uniform, surrounded by his wives and children, and in front of his own house. I made him doubly happy by giving him a copy of the latter photo. Of course I reported the news of these alarming events at once, that very morning, to the officer at Mruli. In the letter I mentioned, that as I was still at liberty, I would endeavour to escape to Masindi and await his further instructions there. But thinking the matter over, I came to the conclusion, that I might do more good by remaining on the spot, and thereby supporting by my presence Surur Effendi's noble effort to suppress the mutinous spirit among the soldiers. I therefore remained, and attended to my medical duties, as if no disloyal meeting had taken place the previous night.

At Fovira it has to be open-air doctoring, as there is no hospital. Should it rain, I see the patients in the small adjoining hut, where I also inquire into such cases as have to be seen in private. The gathering shown in the illustration is a fair sample of an ordinary morning's work among the Soudanese, their women, and children. This lot done with, I attended Swahilies and Lendus, and wound up by treating such of the native Wanyoro population as chose to apply. Urgent cases, of course, are treated at once, and take precedence. I have to act on the principle of "no admittance except on business," in order to prevent gaping crowds of the curious from gathering around us.

The following day I called Surur Effendi and Farijalla Effendi to my room, and I then told Farijalla Effendi what I had heard of his disloyal doings. Of course he denied everything, and professed to be ready to swear on the Koran that he was loyal. I said I would accept his assurance, but that I had spoken thus openly to him on the subject, in order that he might judge by the fact of my having remained at Fovira, that I was not afraid of him or of any disloyal act he might be meditating. I asked both officers to call the soldiers together, and to ascertain openly whether they were prepared to remain loyal, and to warn all the men not to follow the bad example set by the mutineers in Uganda, as the mutineers were bound to be crushed before long by the overwhelming power of the white man. This was done, and I believe it had a very good effect.

In a day or two the disloyal Effendi was summoned to proceed under escort to headquarters; and when I arrived at Misindi, I found he had been promptly imprisoned. That the disloyal spirit had not disappeared, I found out by a conversation of the Soudanese soldiers forming my escort on the return journey to Masindi. My companion, when he left me at Fovira, had taken the Maxim gun away with him. The soldiers, talking this over by the camp-fire, declared that any attempt made by the white man to take away the only other gun remaining at the fort would be resisted by them openly and by force.

The road from Fovira to Masindi was rather dangerous at this time, being raided by hostile hordes, led by the son of ex-king Kabarega. At "Kaligire" we heard that the enemy had raided a village only three hours off, and had killed twelve of our friendlies. Next day at "Kiorbezi" we heard that the enemy had passed the previous night, and had killed the chief of the village. The following day, the 17th of January 1898, I arrived at Masindi; and what happened there the same evening, I am not likely to forget very soon.

I found a letter for me from the commanding military officer, away at the time at Mruli, requesting me to take charge of the fort. The Armenian clerk informed me in the afternoon that a letter had to be sent to Fovira, and accordingly three armed friendlies were sent off with it. I may say at once that next day two only of these men returned alive; they had been met and attacked by the enemy who killed one, but the two others made good their escape back to our fort. I have there-

OPEN-AIR DOCTORING AT FOVIRA

fore reason to feel thankful, that when I travelled the very same road on the preceding day I met with no mishap.

On this evening the Wanyoro chief Bekamba was murdered by the Soudanese. He was one of the six great chiefs of Unyoro, and he ruled over the district around Masindi. His kraal was only a few minutes' walk from the fort. I often saw him, when he paid a state visit to the officer in command. He was an old man with a small curly grey beard. As he was infirm on one leg, the British Government had made him a present of the two-wheeled hand-cart shown in the illustration. He was very proud of this vehicle, his state-carriage, and always rode in it. He would call at the office, leaning on his long staff. When seated in his state-carriage, he always carried a fly-whip in his right hand and a long pipe in his left. I made his acquaintance in rather a curious way, and our first meeting greatly impressed me in his favour. I was out for a walk, and passing near a kraal I inquired of the door-keeper the way to the nearest spot for water and whether it was a river or a swamp. The man hurriedly went in and, to my surprise, an old gentlemanly negro, dressed in white, came limping out on his staff, carrying a bowl of water in his hand. I could see at a glance that he was some great man, but I had no idea it was Bekamba himself, the supreme chief of the district. He had misunderstood his servant; he thought I had asked for some water to drink, and so he had brought it in his own hand, though surrounded by a crowd of servants and of smaller chiefs.

BEKAMBA, THE WANYORO CHIEF, IN HIS STATE-CARRIAGE.

The circumstance brings forcibly to one's mind the Patriarchs who, with true Eastern courtesy, personally waited on the stranger wayfaring past their dwelling! I can never think of Bekamba without recalling his noble and courteous bearing on that first occasion, and I was sorry when I heard subsequently that grave doubts were entertained as to his loyalty to our Government. But we must remember, that he was an old man, and that he could scarcely be expected to love the conquering white man who had reduced his country from an independent kingdom to a mere province of the Uganda Protectorate. Much of his own authority had necessarily vanished by these changes, and his king, Kabarega, was a fugitive and an exile. Furthermore, his own children were in Kabarega's power, and held by that ruthless savage as hostages for their father's good behaviour; Kabarega keeping the threat hanging over poor Bekamba's head, that his children might any day be mutilated or killed.

When I arrived on the 17th of January at Masindi, I noticed premonitory signs that some terrible events were about to happen. We had at Masindi a number of armed Waganda soldiers, our friendly allies. They had been sent by the Protestant Prime Minister of Uganda with the consent of the British Government. The Waganda soldiers took duty in turns with the Soudanese. As long as one of us wihte men was at Masindi, the Waganda felt supported and remained with us; but what made them decamp in a hurry during our absence from Masindi, I do not know, unless they had some inkling of the bloodshed about to happen. The fact remains, that when I arrived at Masindi, all our armed Waganda had secretly fled; and some of the Lendus too had run away, taking their families and belongings with them.

At this time the fate of us two white men—we were but two in Unyoro—was trembling in the balance. That others in the Uganda Protectorate thought so too, would appear from the English missionaries at Kampala assuring me that we were especially remembered by them in their daily prayers. I am convinced, that if a single mutineer had succeeded in personally appearing in Unyoro, this province would have been lost, for a time at least, to the British Government, and it would have entailed hard fighting to reconquer it. We did not know what moment any or all of the Unyoro garrisons might declare openly in favour of their brothers and relatives who were in open mutiny in Uganda, and who had murdered three white men and had killed three more in the subsequent sanguinary fights. That the Soudanese in Unyoro were in heart with the mutineers, we had many instances to convince us of—the disloyal meeting at Fovira, discussing murdering one of us and imprisoning the other; the difficulty that the commanding officer had experienced in getting a Fajao contingent to bring one of their guns into the fort at Masindi; the flat refusal of the Soudanese officer in command at Hoima to obey the order of the commanding officer to guard the western crossing of the Kafu river against the approach of the mutineers; the complaint of Waganda friendlies that one of the Soudanese officers at Mruli had taunted them, and had told them that the Waganda were a bad lot for helping the white man against the Soudanese, and that they ought to let the white man and the mutineers fight it out by themselves.

The feeling of insecurity and impending disaster seemed present with every one; for my four servants, who sleep in huts outside the fort at Masindi, came to me in a body and asked permission to sleep this night inside the fort and near me. I gave, of course, a ready assent.

Darkness had set in, and I was in my hut —the medical officer's residence—in the fort at Masindi,

THE MEDICAL OFFICER'S RESIDENCE AT MASINDI.

entering in a diary by candlelight, the events of the day. This hut consists of mud-walls, a grass-thatched roof, a mud-floor, two apertures serving as windows and closed by wooden shutters, and a wooden door. It was overrun by white-ants, spiders, and rats. It leaked so badly, that whenever a good heavy rain came down, I had to place a pail on each side of my camp-bed to catch the

L.

descending trickle; and though by good luck it did not come down on the top of my bed, it did on the top of my camp-table which I had to move to prevent the raindrops from splashing all over the room.

Suddenly at 8.30 P.M. two men came running into my room—Fadlemula Effendi, the Soudanese officer in command, and the headman of Kajanga, our Wanyoro ally. Both men were armed. The Effendi hurriedly told me that the Soudanese sergeant-major, when doing his round of patrol inspection, had been set upon by hostile Wanyoro and had been killed by a spear-thrust in the back. As I turned to get my Martini rifle and a lantern, the Effendi rushed away, and I did not see him again till after the occurrence of the subsequent sad events. As I hurried towards the entrance of the fort I was accompanied by the Armenian clerk and by my servants, my plucky little Wahima boy keeping close to my side and carrying my rifle for me; my Arab servant had armed himself with my second rifle. Before I could reach the entrance, I was met by a rush of armed Soudanese soldiers and completely surrounded by them near the corn-stores inside the fort.

These corn-stores consist of huge wicker baskets, plastered on the inside and on the outside with mud; they are raised above the ground on wooden trestles about two feet high; and they are protected against sun and rain by a grass-thatched cover resembling a candle-extinguisher. Dry food, such as Indian-corn, is stored up in this manner in anticipation of unforeseen occurrences.

Nearly all the Soudanese soldiers at the time at Masindi were raw recruits. When they surrounded me, they were mad with excitement. They had refused to listen to their officer's voice, and had rushed into the fort against his direct orders. All their rifles were loaded and were pointed at me. They were shouting angrily, but as I did not understand one word, I was fortunately able to remain unmoved. My Arab, however, understood, and he said to me in Swahili: "Master, get back to the house; they mean to do you some harm." Even if I had wanted to retreat, I could not have done so, as I was hemmed in on all sides. It is surprising that one of the rifles in all this pushing and surging crowd did not go off by accident and stretch me dead. A merciful Providence saved my life, and saved thereby the whole of Unyoro; for my death would have committed the men, once for all, to throw in their lot with the mutineers and to fight to the bitter end against the avenging hand of England's might, which was already overtaking the other murderers. I felt that I was appreciably near death, for the bearing of the soldiers was most menacing.

Fortunately, the Effendi's voice was heard shouting over and over again: "It is not war against the fort." This no doubt helped to save us and the fort. None of the soldiers seemed to know exactly what was to be the next step, and whether or not it was to be open mutiny against the Government. They had not yet quite made up their minds whether I was to be killed. Presumably no one had a private grudge to avenge on my person, and not a few of them may have been at one time or another under my hands for medical treatment. I endeavoured to get them under control by pointing out that the fort had to be defended against the supposed common enemy. Gradually I regained some authority over them, and they obeyed me so far, that they went to guard various positions which I indicated, such as the bastions, the powder magazine, and the ammunition store. But when I wanted to leave the fort, to attend to what was happening outside, they firmly but politely refused to let me out, on pretext that my life would be in danger. For a short time I was practically a prisoner inside the fort in the hands of the Soudanese soldiers.

In the meanwhile a number of shots were being fired outside the fort, and the sky had become lurid with burning huts. The first rumour, as brought to me by Fadlemula Effendi, that the sergeant-major had been killed by Wanyoro at Bekamba's kraal, no doubt led to the insubordinate soldiers attacking Bekamba. The unfortunate chief requested to be taken to the fort, and had reached in his cart the open space in front of the fort, when some of the soldiers ordered the man who pulled Bekamba's cart to lie down and submit to a flogging. Knowing that resistance was vain, the poor fellow lay down, and then some one shot him through the back, dead on the spot. Thereupon another soldier blew out Bekamba's brains. The dead bodies were plundered and stripped.

When the Effendi joined me, I managed with him to leave the fort, in order to put a stop to the disturbances going on outside. The burning kraals had made the night as light as day. A dreadful sight met my eyes. There, near the fort, lay the naked bodies of chief Bekamba and of one of his men. Some wretches had set fire to Bekamba's body, and the flesh was burning. As the crackling flames flickered round the abdomen, the frizzling of the flesh was horrible and sickening. It recalled to my mind stories, read in my boyhood, of Red Indians torturing a white man to death by stretching him out on the ground and heaping fire on to his abdomen. With the assistance of my servants I pulled Bekamba's body from the burning brands and extinguished the flames. I looked at his wounds. Death must have been instantaneous, and therefore he was spared the torture of being roasted.

The kraal of Kajanga, our friendly ally, had also been set on fire and had been looted. There were a number of cartridges in his hut, and as these took fire, their cracker-like popping off rendered it dangerous to approach too near his kraal. Some of the bullets fell close to my feet.

I now asked to see the dead body of the sergeant-major, stated to have been killed at the outbreak of these disturbances. I found him lying on a couch in his own hut, encircled by a sympathising crowd of women and friends, all waiting for him to breathe his last. Not one had attempted to

THREE OF THE WOUNDED.

staunch the flow of blood from his wound. I had him quickly removed to the fort, and converted one of the buildings into a temporary hospital. Though he had a dangerous spear-wound in his back below the right shoulder, his life was ultimately saved.

Two other wounded were then brought in. One man had received a bullet in his right arm, and another was shot through the foot. Later on came a woman who had her cheek laid open by a bullet, and I had to dress her wound and stitch up her cheek.

Having attended to the wounded, and more or less restored order, I was informed by the Armenian clerk that he had overheard some of the soldiers belonging to other stations talking amongst themselves of leaving us in the morning. I at once went out to these men, and impressed them with the folly and danger of such an act. I pointed out to them that it was their duty to remain; and I am glad to say they listened to me and did not leave us.

Next morning we buried the dead—Bekamba, one of his wives, and two Wanyoro. But some fugitives carried the news of these occurrences to Hoima, two days' march from us, where a Soudanese captain was in charge of the fort. Yabuswezi, the great Wanyoro chief, has his kraal about a mile from Fort Hoima. Some fugitives reported to him that I too had been killed. He thereupon put himself on the defensive. This led to the Soudanese captain ordering him to come to the fort, and, on his refusal to do so, attacking his kraal. Thus the mere rumour of my death led to further bloodshed; for the Soudanese soldiers killed about fifty of the Wanyoro under Yabuswezi, captured some fifty-four of his women, and looted and burned his kraal. Yabuswezi himself fled over the border, with the intention of proceeding to Kampala.

The military officer in command of Unyoro, having received my letter, speedily joined me. Orders were also received from headquarters that, in view of the advance of the mutineers towards Unyoro, it was necessary to prevent the Government ammunition from falling into their hands. I was ordered thereupon to march, with half a company of the Soudanese soldiers then at Masindi, to a place called Ntuti, in Singo. I was to take charge of twenty-one loads of ammunition, a Maxim gun, and tools and belts for the gun. The two locks of the Maxim gun I hid away amongst my private clothing; my instructions being to destroy the locks, should we fall into the hands of the mutineers, or should my own men throw off their allegiance to the British Government.

On the march to Ntuti I passed through Hoima, and found seven of the Wanyoro women still retained as captives by Soudanese soldiers, although orders had been sent by the commanding officer that all were to be liberated. I therefore had these seven women set free.

I met Yabuswezi, and persuaded him to return to his province.

The ostensible reason of my departure from Masindi with the half company of Soudanese, the Maxim gun, and the ammunition, was supposed to be the necessity of holding Ntuti, in Singo, against the rebel king Mwanga. We arrived at Ntuti. In a couple of days orders from headquarters reached me to march on to Kampala, where the soldiers were promptly disarmed, and the Maxim gun and ammunition safely lodged in the fort. I had an anxious time of it from Masindi to Kampala. First of all, because the soldiers over which I had temporary command were some of the men who a few days previously had murdered Bekamba and had endangered my own life; they were at heart disloyal, and they had very nearly openly mutinied. Secondly, the Maxim gun and the twenty-one loads of ammunition would have strengthened the mutineers enormously, if they could have managed to intercept me on the march.

It was a great relief to me when, on arrival at Kampala, my military command ended. A few days later Captain Harrison gained a final success over the mutineers, which practically ended the mutiny, though it cost the life of one more European, Captain Moloney who was dangerously wounded in the attack and succumbed to his injuries. Captain Fielding and Captain Macdonald fell in the earlier engagements.

Of course everybody must regret the occurrence of the mutiny, with its accompaniment of bloodshed and destruction, but it is doubly to be regretted as the Soudanese seemed ideal troops for a country like Uganda. Being Africans, the Protectorate was a natural home to them; being aliens in the country, they had no sympathy with King Mwanga or any of the indigenous races; being Mohammedans, their creed of "Kismet" or "fate" made them dangerous enemies on the battlefield; being inured to hardships, they could live on native produce and did not require, like Indian troops, to be provided with special articles of diet; and last, but not least, owing to their many wives and followers, they looked after their own transport, and were ready to start for an expedition at a moment's notice, without requiring any special preliminary transport arrangements.

Rumours of the narrow escape I had in Unyoro, preceded me to the coast; for when I met the colonel in command of the Indian troops, then on their way to our assistance in Uganda, he expressed surprise at seeing me alive, having heard that I had been carried off into the interior and then murdered. But "all's well that ends well."

CHAPTER XI.

UNYORO.

UNYORO used to be a separate kingdom under King Kabarega. Casati and Baker Pasha speak of him as King Chua. In the heyday of his power the king held annually a great assembly of all his chiefs, at which he chose haphazard one to be beheaded there and then. He stood by with a bowl to catch the blood and to sprinkle it around; the corpse was ignominiously thrown to the vultures and the hyænas. Casati was persuaded to give up his rifles, and when disarmed, was ordered off to execution; but though he escaped with his life, it was as a hunted fugitive, and with the loss of all his possessions, including his valuable diary and collection. Baker Pasha was received by the king with professions of friendship, and then treacherously attacked at night, so that he had to fight his way step by step out of the country, incessantly harassed on the march, and losing many of his followers in killed and wounded.

When the British Government expelled King Kabarega and drove him into exile, Unyoro ceased to be a kingdom and was annexed as a province to the Uganda Protectorate. This province is bounded on the south by the Kafu River, on the east and on the north by the Nile, and on the west by Lake Albert.

Ex-king Kabarega took refuge on the right bank of the Nile. His presence there became a standing menace, and therefore most of the Protectorate troops were stationed in Unyoro. Fort Masindi was built, and it became, owing to its central position, the headquarters of the province. The other stations are: Mruli on the Kafu River, Kibero and Mahaji on the east and west shore respectively of Lake Albert, Fovira and Fajao on the Nile, Hoima and Kitanwa inland. Fort Masindi is built on the usual lines, with a wooden stockade and a deep trench.

From Kampala to Masindi takes twelve days' easy marching. The first part of the journey through Bulamwezi is very pleasant, but the last bit of the road before reaching Mruli is rather hot and trying, over an uninteresting plain, with rank grass, and scarcely any trees. The caravan route about midway cuts through a forest belt. Here I saw some native elephant-hunters in pursuit of an elephant.

Mruli is the southern frontier station. Its position is assigned wrongly in maps. It lies on the north or left bank of the Kafu River, and not on the south or right bank. The river is almost choked with papyrus opposite the station. The native population consists of a few villages thinly populated. A few fields are cultivated, but the river yields the principal supply of food. Any amount of fish is caught by means of cleverly constructed creels. The most common fish is a small species of perch; it has a delicate flavour, but is terribly packed with scores of slender harpoon-shaped bones. A large herd of Government cattle are kept at Mruli, because there are salt-licks close by the river, and the cattle thrive remarkably well here. In the centre of the small fort there is a large tree, under which the Effendi had directed my tent to be pitched. Towards dusk all the vultures in the neighbourhood came to this tree to roost, and their unpleasant presence soon was made known by the drop, drop, drop, on my fly-tent. We managed, with shouting and throwing stones and sticks, to persuade the birds to select another tree for the night. Not only are powder and shot too valuable to be wasted on carrion birds, but the birds themselves are most useful as Nature's scavengers.

On a subsequent visit something else kept dropping from the tree,—large prickly caterpillars. I collected some, but all except two died. The two which underwent the chrysalis change I took with me to Masindi. Six months later I was delighted one day by the appearance of two magnificent large yellow moths of the Saturniidæ family, my Mruli caterpillar having dropped its pupa sac and entered the imago stage of its existence.

The distance from Mruli to Masindi is usually done in two marches, but it can be done in one day if the caravan does not stop at the Katagrukwa River or "river-camp."

A common sight at the entrance of Fort Masindi, whenever one of the chiefs comes on a visit to the officer in command, is a crowd of Wanyoro. Most of them use a cow-hide as a covering, wrapped round the body and fastened across one shoulder. Some of the men, however, have adopted the Waganda barkcloth, and a few, principally sub-chiefs, are dressed in coloured cotton cloth. None of them wear ornaments of any sort.

AT THE ENTRANCE OF FORT MASINDI.

A curious fact has been pointed out, that now and then a native declares he is bewitched, and that, sure enough, he dies soon after. One gentleman told me, that a Soudanese soldier in perfect health came to him one day and demanded that another Soudanese should be put to death for having bewitched him. Of course the absurdity of the request was pointed out to the applicant, but it did not convince him; and a couple of days later he was found dead in his hut, without any clue as to the cause of his death. In all my African experiences I have come across only one similar case; but I have not the slightest hesitation in saying that the man was poisoned. Chief Amara was the most influential and powerful chief in Unyoro, and as he had joined the English cause from the outset, he was bitterly hated by ex-king Kabarega.

One day last year, Amara informed Major Thruston that some one had bewitched him, and that he was about to die. The Major sent Amara on to me; I found nothing whatever to warrant Amara's gloomy forebodings. He said, that occasionally after taking food he had felt inclined to vomit, and that food seemed to make his stomach swell. I treated him for the indigestion and flatulence, and after a few days he declared he was cured, and he ceased to come to me. Suddenly one night I was called out of bed to see him, as he was said to be dying. I did not stop to dress, but on reaching his hut found life already extinct. A post-mortem examination would have been considered desecration by his subjects. I told the Major, however, that I felt convinced that chief Amara was poisoned.

This made Major Thurston watch for a clue, and he found out that one of the disloyal sub-chiefs had received a present of three cows from ex-king Kabarega as payment for having brought about the death of chief Amara. A punitive expedition followed, in which the sub-chief was killed and his village destroyed. In the meanwhile Major Thruston proclaimed Ajaka, the infant son of Amara, to be chief in succession to his

THE INFANT AJAKA, THE YOUNGEST CHIEF IN UNYORO.

father. Chief Amara left two sons, both of them little boys, who are half-brothers; of these Ajaka is the eldest. Major Thruston appointed Msoga, a nephew of Amara, to be regent during Ajaka's minority; but as Msoga is only a lad, the authority of Kiza, who was Amara's most trusted and confidential adviser, has been considerably increased.

UNYORO

Msoga is a weak character. Chief Yabuswezi, whose province adjoins Ajaka's, had told Msoga that he would have to die. Terrified by this prediction, Msoga determined to spend what was left of life in drink and debauchery. The acting officer in command of Unyoro thereupon ordered him to Masindi, in order to have him more under control.

Kiza, on the other hand, is a shrewd old man. When the Soudanese troubles in Unyoro led to Yabuswezi's kraal being looted and burnt, Kiza managed to prevent any harm happening to Ajaka's kraal.

African mothers are often extremely indifferent about their offspring. Ajaka's mother is such a one. She is a Lendu woman, and since Amara's death she has neglected and deserted her son. Major Thruston found her at Masindi and sent her back to Hoima. She again deserted her child, and this time she persuaded the woman who acted as Ajaka's nurse to accompany her. Another woman made a request to leave her present husband who, though he had bought her originally as a slave, had afterwards married her. She now asked for permission to live with another man she had taken a fancy to. She brought her child, a nice little girl between three and four years old, and she declared with great indifference that her husband might have it, as she did not want it. Some of these women have less affection for their offspring than is found among the lower animals.

WANYORO WOMEN WITH NATIVE HOES.

Wanyoro women wear a short petticoat of bark-cloth, but

leave the upper part of the body uncovered. Girls as a rule go uncovered; they never wear the curious grass-ring seen in Uganda. The native hoe is the ordinary pointed heart-shaped piece of iron, tied on to a wooden handle which looks bent, but is cut out of a solid block of wood. The women do nearly all the field labour. A few of them occasionally wear ornaments of beads.

During my stay in Unyoro I never once suffered from "jiggers," and the number of cases I had to treat among the natives was comparatively small. But when I first arrived at Kampala in 1894 the jiggers were at their worst. The jigger is a tiny parasite which burrows in preference under the toe-nails. It may attack the finger-nails, and sometimes it may be found on other parts of the body. In Nyassa-land one was removed from the neck of a European, and in Kavirondo I saw a Swahili whose body was covered all over with them. The missionaries in Uganda told me, that many of the Waganda had succumbed to this parasite, and that one chief lost eighty of his men. One of the cases I was asked to see at Kampala was so bad that I offered to amputate the foot, as the greater part of the ankle was rotten, blood-vessels, nerves, muscle, bone, all one mass of corruption. The patient refused amputation and died a week or two later from exhaustion, owing to the incessant drain on the system.

Since then cleanliness and early medical treatment have effected a great change. I have removed as many as four jiggers in one day from my feet, when I first lived at Port Alice. Since I discontinued wearing slippers in Uganda, and paid attention to using sound socks and sound boots, besides scrubbing my feet every morning and evening with soap and warm water, I have enjoyed considerable immunity. During the last thirty months I have been troubled only once by a jigger. It was at Port Alice. I woke up in the night with a throbbing sensation under a toe-nail, lit a candle, extracted the parasite, and have been free ever since. That night I had neglected to give the feet their usual evening scrub with soap and water.

Cleanliness I believe goes a long way toward securing exemption. Europeans are made aware of the presence of the parasite by the throbbing sensation which it sets up locally, and a tiny black spot on the white skin indicates its position, whence it may be dislodged with the point of a needle. It lies between the epidermis and the cutis vera, and when it has been removed with its bag of eggs, the air comes in contact with the exposed surface and causes a smarting sensation. A little unguentum acidi borici, iodoform, or any other antiseptic, effects a speedy cure.

With very foul ulcers on natives, I have found direct application of pure carbolic acid to answer best, followed by ordinary antiseptic dressings.

I found the hospital arrangements at Masindi thoroughly suitable for native requirements, but the grass-thatched fence which enclosed the hospital grounds was very short-lived and

A HOSPITAL-HUT AT MASINDI.

required constant repair. Major Thruston, with his usual courtesy, at once placed a number of labourers on daily duty at the hospital and thus kept the place in good condition. He added a new wing for all the contagious cases, besides putting up a separate enclosure and hut, some distance off, for small-pox patients.

Small-pox is endemic in Uganda, and every now and again becomes epidemic. I lost one patient, a Soudanese soldier, during the epidemic of 1894 at Kampala; his was confluent variola. I had several cases in Unyoro, but they were all of a mild type.

During my stay in Unyoro we had armed friendly Waganda; one of them was always on duty at the hospital entrance. The hospital orderly was a Soudanese sergeant of the name of Farijalla Memvu; he had already served in this capacity under Emin Pacha. The name "Memvu" means "Ripe Banana." Other curious names are found amongst the Soudanese soldiers. One of my patients at Fajao was named "Timsah Omar," that is, "Crocodile Donkey."

Speaking of names, there are peculiar ones met with amongst the Wanyamwezi porters. In one of my caravans I had men whose names, translated into English, were: Half-Rupee, One-Rupee, Never-Mind, Hard-Work, Bad-Work, War, Cannon, Hippopotamus.

With Swahilies the two favourite names are "Juma," which means "Friday," and "Hamis," "Thursday," and combinations of these two names, such as "Friday the Son of Thursday," "Thursday the Son of Friday." Very often there are so many who have the same name, that the men themselves take or are given some sobriquet, such as "Tumbusi" (vulture), if he had a bald spot on the top of his head, or "Fundi" (artisan), if he showed aptitude for carpentering or other work.

The seven hospital huts at Masindi have been gradually increased in number. They are grass-huts, and are constructed on the Soudanese pattern. Each has a fireplace in the centre and holds three native bedsteads.

Last September some very heavy thunder-storms burst over Masindi. The ammunition store was above-ground and about fifteen yards from my hut. The knowledge of this fact did not add to one's equanimity, when blinding flash and crashing thunderclap, apparently synchronous in time, occurred every minute. One night I was hurriedly sent for, as the lightning had struck two huts. One grass-hut it pierced sideways without setting fire to it, and a Soudanese woman who was inside the hut at the time escaped unhurt. Another grass-hut the lightning struck vertically through the top and down the middle, and neither was this one set on fire. But of the five men who were in the hut, two were killed on the spot and the three others were brought to me for treatment. The two dead men showed not the slightest sign of external injury, but their bodies were icy-cold, as if just taken out of ice, though the limbs were perfectly supple. Of my three patients, one was more or less dazed, but not otherwise injured, and he soon recovered; the two others were in a bad plight. One of them, moaning incessantly, had several patches burnt down his left side, though his clothes were not injured in any way; he seemed to be in great pain and to have been rendered silly and stupid. The third man had no sign of external injury, but was quite demented for the time. He was a big strong fellow and required five men to hold him, whilst I administered restoratives. He rolled about on the ground in a paroxysm of pain, and had to be held to prevent his hurting himself. He uttered deep groans, whilst blood-stained froth issued from his mouth and nostrils; his eyes were closed and his hands tightly clenched. I feared the worst; but the warmth of the fire, warm blankets, hot drinks, and restoratives pulled him through the night, and in three weeks time he was perfectly cured. His throat hurt him at first so much, that I had great difficulty in feeding him.

PATIENTS AT THE HOSPITAL DISPENSARY.

In the illustration, representing patients at the hospital dispensary, he is the tall man supported by his fellow-sufferer from the lightning; both men were then convalescent.

The herd of Government cattle were also struck. One animal was transfixed and killed on the spot, two others were injured and had to be slaughtered. The meat was distributed by the officer in command, and thus a portion fell to me, the first beef within the last six months. At Christmas the officer slaughtered a young bullock and an old cow, and for the second and last time I had beef in Unyoro.

One of my duties was to visit the other forts. Fort Hoima stood first on the list. It was the principal station in Unyoro prior to the transfer of head-quarters to Masindi. It is not surrounded by a trench, but has simply a stockade. A good many of the poles have sprouted, and a green leafy belt now encircles the fort. When I first saw it, it was garrisoned by friendly Waganda. Subsequently I received instructions to bring Soudanese from Mahaji, relieve the Waganda, and give them permission to return to Uganda.

The sub-chief in charge of the Waganda garrison insisted, however, on my giving him this permission in writing. Many of the natives have a great faith in anything written. Once in Usoga a chief visited me; as a sort of introduction he pulled out a piece of paper carefully wrapped up in a clean cloth and presented it. On it was written that the said chief had been imprisoned for a while, but by the clemency of the Government had been permitted to return to his chieftainship.

At Hoima there is a Makraka settlement. They belong to a cannibal tribe. So convinced are the Soudanese that these settlers still have a predilection for human flesh, especially for tender children, that they do not allow their offspring to wander near the village of these supposed ogres. The chief of the settlement is a handy blacksmith. He wears a lot of iron ornaments. He is particularly proud of his beard, because the Soudanese, Lendu, Wanyoro, and Waganda who live around him never can grow either beard or moustache. He carefully plaits his beard and lubricates it with grease. He wears a cloth apron; but all his wives are very conservative, and still adhere to Eve's first raiment of leaves. As the fig-tree in this region is rather difficult to climb, the Makraka ladies find it easier to clothe themselves with the first handful of grass or leaves they meet with, as long as the leaves are not prickly and do not sting. Most of these women wear ornaments, ear-rings, bracelets, and necklaces, either of beads or of iron-wire; they plait their wool, which is somewhat longer than what the Wanyoro or Waganda grow. The huts are perfectly defenceless. The community lives by agriculture, chiefly maize, kaffre-corn, sweet-potatoes, and locusts. The locusts provide their otherwise vegetarian diet with an occasional change. As soon as ever a swarm visits them, old and young are busy collecting locusts which can be stored for a considerable length of time if previously dried in the sun.

ENTRANCE OF FORT HOIMA

Kites feed also on these locusts, and may be seen accompanying a locust swarm. I have watched them catching a locust in the air, holding it in their claws, and without stopping in their flight, feed by taking a bite at it now and again. These birds become at times very impudent. Twice has a kite swooped down on me and flown off with my cap. I recovered the cap by watching where the disillusioned bird dropped it. I have seen them snatch meat out of the hand of a native returning from market; and once a kite flew

A MAKRAKA FAMILY.

off with several bird-skins which I had put out to dry. I wonder what the carnivorous bird thought of it, when he found that the birds he had stolen contained cotton-wool instead of flesh and bone.

Near the Makraka village I saw a native dog catching locusts and eating them. The dog just gave a snap right and left as the swarm flew up; occasionally he caught one, but more often he missed and had to try again.

Baboons came in foraging-parties to raid and plunder the fields of the Makraka. I tried to shoot some of these robbers;

but they distrusted my appearance and scampered off without my getting within range, though they did not mind the Makraka in the least.

At Hoima I had a case of sporadic small-pox, and quite a crowd of itch patients. It is the female itch parasite which causes all the trouble. She burrows under the skin to deposit her eggs; her favourite site is between the fingers, but I have had patients with the whole of the lower part of their body one mass of sores. Cleanliness is a great preventive. The eggs take three days to hatch, consequently a single application of unguentum sulphuris is not enough to cure; it is as well to repeat the treatment to make quite sure of destroying the whole brood. The male parasite only wanders about the human body in search of a spouse.

On the 9th of September 1897, at 12.30 noon, at Masindi Fort, in Unyoro, a very powerful shock of earthquake occurred. I was sitting in my room, and the officer commanding the district was at the open door, leaning against one of the doorposts and chatting with me. My tent-loads, to be out of reach of white-ants, happened to be slung from a bamboo-pole stretched across the room. My companion first became aware of the earthquake. He saw the suspended loads swaying pendulum-fashion, and the next moment the whole house rocked and shook. To me, sitting in a chair, the sensation communicated to the feet was exactly the same tremulous movement which one experiences in an express train going at full speed. The illusion was the stronger, owing to a rumbling noise very similar in sound, which accompanied the shock. It lasted perhaps a minute. The natives in the fort also noticed it. I was told that in September 1896 a similar shock was experienced in this very hut.

My hut at Hoima was more picturesque than comfortable. A number of the props which supported the narrow verandah had sprouted and formed a living enclosure of young trees. The reed-work which closed up the verandah breast-high prevented access of air, and the condition of the interior could be gathered by the many toad-stools which were flourishing in the room. The hut was rendered still more damp, dark, and dismal by a reed-screen run across the room to screen off a recess to serve as a bedroom.

Amongst the prisoners at Hoima there was a man sent

UNYORO

by chief Yabuswezi who wished the man to be punished for having bewitched the village, thereby causing a hyæna to carry off three of the inhabitants. I liberated the man, and explained to Yabuswezi that white men do not believe in such superstitions.

I went to Unyoro by the new caravan road, and I returned to Uganda by the old route which passes by Hoima, the upper crossing of the Kafu River, and through Singo. The number and size of the swamps, through which the old caravan road

MY HUT AT HOIMA.

leads, surprised me. In some parts, attempts had been made to bridge a swamp, but not being kept in repair, the scaffolding had tumbled down. This made it impossible to use the bridge and, owing to the débris, made it most difficult to pass even alongside of it.

I had in my caravan several Wanyoro porters wearing a petticoat made of strips of leaves of the wild date-palm.

A favourite shape of gourd-bottle for a journey consists of two bulbs with a narrow neck or constriction joining them. The upper bulb is small and acts as a sort of funnel for filling the bottle; the neck serves to hold the gourd or to tie it to the girdle when marching.

The upper crossing of the Kafu River is shallow compared to the lower crossing at Mruli; it is also more open. Hundreds of wild duck were disturbed at our approach; some splashed and fluttered noisily down-stream, others flew up, and, after circling above our heads, went up-stream. On the opposite bank friendly Waganda were waiting to ferry us across in dug-outs; and when the last of my caravan had crossed the Kafu, we had left Unyoro.

CHAPTER XII.

OUR STATIONS ON THE NILE.

SHULI NATIVES.

THE Nile! What a marvellous panorama the name conjures up! A nation arising out of pre-historic haze, flourishing for thousands of years, disappearing for ever! The vanished splendour of the Pharaohs, the lost lore of the Egyptians, the hidden mysteries of the Pyramids! A babe cradled on its bosom, destined to become the Lawgiver of the world, whose divinely-inspired message, "Thou shalt love the Lord thy God, and thou shalt love thy neighbour as thyself," sounds through all eternity!

Recalling the stupendous structures erected by the mighty race which the hand of Fate has swept away, and glancing at the puny fort at Fovira, the river might apply to us Byron's lines:—

> "Creatures of clay—vain dwellers in the dust!
> The moth survives you, and are ye more just?
> Things of a day! you wither ere the night,
> Heedless and blind to Wisdom's wasted light!"

Seen from the fort at Fovira, the huge expanse of water might be taken for a tranquil lake, for there is not a sound to betray the motion. But the resistless current which is ever sweeping onward becomes apparent by the islands floating past. Noiselessly and swiftly they glide into view and pass out of sight. Relentless as Fate, silent as death, ceaseless as time, the ancient river pursues its majestic course.

The river scenery at Fovira is striking. The wild date-palm waves a gentle greeting with its graceful many-fingered leaves, the welcome banana holds out its luscious fruit, and the dark green of the papyrus contrasts with the lighter green of the various shrubs and trees around.

Fovira is purely and simply a military frontier station; it is quite out of the track of the ivory dealers and consequently there is practically no business whatever. To be in receipt of

RIVER SCENERY AT FOVIRA.

a comfortable salary, and yet have no other European near to criticise one's shabbiest attire or most frugal meal; to have a few humdrum daily routine duties to attend to and yet abundance of leisure to gratify one's hobbies of gardening or carpentering; to live in a perennial warm English summer with the thermometer on an average at 75° F., and yet have the nights pleasantly cool to enjoy a crackling wood-fire; to have boating and fishing on one side and partridge and guinea-fowl shooting on the other, with an occasional reed-buck or water-buck thrown in to enliven the sport; to enjoy splendid health year in year out, and yet be accredited with heroism for continuing to hold the appointment; to delight neighbouring chiefs with handsome presents and yet have not a penny of the expense to bear, as these gifts are provided for in the Budget; to have a nominal and minimum share of Government responsibility and yet locally "to boss the show," as the Yankee tersely expresses the wielding of supreme authority,—to combine all these at the same time, one has to be appointed officer in charge of Fovira, and then one has in addition a sabbath stillness throughout the week, lovely scenery, a timid and peaceful native population, and last but not least, a regular monthly service with England, bringing a fresh supply of letters, newspapers, periodicals and books.

The resident must keep his own garden, his own poultry, his own sheep and goats; but the cost of this is practically nil, and may afford him a pleasant occupation. This *dolce far niente* and truly rural existence suits best the sort of man who can find absorbing interest in the progress of his rice crops, the size of his onions, the goodness of his potatoes, the delicacy of his peas and beans, the number of his carrots and beet-roots, the mellowness of his melons, the succulence of his papayes, the fragrance of his mignonette, and the rich display of colour of his pansies, pinks, marigolds, zenias, and nasturtiums, and who is not above taking pleasure in hearing of the last lamb or kid born to his flock and the last batch of chickens reared. Government has gratuitously supplied the station with some forty head of cattle; as none are slaughtered and the herd steadily multiplies, there need be no lack of milk and cream and butter, to complete the happiness of this Arcadian life.

The fort stands about 20 feet above the level of the river. One side slopes down to the water, the other three sides have an earth wall, a stockade, and a deep trench to protect them. There are two entrances, one on each side of the fort. Of these, one is by means of a narrow drawbridge, looking somewhat like a ladder when drawn up; its length gauges the width of the trench. A good many of the poles which were used for the stockade belong to a juicy-stemmed plant. These have sprouted, and with their crowns of tropical leaves they lend a picturesque charm to the surroundings. Their presence has probably attracted the scores of brilliantly coloured beetles which on my first visit I saw buzzing about. Most of them were longicorns, some flaunting a conspicuous blue and **white dress, others a sombre red and black.** Other species, however, were also represented. I picked up a fine specimen of the **rhinoceros-beetle, and the shining black cetonia burrowed in and out amongst the thatch.**

To prevent the river-side of the fort from gently sliding one day into the river, a part of it has been banked up. This spot, with the grateful shade of an adjoining tree, seems indicated

DRAWBRIDGE OF FORT FOVIRA.

by Nature as the very place for the afternoon cup of tea. Here, in the soft balmy atmosphere, with the silver sheen of the silent river at one's feet, and the deep blue of heaven's endless space overhead, with the sleepy drone of beetles humming around, and the ringdoves cooing from the stately palms, one yields to the gentle spirit of poetry which breathes around the scene, and one welcomes :—

> This hour of restful pleasure
> As a foretaste of pleasures to come,
> Which angels of God cannot measure,
> Which mind of man cannot sum !

It was at Fovira that I first saw a small species of crow with a long, brown, and pointed tail. It was present in large numbers, and busy on the newly-tilled fields in search of grubs. At first I thought there must be two distinct species, as the beak of some was black and of others blood-red; but when I saw the black-billed feeding the red-billed, I knew that one was but the young of the other. The red colour was due to the presence of blood shining through the horny substance, and exactly in the same way that a finger-nail becomes pale when pressed, the red beak became colourless under pressure. I saw here, too, the pretty green pigeon called "ninga" by the Swahilies. Its feet and bill are orange-red. It lives on berries. When perched in the green foliage it is most difficult to distinguish from its surroundings.

There are pleasant walks in the neighbourhood, and since the Government road leading to Masindi has been finished, the pedestrian can walk for hours without being bothered by the prickly darts of the rank grass, or the thorns, thistles, and burrs, which obstructed the path on my first visit to Fovira.

Everybody has not a talent for building a house, but the officer in charge of Fovira knew what he was about when he built the neat bungalow inside the fort. It is a combination of two Soudanese circular huts joined on to a small central Swahili hut. A narrow verandah runs all round the building. Each of the three rooms has three small square windows with wooden shutters. The mud walls, of the usual wattle and daub style, are washed over with some whitish clay, the nearest approach to white-washing which can be locally obtained.

My host courteously placed one of the rooms at my disposal. He was busy superintending the construction of a seine or casting-net for supplying his table more easily with fish; in the meantime he persuaded me to while away an hour on the river with hook and line. I have never been a devotee of Izaac Walton's "gentle art," and it is years since I baited a hook and threw a line; nor have I gone in for boating since I feathered an oar at college; but I accepted the invitation as offering a better chance of seeing a species of kingfisher which my host, not knowing its name, called the "golden kingfisher," and which, according to him, did not answer the description of any of the different sorts of kingfishers one usually meets with in Africa. It was not the large black and white sort, which hovers with incessant flutter of wings above one spot, keenly watching for its prey, and then suddenly drops like a stone with a splash into the water and emerges with a wriggling fish newly caught; nor was it the tiny many-coloured bird, the weight of whose brilliant-hued body scarcely bends the water-reeds on which it perches; nor was it the glorious blue-backed species with the black shoulders; nor any other that I could think of. To see the "golden kingfisher" I went. The current swept my line into the form of a huge arc, the hooks got entangled in the reeds and lost, and it was sweating hard work to row against the stream for even a short distance

THE WANYORO CHIEF LEJUMBA.

back to our landing-place. As for the "golden kingfisher"—it refused to show itself. Another long spell of time will have to elapse before I am persuaded to try again the enthusiastic angler's absorbing pursuit.

About a quarter of an hour's walk from the fort, the Wanyoro chief, Lejumba, has pitched his kraal. It is interesting to know that he is the son and successor of chief Rionga, with whom Baker Pasha made blood-brotherhood. Lejumba allowed me to photograph him with some of his sub-chiefs and leading men, and he was as pleased as Punch when I presented him with a copy of his likeness on the day I left. He made recently a successful punitive raid against some tribe living higher up the river and on the opposite bank, and brought back some hundreds of sheep and goats. A handsome share of his spoil, I am told, he gave as a present to the fort. A good many of his patients were treated by me gratis, and his present to me of a couple of chickens was not meant as an acknowledgment for the scores of cases I had attended, but was simply the native style of greeting which a courteous African chief usually gives to every

THE LANGO CHIEF AMIEN.

European traveller, whether he be clerk or commissioner. I believe even missionaries have been driven to the conclusion, that gratitude is a stage in mental development which the African savage, whether he be peasant or chief, has not yet attained to. Lejumba is closely related to the royal house of Unyoro, for his father was the nephew of the late king, but a bitter blood-feud existed already then between the two families. He is, therefore, bound to be a faithful ally of the white man, for if he fell into the hands of ex-king Kabarega's sons, his doom would be sealed. He did not strike me as being particularly intelligent, but he is neither better nor worse than the average Wanyoro chief, though his face expresses cunning and self-indulgence.

On the opposite or northern bank of the Nile dwells the Lango race. They are not under British rule, but now and then they come across in dug-outs and barter native produce (sweet-potatoes and matama flour) in exchange for cloth and beads. I had an opportunity of seeing them, when their chief Amien came over with sons and followers to receive a Government present of cotton cloth, white and coloured. He has a fine and stately figure, though already "in the sere and yellow leaf" of age. He wore a serval skin girt round his loins, an amulet or charm round his neck, some bracelets, and an anklet. In spite of his wrinkles there was a manly, hardy expression on his face. One glance at him and his followers, would suffice to pick him out as the ἄναξ ἀνδρῶν of his tribe, as Kingsley would express it. It is noteworthy, that he did not affect the curious headgear adopted by his tribe. Most of his men, including his two sons, had their wool plaited into a bun-shaped excrescence on the occiput, ornamented with beads and well-lubricated with grease and mud. Some of the warrior dandies wore huge wigs of bright-coloured feathers. Every one, man or boy, was clothed with a small apron of cloth or goat-skin. The women go about naked, but are fond of decking themselves with ornaments.

The serval is a carnivorous animal of the cat tribe. Judging by the skins brought for sale, there must be a great many different species of it. Some have tiny spots set close together, and are of a brown colour; others are bright orange-yellow, with large handsome black spots. I have seen them sold at Kampala brand-new at two shillings each.

One day two Lango natives, a boy and a man, evidently father and son, crossed to our side. The boy wore already the national ornament, a tiny bun on his occiput; in his arms he held a long-legged white chicken which he wanted to barter for cloth.

Government officials, I have been told, are prohibited from crossing the Nile at Fovira, but judging from what one can see of the opposite bank from a distance, the Lango are a thriving agricultural race, with numerous and well-peopled hamlets. With the exception of certain landing-places, the dense papyrus growth draws an impenetrable barrier some hundreds of yards wide along both sides of the river.

OUR STATIONS ON THE NILE 189

I saw neither crocodiles nor hippos at Fovira, though no doubt they are present. There are a good many white-ant hills about, though the fort itself is singularly free from this nuisance.

About an hour's walk from Fovira I came upon a different race. They call themselves the "Falua," and differ from the Wanyoro in every respect. Wanyoro women never go naked, but here I came upon not a few as nude as the Wakavirondo. It

SEM-SEM DRYING-STACK.

was the time of the sem-sem crop. The sem-sem plant grows somewhat like flax, but it bears a number of vertical pods which, when ripe, burst at the top and form a deep miniature cup surmounted by a miniature crown. The plants are reaped with an ordinary knife, tied into small bundles, and then attached to the sem-sem drying-stack.

The drying-stack consists of a reed-screen resting slantingly against a horizontal pole supported on two vertical props with forked ends. The screen is made of interlacing reeds, and is placed so as to receive as many as possible of the direct rays of the sun. On this reed-screen the sem-sem crop is allowed to dry thoroughly, when the plants, held with the open mouth of the pods pointing downwards, at the slightest shake will shower all their tiny seeds on to the cloth or mat spread out to receive them. The sem-sem is an oil-giving seed, and is of immense importance to agricultural races living almost exclusively on a vegetable diet. A very simple method of extracting the oil is to toast the sem-sem slightly and then boil it; the oil rises to the surface and can be skimmed off. If properly prepared, the oil is equal to the finest olive-oil, and very useful for culinary purposes. A pint of it at Masindi could be bought for two shillings.

The monkey-nut, which forms such an important trade between Mozambique and Marseilles, where it is used in the manufacture of the so-called olive-oil of commerce, thrives at Fovira; but the natives find it easier to extract their oil from the sem-sem grain.

Amongst the Falua neither men nor boys go uncovered. The Falua spear has a very small but sharp spear-head. The villages lie quite unprotected; they seemed to be well stocked with sheep, goats, and poultry. Spiral coils of brass wire round the wrists were worn by the wealthier ladies, and ornaments of beads by the poorer class.

A curious corn-bin is manufactured by the villagers. It consists of wicker-work, and resembles somewhat a soiled linen-basket with a thick rim. It is well plastered with red clay both inside and out, and probably answers its purpose of protecting the grain from insects and rats.

Wimbi is another grain largely cultivated by the natives. It is used principally in the preparation of their native brew. Wimbi is a species of grass, the stalk of which bears several tufts of seeds. When ripe, the tufts are nipped off by hand or cropped with a short knife; they are then thoroughly dried in the sun, and finally threshed out in a very primitive way with sticks.

From a shrub which grows six to eight feet high the natives gather a small kind of bean. This, too, is largely cultivated here. In the illustration one of the women has a grass-platter with a lot of these tiny pods collected, preparatory to shelling them for their frugal meal. Most of the huts were of the ordinary type, but a few amongst them were of superior workmanship. The hut resembled in shape half an orange, with the thatch reaching to the ground, except for a

A FALUA FAMILY

small space in front, where it was cut to expose the mud-wall with its neatly finished arched entrance. Like most of the natives, men and women smoke.

Many of the small children have a very large abdomen, and remind one of nestlings. In one village over a score of these children were marched up to me for treatment. It was a sight! In not a few cases the condition is natural, the child devouring whatever it can lay its hands on; in other cases it is due to ailments which readily yield to treatment.

A FALUA DWELLING.

One of the difficulties with which the medical man has to contend in these regions is the impossibility of finding out the exact ailment of the patient, owing to the interpreter's limited knowledge of the language. A ludicrous, though rather unpleasant, occurrence once happened to me in this connection. I was attending a number of Wakavirondo captives, women and children. The patient had some gastric trouble. I do not know, of course, how the interpreter translated my question, but the patient, together with eight or ten other women, proceeded to give me a visible proof of the form her indisposition took.

Another difficulty is, that natives often come for treatment for imaginary complaints. One of the great Waganda chiefs, the Kago, used to come to me regularly with his story of the "worm." One day the "worm" was in his heart, another day in the small of his back, another time it had travelled to his arm, and so on. I gave him the benefit of the doubt, and treated him for rheumatism, oppression, or anything rational bearing on his symptoms. In spite of all his ailments he grew daily more stout and strong. One day I gave him a strong purgative. He did not reappear for a week; when he came, he was accompanied by one of his men leading a fat sheep. He had never given me the slightest acknowledgment for the scores and scores of times he had come to me for the treatment which he was receiving gratis. This day he solemnly made me a present of a fat sheep. He assured me that my last medicine was splendid. The effect was such, he said, that he really thought that he was about to die, and that it had utterly prostrated him for days. He felt, however, that he was cured, and he came to thank me publicly. It was many months, before he was troubled again by his old enemy the "worm." I was interested when one day the Mission doctor, Dr. A. Cook, incidentally mentioned to me that some natives came to him with imaginary diseases. They cause a serious loss of time to him whom I know to be one of the most able and hard-working men I have had the privilege of meeting either in professional consultation or in private life.

The Falua not only use the ordinary type of corn-store seen everywhere, but have a peculiar one of their own. Instead of the basket being very deep and the cover over it removable, the basket is wide but shallow, and the cover over it is a fixture with an opening in front permitting access to the store. The corn is therefore much more handy to get at, and the opening is readily closed again with dry banana-leaves or grass.

The Falua have a good many banana plantations, but the banana does not play here as important a part in every-day life as in Uganda, though a banana plantation can provide the native with everything he requires—shelter, clothing, fuel, food.

Returning from the Falua village to the fort, my boy uttered an exclamation of alarm; he had seen me pass and almost touch a deadly puff-adder lying coiled up in the grass. As it had disappeared, we did not stay to look for it, but left the dangerous spot as quickly as possible.

I was shown at Fovira some exquisitely delicate white feathers obtained from under the tail of a large bird. From the description of the bird I felt satisfied it belonged to the stork species—it is, in fact, the well-known marabou. The feathers are extremely valuable, almost worth their weight in gold. I saw scores and scores of these birds solemnly sitting on the trees, when I journeyed from Fovira to Mruli by the road which gives a view of the Nile almost the whole way. It was here, that I shot a specimen of the Unyoro guinea-fowl. I was anxious to secure it; but two of the Soudanese soldiers, eager to bring me the bird, managed to pull out the whole of its tail and a handful or two of other feathers. This brings to my mind, that I once saw a Swahili porter carrying a chicken ready plucked but left alive, and tied to his belt. I had the chicken at once killed and the porter punished.

I have noticed at times diametrically opposite qualities in a Swahili. He will share whatever he is eating with anybody who holds out his hand for a portion of it, and he will allow his sick companion to die of hunger and thirst before his very eyes. He will follow bravely into the very thickest of the fight, with death staring him in the face, and he will run away and hide himself when a few shots are fired near him. He will fight and quarrel to be allowed to carry the heaviest tusk of ivory, and he will be equally quarrelsome to get the lightest load. And yet, when I said good-bye to Fort Fovira and returned to Masindi, I was glad that at least half of my porters were Swahilies, for they are well-accustomed to caravan work.

Fajao, the other Government station on the Nile, is not a fort; it is purely and simply a military settlement. The scenery at Fajao is the very opposite of what one sees at Fovira. Instead of having a silent river, one hears the ceaseless roar of the Murchison Falls; instead of the open flat country, one sees steep hills and lofty forest trees; instead of having the peaceful Lango as neighbours, the hostile Shuli hold the opposite bank. Crocs and hippos swarm in the river, and lions infest the neighbourhood. Instead of a healthy station, the climate must try every white man's constitution, if stationed here for any length of time; death and danger surround him by land and by water, and all his energies are called forth to guard against them.

There was no hospital at Fajao, but Major Thruston most kindly gave me *carte blanche* to build one. "Build it where you like, how you like, what you like, and stay as long as you like," was his way of summing it up. Thereupon I set to work, and in twelve days had built the hospital shown in the illustration. A row of patients may be seen calling at the hut which serves as dispensary; next to it is an open shed which answers the purpose of a waiting-room for the patients. Four hospital huts have been erected, similar to what has answered so well at Masindi, and the hospital grounds are similarly enclosed by a grass-fence. On my second visit to Fajao, I was very thankful to have a hut ready to receive the poor soldier who was so badly mauled by the man-eating lioness. It is always well to have a special place for patients.

A male or female negro in the full bloom of lusty adoles-

THE HOSPITAL AT FAJAO.

cence has a strong peculiar odour which European olfactory nerves fail to appreciate. When unwashed feet and foul ulcers are superadded, the effect is overpowering. A whiff from the bottomless pit with the lid off is what one imagines, if popular notions respecting that undesirable place are to be relied on, the only thing that can possibly equal it.

Abura, one of the Shuli chiefs, came to me to be treated. He was suffering from a complication of diseases. For one of these I had to perform the operation which Jews and Mohammedans practise as a religious rite. Amongst Africans some races perform it also as a national custom, other races abhor it. To the latter belong the Shuli, and Abura became seriously alarmed whether his subjects might not depose him on hearing to what he had submitted. He arranged in that case to return with all his family and followers, and settle on the British side of the Nile. However, his fears proved groundless. Another of his complications was ringworm. Of this disease I saw several cases at Fajao on our side of the river. Abura had only brought two of his wives with him; they were absolutely nude. He, however, and all his men were covered, wearing an apron of goat-skin.

The Shuli wear anklets, bracelets, armlets, and necklets of brass wire or beads; but a remarkable fashion with many of them is to pierce the under-lip and stick through it a short blunt pencil of glass one to two inches long. They push it through from inside, so that the thick end of the pencil touches the teeth.

They are expert fishermen with hook and line and, in spite of the hundreds of crocodiles, fearlessly paddle in their fragile dug-outs amid the foaming and whirling backwash of the river, where it forms the deep bay-like indentations. They have neither float nor lead to their line, and the hook is only a most ridiculous bent piece of soft iron-wire, and yet I saw them catch fish after fish, a species of large delicious mullet. Two other species of fish caught here are a large mud-fish and the small bony perch one sees at Mruli.

On my second visit to Fajao, Abura sent word that he would like very much to see me, but that he had received orders from the supreme chief at Wadelai that neither he nor the other Shuli chiefs were to be friendly with the English, but were to support the cause of ex-king Kabarega.

The Fajao garrison were going through a trying time with their crops; drought, locusts, hippos, and baboons uniting to impoverish the settlement. As might be expected from its being a settlement in a tropical forest, all sorts of interesting zoological specimens frequent these woods. The black and white Colobus and several other species of monkey, a green squirrel with three black stripes from head to tail, a red-nosed rat with a red patch near the tail, and lovely specimens of papilio and charaxes. A little lower down the river the pepper-plant, bearing the small red chili pods, grows wild in profusion as a common shrub eight feet high.

The road from Fajao to Masindi, lying through the late chief

Amara's country, was in excellent condition, and half-a-dozen men could have walked abreast. Caravans, however, always travel in Indian file, one behind the other. With natives on the march, the head of a family usually walks first, armed with a spear. The others follow more or less according to the lightness of their burdens; the poor drudge of the family has the biggest and heaviest load and comes last.

NATIVES ON THE MARCH.

On my last visit to Fajoa a Shuli spy was brought to me. The Effendi thought the man was a friend to the English, because he came from time to time pretending to bring news that ex-king Kabarega was about to attack the settlement. Such attack never happened, and the man only came to collect information for Kabarega. I questioned the man closely, and soon found out what he had really come for. According to him, the ex-king was about to attack us with an army of which one thousand men were armed with guns. He said the king had heard that we were all terrified by the news, and that the Soudanese captain in command had run away to Masindi and the white medicine-man had fled down the Nile. I saw at once what this garbled news evidently referred to, as I had gone one day in a dug-out downstream to shoot a hippo, and the captain had left Fajao for Masindi on business. I told the spy to let Kabarega know we were ready for him, and that if he did come, in all probability he would never return again. The Shuli then remarked, that Kabarega would probably not come on hearing we were ready for him. In order that the man might not guess what we wished him to tell his master, I now strongly recommended he should not let the ex-king know, that we were hoping he would come and that the white medicine-man was still here.

After the spy had been allowed to re-cross the river, I consulted with the three Soudanese officers, and we got everything ready to give Kabarega a warm reception if he did venture to attack us. However, he did not come near us; he sent instead an armed band to raid our friendlies and to capture slaves. It happened, that the Shuli had also sent an armed raiding band for the same purpose. These two bands, having crossed the river unknown to each other, met, and taking each other for the enemy, they at once had a hotly contested fight. Under cover of darkness each party escaped and re-crossed the river, leaving their dead on the field. About twenty men were killed on each side. This extraordinary mistake, that friends should turn their weapons against each other and slaughter each other, was attributed by the superstitious natives to the magic arts of the white medicine-man. It had, however, one good result, our friendlies were left for a while unmolested by ex-king Kabarega and his Shuli allies.

CHAPTER XIII.

ON THE SHORES OF LAKE ALBERT.

LUR CHILDREN.

THERE are two Government stations on Lake Albert, almost opposite to each other,—Kibero on the east shore, Mahaji on the west. The former is inhabited by Wanyoro, the latter by the Lur. These are two distinct races, differing in language, dress, and mode of life. The native village at Kibero is a thriving place, and it possesses a paying industry; but Major Thruston, who saw it in King Kabarega's days and before it fell into British hands, told me that formerly it was three times the size it is now. It has therefore not yet recovered from the effects of the war waged against King Kabarega. A few of the men wear bark-cloth, but the majority are dressed in cowhides thrown like a cloak about the body. The women have short petticoats of bark-cloth reaching from the waist to below the knees. The covering of boys is usually a mantle of goat-skin, but girls up to puberty go uncovered. Babies are carried on the back in a sort of leathern sling supported by the mother's shoulders and waist. This leaves the legs, arms, and head of the baby free. Almost every family owns a few goats or sheep. The boys work as goatherds or shepherds, but the girls help their mothers in the great local salt-industry.

There seems to be an inexhaustible wealth of salt here. Some day European appliances and European enterprise may turn this industry into a most valuable and paying concern. In King Kabarega's reign one of the chiefs secured for himself and his followers the monopoly of the manufacture, and paid for the concession a tribute or rent of one thousand loads of salt annually. When the British Government, having expelled King Kabarega, took over Kibero, this tribute or rent was reduced, owing to the great diminution in the population, to three hundred

IN THE NATIVE VILLAGE AT KIBERO.

loads of salt annually, each load to weigh 30 lbs., in other words, 9000 lbs. of salt per annum. The salt-industry is worked exclusively by women and girls. A brisk trade is carried on. At Hoima one Mganda asked me for a "permit" to send sixty of his men to buy salt at Kibero. There is no other industry in this locality. Agriculture proved a failure owing to the excessive amount of salt in the soil. The salt is bartered in exchange for food supplies, cloth, and shells. Fishing would be sure to pay. I saw Soudanese boys constantly catching fish, but the natives are either too lazy or find it easier to purchase canoe-loads of fish from the lake-dwellers higher up, who bring their catch to the Kibero market. The Kibero salt is greyish-white, but not at all unpleasant to eat, though prepared in the crudest possible manner. The European naturally prefers the white table-salt from England, if he has any left among his provisions, but should he have run out of it, there would be no hardship in using the native salt.

The salt is extracted by a very simple process. The soil is

first of all scraped together into small mounds about a foot high. It is then loosely scattered over the surface, apparently to let it dry in the sun, and all obvious impurities are removed. Two earthen vessels are required, one large, the other small. A few stones are arranged so as to support the larger vessel, and the smaller vessel is then placed underneath it. The larger acts as a percolator, the smaller as a receiver. There is a hole in the bottom of the percolator, blocked with tiny pebbles in such a manner, that the fluid can only pass through in drops. The scraped-up soil is now placed in the percolator and slightly oversaturated with water, and the mass is stirred about with the hands. The slight excess of water trickles past the pebbles and drips into the lower vessel, carrying with it a certain proportion of the salt which it has dissolved out. From time to time, knowing by experience when to do so, the woman scoops out the soil which has yielded up its share of salt, and throws it

THE SALT-INDUSTRY AT KIBERO.

on the adjoining refuse-heap which in course of time becomes a regular wall of earth. As a rule, each woman attends to but one set of earthen vessels. When the day's work is done, the saline water, earthen vessels, and scoop are carried home in a narrow wooden trough which no doubt has come into use to prevent the loss of any of the precious saline fluid, should it happen to splash out on the way home. This saline water is boiled down at home and yields up its salt.

It is obvious that the process of manufacture is so crude,

that only a small portion of the salt is really extracted, and the waste is considerable; but there is such a superabundance of fresh material to work upon, that it would not pay to waste more time on each potful of soil subjected to this treatment. In hot sunny weather the whole female community is as busy as bees; but rainy weather puts at once a temporary stop to the work, because the natives do not even take the trouble to put up a slight shed to protect from the rain the particular spot which they happen to be working at. Should the hollow, where they work, get swamped by the rain, they abandon it for the time and proceed to tackle a fresh patch. When the salt is ready, it is made up into small loads weighing from 5 lbs. to 30 lbs., and is then carried by the men to the different markets. The men have apparently no other work to do, and in the meanwhile smoke and loaf about all day in an open shed, evidently their African club-room.

Melindwa, the chief, brought me a present of salt which I distributed among my Soudanese escort and Swahili porters.

Close to where the salt-industry is carried on, there are a dozen or more hot sulphur-springs which bubble out of the ground at the foot of the range of hills east of Kibero. Where it emerges from the soil, the water is boiling hot, but even a short run of a hundred yards in the open air cools the water sufficiently to enable one to enjoy a warm bath. Just for the novelty of the thing I indulged on the spot in such a bath, a cosy corner rendering the place absolutely private; but I found it more convenient afterwards to have the hot water brought to my tent. The water forms narrow channels, and has only to flow a few hundred yards to reach Lake Albert. There is a yellowish slimy incrustation on the pebbles over which the hot water flows.

I discovered some similar hot springs, six of them, all lying close together, on the west shore of Lake Albert, about two and a half hours from Mahaji; they have only three to five feet to run to reach the lake. They issue from the grassy foot of the hills which border the lake. I do not know if Emin Pasha was aware of their existence. It is rather curious that there should be hot springs on both sides of the lake. The water of the lake has a slightly mawkish taste.

During my stay at Kibero I succeeded, but not till I had put some pressure on chief Melindwa, in getting sanitary requirements added to every dwelling, and suitably screened off. The

Soudanese settlement was already provided, but to the native population it was a novelty. For generations they had used the adjoining scrub, the condition of which may be imagined. If plague germs by any chance had been conveyed to this locality, they would have found the exisiting insanitary condition the very thing for fostering their dissemination.

The official quarters at Kibero consist of three grass-huts. The two larger huts are built in the Swahili style; one for the European and the other for his servants. On my second visit I found a third hut erected. It was in the Soudanese pattern, circular, and sufficiently large to serve as a kitchen. Of all the methods of thatching, the Swahili is the worst. The roof often

MY QUARTERS AT KIBERO.

leaks when quite new, and after a very short exposure to the weather it is almost certain to let the rain pass freely. On my first visit a thunder-storm broke over the place during the night. I woke up with the drip-drip-drip of the rain falling on me. With difficulty I managed to light a candle, as some of the drops had splashed on the wick, and for some time it only spluttered in response to the match. My bed was soaked, and a score of leaks in other parts of the hut did not hold out much chance of a dry corner to sleep in. My umbrella was not large enough to crouch under and sleep. Looking around in search of some sort of shelter, I caught sight of the ground-sheet of my tent. At once I crept under it. It was rather an undignified position, but a welcome protection all the same. Though not the most cheerful way of spending the night, I knew from experience that it is possible to fare worse.

These huts are only 25 yards from the water. Imagination might draw quite a pleasant picture from certain given facts:— a private hut close to the sea, the only European within hundreds of miles, summer heat, shallow water, and patches of sandy beach. But the reality is a climb down from any lofty flights indulged in by the imagination: the hut leaks like a sieve, no European help is near in case of danger or illness, every precaution is necessary to avoid sun-stroke, the water harbours crocodiles, and the beach is rendered offensive and injurious by savages untrammelled by hygienic or any other considerations.

On my third journey across Lake Albert, I was entrusted with the duty of taking arrears of pay and rations to the Mahaji garrison, and of installing Nur Abdel Baïn Effendi as officer in command. I was also to select a number of men to form the new garrison under Nur Effendi, and to bring the others back with me. For this purpose some native dug-outs were to accompany me. The weather was unsettled and threatening, and Imam Effendi advised us to wait for a day or two. Both sides of the lake are bordered by mountains, and until the weather is sufficiently clear to see the opposite mountains, it is considered unsafe to venture across the lake in an open boat. On the first fine day, we embarked. As the dug-outs take longer to cross, we gave them a start of four hours. At 5 P.M. I followed in Her Majesty's steel-boat *Alexandra*. Sixteen men are required to row this boat across the lake, eight on, eight off alternately, four men to each side. A little grass-thatch awning, supported on four sticks, is put up near the stern, in order to provide the European with some shelter against the tropical sun. I had shot that afternoon a young crocodile, and some of the Soudanese had asked me to let them eat it. This inspired my Swahilies with an impromptu boat-song, the chorus of which was—

"Wanubi Kula mamba,
    Kula mamba, Kula mamba,
Wanubi Kula mamba!"

The last syllable of each word was yelled out *fortissimo*, with the mouth as wide open as possible; what Milton would call "linked sweetness long drawn out." The translation is—

"The Soudanese eat crocodiles,
    Eat crocodiles, eat crocodiles,
The Soudanese eat crocodiles!"

I had eight Swahili porters and eight Soudanese soldiers, each set taking it in turn to row for an hour. The boat was heavily laden with the bales of cloth, representing the arrears of pay for the Mahaji garrison.

All went well until about midnight, and it was nearly full moon. I was peacefully slumbering, when all of a sudden a terrific thunder-storm burst over us and covered us with dense

HER MAJESTY'S STEEL-BOAT "ALEXANDRA" ON LAKE ALBERT NYANZA.

darkness, illumined by fearfully vivid flashes of lightning, the glare of which blinded us. It is usually easy to steer the boat by keeping the opposite mountain-chain in view, but now the man at the helm could only steer according as the fitful lightning disclosed the tops of the distant mountain-range. The waves were tumultuous, and the boat danced like a cork on the top of the billows. Every now and again a big wave washed over us and threatened to engulf us. The boat was steadily filling, and every man toiled for dear life, either rowing, or baling out the water. I was miserably sea-sick. Most of the men were very ill, one of them even bringing up blood. In the morning the storm abated somewhat. We made for the nearest land and got ashore, thankful to Providence that the boat had outlived the storm. We did not quite know where we were, but felt sure that if we kept straight towards the mountains, we must cut across some footpath between the mountains and the lake. We had a nasty scramble through thorny jungle, but luckily found the footpath and now toiled along it. We were all wet through, and chilled with the bath in which we had sat for so many hours with our clothes on. A couple of men hurried ahead to have a fire ready for us. What was our surprise, when we found we were nowhere near Mahaji, and that we had returned to Kibero! The storm overtook us, when we were about half-way across the lake; in the darkness we must have moved round in a circle and finally steered back towards Kibero.

A grilling hot day succeeded. We were able to dry our belongings and such of the Government bales, as had got soaked. Most of my men were ill and exhausted; but to my surprise no attack of fever fell on me, though I fully expected it.

A somewhat similar misadventure once happened to me in my boyhood, when my brother and I were on a walking tour in Scotland. We had rested in an inn at the foot of a range of hills, and we decided to cross to the other side of the hills before night. The guide led us along a sheep track, but when it grew dusk he deserted us. We pushed on steadily in the direction indicated, lost the path, and floundered every now and again up to our knees in boggy mud-holes. When we reached the precipitous descent, we saw in the valley below us an inn, and we thought that it looked very much like the one we had left in the afternoon; but we attributed this to fancy, because we had to be ferried across a small stream which we had not noticed when we started. It was not till we were greeted by the same landlord, that we realised we had moved in a circle back to our starting-point.

It is singular to have had a repetition of such an experience in the heart of Africa, on one of the great lakes, and with suitable accompaniment of tumultuous waves, thunder, lightning, and rain.

As soon as the weather permitted it, we made another attempt to cross the lake, but this time during the day. We reached

Mahaji safely, and in time for an afternoon cup of tea in front of the hut built for the use of European officials on the slope of the hill.

In the steel-boat it took me ten hours, twelve hours, and eight and a half hours respectively to cross Lake Albert. I believe the quickest passage recorded has been a few minutes under eight hours.

Mahaji is perched on the top of a hill; Kibero is built on a plain. At Kibero no attempt is made at agriculture. At Mahaji banana groves and fields of Kaffre-corn supply the natives with

AFTERNOON TEA AT MAHAJI.

food and labour. At Kibero only scrub and undergrowth is found; Mahaji is well wooded.

Nur Effendi had safely crossed in the dug-out, but told me that he and his were very nearly drowned. He must indeed have had an awful time of it, remembering what we had experienced in the large steel-boat. Two other dug-outs with Swahilies had also succeeded in crossing; but the officer at Mahaji had promptly placed the men under supervision, in case they should turn out to be fugitive deserters. The other canoes had all speedily returned to Kibero, fearing to face the elements. Therefore no loss of life at sea resulted from the storm.

Having selected the twenty-five men to form the new garrison, I made arrangements to ship the others to Kibero with their women, children, followers, and belongings.

There was great rejoicing among the garrison on receiving their arrears of pay. The Effendi had quite a tidy sum owing to him, represented by a good many bales of cloth.

The native chief brought me a couple of chickens and a few eggs. I went to visit his village, and at the very entrance I came across a most interesting group. A young man, tall, well-built, and muscular, stood with a spear in his hand; by the door of the hut was his wife in the full bloom of youth; an urchin was playing on the ground. The whole scene, full of tranquil peace, recalled the condition of mankind at the dawn of history. The sort of leathern sling, in which Lur babies are carried, is a strong support to the weak spine of babyhood, and at the same time allows a full and free motion to head, arms, and legs. The baby partly sits in this leathern support. There are no crooked or bandy-legged individuals in the whole race. Only small children go about uncovered.

The spear carried by every adult male, is a business-like weapon, evidently not meant for show. I saw neither shields, nor bows, nor swords. The spear-head is somewhat like the Kavirondo one, small and narrow; it is continuous with a tubular iron prolongation one to two feet in length, into which the wooden shaft of the spear is inserted.

A queer fashion with many of the young warriors was the chignon-like bunch of gay feathers attached to the occiput. The men wore more ornaments than the women. Necklaces and bracelets of bright-coloured beads were very fashionable with the men. A few of the elders wore ivory bracelets and anklets. The men never went uncovered, and in this respect were much more particular than the women. Many of the women had their heads clean shaved.

The Lur women occupy, as regards dress, a position midway between the Makraka with their bunches of leaves and the Kavirondo with their tails of plaited strings. They wear the Makraka leaves and the Kavirondo tails. In the Lur village I saw a woman carrying an enormous burden of firewood on her head. It was a proof of the abundance of firewood in the neighbourhood. The logs of wood are tied into a long cone-shaped bundle eight to ten feet long. By this arrangement the huge load can be raised to the head without requiring any great muscular exertion of the arms. The load is first of all propped against the nearest tree, but with the narrow end resting on the ground. By bending the head, covered with a protective grass-pad, towards the load, but nearer its top-heavy end, only a slight effort is necessary to balance the whole mass on the head. With a little practice the women know exactly where the wood should be balanced, so as not to require the support of a hand to keep it on the head, as she walks home with it. The woman carries a staff in her hand, and leans against it when she stops to have a chat; she does not trouble to unburden herself of her load.

LUR WOMAN CARRYING A LOAD OF WOOD.

Most of the women carried a knife without a protective sheath; it is passed through the waist-belt, and usually worn on the right thigh. It is curved and fairly sharp, but is not meant for offence or defence. It is probably next to the cooking-pot the most necessary household article. With it the woman harvests the ears of matama-corn, peels sweet-potatoes or green bananas for dinner, slices the grass fibres for plaiting the fashionable tail, and uses it surgically to extract thorns and splinters of wood.

The Lur at Mahaji are a quiet, industrious, and well-to-do community. Their fields and banana-groves, their fowls, goats, and sheep, provide them with every necessary and luxury they can think of; and hence they pass a happy and peaceful existence, protected by the Soudanese garrison from being molested by hostile or envious neighbours.

Whilst I was at Mahaji, another severe thunder-storm occurred.

A LUR FAMILY AT MAHAJI

I passed a very unpleasant night; for although the hut in this case was water-tight, I fully expected either that the hut would be blown down or the tree behind it would be uprooted and fall on the top of it. More than once I was on the point of leaving the hut and exposing myself to the fury of the elements outside, in preference to being squashed inside the hut. In the morning the news was brought to us that the steel-boat *Alexandra* was a wreck. The force of the waves had caused a number of screws which bound the transverse sections together, to snap off, and the boat had parted amid-ships. What a blessing my crew and I were safe ashore! And what a singular proof how near we had been to death on that fearful night-storm at sea! What a piece of good luck that the boat should have held together long enough to enable us to reach Mahaji! Other local disasters were reported, amongst them the death of one native woman. The force of the wind must have been very great, to have overthrown the big tree which I saw lying uprooted in the village.

Very little damage was done, however, to the dwellings. Some of the grass-thatch of the Lur corn-stores was blown about a bit. The Lur dwellings are oval and low, the grass-thatch reaches right down to the ground, and the entrance projects slightly forward like a portico.

One of the objects of my visit to Mahaji was the selection of a site for a leper establishment. I had met with cases of leprosy in different parts of Unyoro, and my suggestion to collect the lepers, and to isolate them at Mahaji, was favourably received by the officer in command of Unyoro. The advantages offered by Mahaji were: removal of the lepers from Unyoro, their isolation, and an abundant local supply of food for them. A hill near the Lur village was selected and the ground cleared. Huts were being erected, and two women had already been transferred to the new leper station, when, owing to the Soudanese mutiny, the work had to be discontinued and I was recalled in a hurry to Masindi. But the difficulty was how to get back to Kibero, as the steel-boat was a wreck, and storms were of daily occurrence. Acting on the advice of Kiza, in charge of the Wanyoro dug-outs, it was decided to proceed in a dug-out to Tukwenda's, and from there to cross the lake at its narrow northern end. This proved, indeed, a quicker way of reaching Kibero than waiting at Mahaji for the weather to clear sufficiently to risk crossing the lake in a dug-out direct from Mahaji to Kibero. The steel-boat had of course to be abandoned at Mahaji. Tukwenda is a friendly Lur chief on the north-west shore of the lake.

The rapidity with which these thunder-storms appear on Lake Albert, reminds one of the warning sent by the prophet to king Ahab, as soon as ever a cloud of the size of a man's hand appeared on the horizon, lest the rain should stop him. Experience had taught us to keep close to the shore, to be able

LUR CORN-STORES.

to take refuge on land in case a storm should burst upon us. However, we reached our camp without a mishap, and the Lur chief Tukwenda at once paid me a visit.

He is a tall elderly man, of courteous and noble bearing, simply clad in a cowhide mantle with his muscular arms left bare. He wore no ornaments, and his example had evidently influenced his tribe. The men were all more or less well-covered. Tukwenda brought me a present of a splendid fat-tailed sheep; as African etiquette requires a return present of at least the same value, I delighted Tukwenda and his whole tribe by my gift of a bright yellow cotton cloth known locally as a "kanga." This piece of cloth had cost me originally at Kampala two and a half rupees, about three shillings, here it was worth double that amount. I could have bought the fattest sheep at Tukwenda's for about half-a-crown; my gift was therefore appreciated, and Tukwenda became exceedingly friendly and invited me to visit him at his kraal.

The mountain-chain, which at Mahaji abuts on the lake, gradually recedes from the shore in a north-westerly direction, and thus leaves a large and gradually broadening out plain between it and the lake. This plain is Tukwenda's realm. It is a most fertile and prosperous country, as the numerous and thriving kraals testify. Pleasant trees dot the surface, and in some parts, as at Pongo, where I shot my first elephant, there are virgin forests, visited by herds of elephants. The lake, one would imagine, would cause these lake-dwellers to be fishermen; but, with the exception of a few fish-baskets sunk to trap the fish, no attempt is made at fishing, either with a net or with hook and line. A number of small dug-outs go out daily in search of dead fish, which are picked up floating on the water. A huge fish carried on a pole by two men was brought to me. It was mottled with green and black spots and had a big head. The jaws displayed a ferocious set of teeth which could easily snap off a man's foot or arm. My men called it the Kambari-ya-fisi or hyæna-fish, a suggestive and appropriate name. I felt no inclination to taste such a horrid-looking creature, especially as it was picked up dead; I therefore declined the present which Lur taste considered a delicacy.

On visiting Tukwenda's kraal he introduced to me his three daughters, fine young girls, wearing the customary tail and bunch of leaves. The youngest had her upper lip pierced, and wore in it a small ring of red, blue, and white beads. The second had pierced her lower lip instead, and wore in it what looked like a cribbage-peg. The eldest girl had shaved her head, excepting a patch on the top, which looked as if she sported a woollen skull-cap; the second girl had made a clean shave of it altogether, and the youngest had left a tiny top-knot of wool. These three girls were apparently his favourite daughters; for he had such a vast number of wives, that one kraal was insufficient to house them all, and he had to build several kraals or villages for them. He certainly had a good number of babies. There was one in particular, which I wanted to photograph in the sling on its mother's back, because the mother had decorated the child's leathern receptacle with long streamers which looked very picturesque and reminded me of young English mothers decking their baby's cot with bright-coloured ribbons and lace. Photographers in England could not get on without mothers who want their children to be

MY TENT.

photographed. But this African mother was terrified for her baby's life, in presence of the white medicine-man's mysterious camera; she fled, and hid herself and her baby.

Tukwenda, too, made diligent inquiry amongst my men to know, if my magic was likely to have any injurious effects upon his own life; whereupon my boys assured him that it would produce untold blessings. I sincerely hope he has not been visited by famine, pestilence, or hostile slave-hunters since I left, or the next European calling on him with a camera might receive anything but a friendly welcome.

Both at Kibero and Mahaji I saw but few water-fowl, but at Tukwenda's there were a good many. The very day I arrived, as my boat drew near the landing-place, I bowled over two wild

ON THE SHORES OF LAKE ALBERT 213

geese with one shot. They were exceptionally tender and unusually good eating.

I have often seen pictures of a bull making a hostile demonstration, but my first personal experience, of what the situation is like, I was to have at Tukwenda's. A magnificent black bull was returning to his kraal past my camp, and was greatly upset by the presence of the tent and the strangers. Uttering loud bellowings he came on in a sharp trot for a visit of inspection. In a moment the camp was empty. I hurriedly snatched up my rifle and loaded it; but what did the bull know about a loaded rifle or any possible harm from it to himself! Even Tukwenda's men had bolted, calling out that it was a most dangerous brute. Little knots of men stood at respectful distances, all excitement and curiosity to know what would happen next. It was a striking picture; this fine animal, standing there in its glorious strength, with its powerful neck, fiercely lashing its tail, occasionally pawing the ground with its fore-feet, tossing its proud head and bellowing; and there was weak humanity, but armed with the loaded rifle, a dangerous foe for the strongest of the brute creation to encounter. I wished myself a few hundred yards farther off; but as I had to face the situation, I held my rifle ready to fire the moment the bull should lower its head and charge. It would never have done to have shot the bull at once, as it would most certainly have severed all friendly intercourse with Tukwenda.

Fortunately some one had hurriedly sent for the bull's keeper, a six-year old, naked little urchin. He came on the scene, and before the bull was aware—switch!—gave the brute a whack across the flank with a long lithe reed wand. The effect was magical. The bull became most humble, and with a deprecatory toss of the head in my direction, to draw the urchin's attention to my uncalled-for intrusion on the plain, and with a sort of silent request to be allowed to finish the job in hand, the bull turned away from my camp and slowly and regretfully walked away. The longing to have one more stare at me and my tent was too great; but, switch! switch! a double-hander against each flank drove the last spark of fighting out of the brute, and it fairly galloped off, amid the jeers and laughter of the hundreds who a few minutes before had fled helter-skelter in every direction.

Outside the village, at a little distance from the "madding

crowd." I came upon two Lur men playing the native game "soko." This game seems common to a great part of Africa; the Swahilies at the coast call it "bau," the Soudanese call it "lohe"; but though the name may change, the game remains the same. Its nearest relatives in the family of games are chess and draughts; it is neither the one nor the other, but maintains a dignified individuality. The board and stand were carved, in the present instance, out of a single solid lump of wood. There were ten rows of circular depressions and four of these depressions in each row. At either end was a large cup-shaped hollow to hold each player's pellets.

If introduced into Europe, we should probably have the game as a polished piece of walnut-wood and pretty glass marbles to play it with. But native ingenuity was at no loss to supply the necessary counters for the

LUR PLAYING THE NATIVE GAME "SOKO."

game. The men were using the dry pellets of goat droppings! They were deeply absorbed in the game. It consists in placing a pellet into each depression in turn, first on your own side and then invading the enemy's rows. When the game is in full swing, the player takes the pellets out of any one of his spaces, and distributes them always in the same single fashion. If his last pellet drops into a space belonging to the enemy, he scoops all in the adjoining depression, till the game ends somewhat in the style of "Beggar my neighbour." That there is a certain amount of skill necessary is self-evident; and to judge from its being a universal favourite amongst totally different races, the game must have some popular attraction. It was a curious sight to watch these two savages, almost naked, and with a curious tuft of feathers stuck on the head, interested in a peaceful homely game. "One touch of Nature makes the world akin!"

From Tukwenda's we went on to Pongo, where we passed the night. From Mahaji to Tukwenda's we had high mountains, densely wooded from summit to base, flanking the lake; with mountain streamlets tossing themselves from the heights above into the lake in sparkling noisy cascades; with birds singing, twittering, screaming amid the green foliage; with monkeys of different species going through their amusing antics and gymnastics from branch to branch, and with a wild-cat darting from boulder to boulder along the rock-bound shore.

From Tukwenda's to Pongo we had sunny plains, with tall reeds intercepting the view, with startled water-fowl of many a species noisily rising on the wing, with many a "deep and glassy bay," with cultivated fields stretching almost to the water's edge, with nestling hamlets, and with sombre forests.

At Pongo I shot some of the black-and-white Colobus monkeys; their skins are much sought after, and form an article of commerce. I remember, at the north end of Lake Nyassa, some one buying forty of them. A gentleman at Kampala showed me a dozen of these skins which the officer at Nandi had bought for him. These monkeys are found from the Eldoma Ravine right up to Kavirondo. I have also come across them from Fajao on the Victoria Nile, across Unyoro, as far as the west coast of Lake Albert. They are black with the exception of a white face, a white tuft to the tail, and a fringe of long white hairs across the lower part of the back and along the flanks up to the armpits. They have only four fingers to each hand, with just an indication of the missing thumb, but five toes to each foot.

The natives of Pongo were harassed by different species of animal marauders. Elephants would walk across their cultivations and leave huge tracks in the soft soil of the fields. Then baboons would come in troops, not only to plunder the ripe corn, but to cause mischievous and wanton injury to the young green plants.

The villagers were afraid to encounter these huge fierce baboons which were not a bit afraid of them. My appearance on the scene caused the brutes reluctantly to move off, fiercely gnashing their teeth, and uttering shrill angry screams mingled with sounds somewhat like a dog's bark. The ringleader, a monstrous big fellow, was the last to leave the field which they were plundering not a hundred yards from my tent. I aimed at the big rascal, with his hands full of stolen corn-heads. I gave him a Martini bullet. He threw up his hands and fell backwards, exactly as I remember seeing a man do who was shot through the chest in battle. The baboon picked himself up and crawled towards the sheltering jungle, again exactly like the wounded

COLOBUS MONKEYS.

man did, who was thus vividly recalled to my mind. I had no chance of firing another shot, as a crowd of natives rushed towards the wounded animal; but the moment it had got into the long grass of the jungle, not a native had the courage to follow.

The heavy blood-spoor proved that the fierce brute must be *in extremis;* I therefore went in pursuit. My own men accompanied me, and thereupon some natives, thus encouraged, joined us too. The thorny, impenetrable nature of the jungle delayed us for a long while, and when we had scrambled through and reached the forest, the blood-spoor was lost.

Just then my attention was drawn to some beautiful Colobus monkeys scampering off in the very topmost boughs of the highest trees. I secured one specimen with my first bullet. My second shot badly wounded another, which, to my regret, dropped from her arms her baby, of whose existence I was unaware till then. I had to fire once more to put her also out of pain. I felt very sorry to have cut short the baby-monkey's life; it was, however, interesting to see that the fringe of long white hairs round the back of the adult was only represented by a patch of grey woolly hair in the baby.

My Soudanese escort begged me to let them have the monkeys to eat, and they proceeded to have a grand feast. Monkeys, when skinned, have an unpleasant smell, which has rather prejudiced me. I have therefore not tasted this dish which so many natives enjoy with relish. Swahilies, however, will not eat monkeys, but with them the prejudice is, as they told me themselves, that they consider it cannibalism to eat either monkeys or human beings. They hold, untaught by Darwin, the doctrine that monkeys are but a lower type of human beings.

The daily thunder-storm at Pongo, for a change, started at early dawn, and all my men had to hold on to the poles and ropes of my tent to prevent its being blown to pieces. It was a short but sharp storm, and the condition of the lake afterwards was such that no canoe could have lived on it.

As soon as the waves had calmed down, we embarked in the dug-outs to cross the lake from Pongo in the Lur country to Rukuya in Unyoro. The Wanyoro canoe-men wore a sort of eye-shade, made of reeds, to protect their eyes from the fierce glare of a tropical sun shining on the mirror-like surface of this treacherous lake which now lay as calm as if it were but a small sheltered village pool.

I noticed something white floating on the water some distance off, and suggested it might be a dead fish, which it turned out to be when we had paddled up to it. It was a big fish, and my Wanyoro gloated over the feast it would provide for them on shore. The prize was at once hoisted into the dug-out; but when the Wanyoro probed its goodness with their fingers, the squashy sound nearly made me sick. The breeze fortunately blew the overpowering aroma away from me, or I should have had to insist on its being consigned back to the deep. It proved to me that neither Lur nor Wanyoro are particular, when it comes to feeding on picked-up dead fish.

The Wanyoro have pleasant-sounding boat-songs; the tune

WANYORO CANOEMEN OF LAKE ALBERT WEARING REED EYE-SHADES.

remains the same, though the words are generally impromptu, with the exception of the chorus. A favourite chorus was—

"Nakluvere voia, voia,
Nakluvere, voia, voia!"

Whatever that may mean. In one solo there were constant allusions to various articles of food; the song was evidently depicting a Sybarite native feast, and must have made the mouths of the men water, knowing that a big dead fish was lying safely in the dug-out ready to be cooked and eaten.

ON THE SHORES OF LAKE ALBERT 219

We saw a huge pelican on the water, and my Wanyoro begged me for it. I fired, but missed, and the ungainly-looking bird flew up and swiftly disappeared in the dim distance.

From Rukuya we hugged the east shore of the lake till we reached Kibero. Next day I said a long good-bye to Kibero and Lake Albert.

THE DAUGHTERS OF TUKWENDA.

CHAPTER XIV.

ELEPHANT-HUNTING.

THE Uganda Protectorate begins at the Kedong. Elephants are occasionally met with here; for on one journey I came upon fresh elephant-spoor, and on a subsequent visit upon the remains of a recently killed elephant. Birds and beasts of prey had left little of the huge carcase besides the skull, the heavier bones, and some lumps of putrefying hide; yet my Wanyamwezi porters cooked this mal-odorous offal over their camp-fires, and gorged themselves with as much gusto, as any hyæna or vulture might display. But it was in Unyoro, the northern limit of the Protectorate, that I saw, for the first time, wild elephants. This happened at Kibero, on the east shore of Lake Albert. I had gone in a dug-out canoe to look out for hippos, said to be present about here in large numbers.

A dug-out canoe is simply a hollowed-out tree-trunk. The natives use rather peculiar paddles which look somewhat like a huge spade with a slight curve backwards. There are usually five to six canoe-men. One man sits at the stern and steers with his paddle.

We pulled along for perhaps an hour, but saw only one solitary hippo; and he did not wait for us to get nearer than a quarter of a mile before he popped his head under water, and we saw no more of him. We had selected a sandy bit of beach to land, when a Soudanese was the first to notice the unmistakable signs that a herd of elephants had recently visited this very spot. We decided to follow them up, and we came upon the herd in about two hours.

But before we started, I sent the dug-out to fetch the cook and some provisions, and to bring my camp-bedstead and blankets; and another of my men I told off, to put up a grass-

hut on the spot to shelter me for the night. These grass-huts can be run up in half-an-hour or less, and are very primitive. About a dozen long, lithe wands are cut from the nearest shrubs, or from the reed-stalks of the elephant-grass, and are stuck an inch or two into the ground in a circle. By bending the reeds towards each other, and fastening the ends together with wisps of grass, and then piling grass over this beehive frame, leaving a small hole open to serve as entrance, the hut is ready.

At first the elephant track through the jungle was easy enough to follow, but soon we had to keep to the spoor of one animal only, because the herd had spread itself out, where the bush grew denser and more difficult to pass. By-and-by we heard the peculiar rumbling noise made by elephants feeding in security and unalarmed. We made straight for it, till it became the clear "hurr-hurr," a sure sign that the elephant is very comfortable and quite unconscious of danger.

As the bush became so dense that we could barely see three or four yards ahead of us, we got, quite unintentionally, right into the very middle of the herd. For we suddenly heard one of the elephants rumbling behind us, and two others answering to our right and left. To find one's self unexpectedly surrounded by these dangerous animals is rather unpleasant; but having placed ourselves in the dilemma, we had to make the best of it.

Elephant-hunting is considered out here a much more dangerous sport than hunting lions. The elephant and the buffalo are exceedingly vindictive and revengeful, especially if wounded, and they then offer a more exciting sport to the hunter, as they usually go for their enemy, if they see him, and try to kill him. We therefore pushed forward with great caution towards the elephant we knew to be somewhere in front of us, when suddenly my Soudanese guide dropped on his knee and pointed silently ahead. Kneeling down by his side and peering into the obscurity of the bush, I had just realised that two elephants were standing motionless within a few yards of us, when one of the animals swung round. I rapidly aimed half-way between ear and eye, and gave him a solid bullet from the Lee-Speed rifle. The shot was instantly followed by the whole herd, over fifty probably, setting up the most awe-inspiring screaming, hissing, snorting, and trumpeting imaginable. It was something really awful and fearful, and it did shake our nerves.

The next instant my men and I were running away like mad for our lives, as branches, and even trees, fell crashing, torn down by the infuriated, but to us invisible, animals. Somehow we escaped without encountering any. When we stopped to recover our breath, our courage returned. We went back, and found that the wounded elephant must have fallen down and been trampled on by others, for we picked up a handful of the long bristles which fringe the tip of the tail.

There was very little blood, but we followed it up for perhaps a quarter of an hour, when, in the obscurity of the bush, we almost walked into the finest elephant I have ever seen. His legs I had taken for tree-trunks. When they moved, I felt a thrill like an electric shock; and the eye involuntarily travelled upwards to the huge body. It was a splendid chance to have hamstrung this gigantic tusker and thus made absolutely sure of him. I did not do it, but preferred the shot at the head, and thus lost tusks worth fully a couple of hundred pounds. As he turned his head, the intervening branches and leaves made the aim very difficult. The bullet hit him behind the eye, and he fell almost on top of us.

This second shot was succeeded by such horrible screams of rage and fury, that we became again utterly demoralised and unnerved. Once more we stampeded, and such of the Wanyoro natives as had accompanied me never stopped running till they had reached our camp. The Soudanese stuck to me. One vicious brute chased us for some distance, but was baffled by the trees and the shrubs. As we doubled, he just missed us, and rushed off at right angles, crashing through the underwood like a steam-engine. I had to throw myself on the ground, exhausted by the overpowering emotion, the rifle shaking in my trembling hands.

When sufficiently recovered, the two or three of us that remained, once more went in pursuit. The fallen elephant had not been killed outright, but had got away. Patches of blood about the size of a plate showed that he was badly wounded. He had left the herd, and had gone off by himself out of the bush and towards the hills. The blood-trail was easy to follow, and his head must have been drooping towards the wounded side, as the left-hand tusk had occasionally scraped the ground.

Just then a heavy thunder-storm broke over us, and the torrent of rain soon obliterated every trace of the trail.

Soaked to the skin, we had to return to the camp disheartened. My camp-bedstead and a blanket had turned up, but not a change of dry clothing. A glorious camp-fire, in spite of the rain, awaited us; and we steamed ourselves at it. My cook had brought a chicken, but no other provisions, and he proceeded to roast it over the fire.

It was getting dark, when five hippos were noticed in the lake, some four or five hundred yards higher up. Being wet through, it was impossible for me to get more wet. I therefore went stalking through the dripping elephant-grass to within two hundred yards of the hippos. This time I used my Martini-Henri rifle. I fired but one shot. The wounded hippopotamus reared himself half out of the water and then fell heavily backwards. The Soudanese by my side called out "Eiva, kalass, mut." I know but a few words of Arabic, but understood this to mean "Yes, he is done for, he is dead." For all this, the wounded hippo escaped that day; about a fortnight later the natives brought me the four large tusks. They had found the dying animal, and had despatched it with their spears, keeping the meat and hide for their own use.

Having divested myself of my wet clothes and rolled myself up in a blanket, I sought the shelter of the grass-hut. It was not pleasant to be roused more than once that night by the lugubrious howling of a hungry hyæna close to me, as I have had to attend to more than one patient who has been seized in his sleep by one of these cowardly brutes. This one need only have poked its nose through my grass shelter to have grabbed me. Early next morning we returned to Kibero.

My second adventure with elephants was on the west shore of Lake Albert, in the Lur country. We were about to re-cross the lake, when a severe storm burst over us and prevented us. I was sitting in my tent, annoyed at the delay, when natives brought word that a herd of elephants were browsing in the adjoining forest. We tracked the animals through the forest to a grass plain just beyond it. They had evidently been alarmed. As the wind was in our favour, I got to within sixty yards; but, owing to the grass being some ten feet high, I had to climb a tree to see the animals. My head-servant and another man climbed up after me, but the others decamped to a little knoll farther off. The elephants at once noticed us, but, though evidently on the alert as to any possible mischief on our part, they showed no alarm, and probably took us for monkeys.

The tree was not high enough nor strong enough to have afforded us safety, and, standing by itself, it was much too isolated and exposed. My head-servant predicted our death if, conspicuous as we were, the fury of the herd should be drawn towards us; he entreated me not to fire. We quickly scrambled down the tree, and, under the protection of the long grass, retreated to the knoll. As we retreated in one direction, the elephants moved off in the opposite direction, suspicious of our presence. But, as flight of the enemy is a wonderful factor in rousing courage, we became again most courageous, and at once followed in pursuit.

This time I got to within what I estimated to be eighty yards; measuring it out afterwards, it was found to be exactly 102 yards. From here I took a steady aim at the eye of the elephant most exposed. I used the Lee-Speed rifle and solid bullet, with smokeless powder. The elephant was hit; he turned and disappeared among the others. We had now a very interesting sight. The elephants were evidently puzzled; their comrade was attacked apparently from one direction, whereas the sound of the shot came from another. They now formed a sort of ring, most of them facing us, but others facing the flank attacked. I fired one more shot and heard it strike.

Then we witnessed a splendid display of defiance. We were safely hidden by the protecting screen of leaves. With screams of rage and fear, the elephants facing us would advance five or ten yards in our direction in line of battle, waving their trunks, and then would retrace their steps backwards, swaying their huge bodies. A similar movement was made by others towards the flank they imagined to have been also attacked. Behind these advancing elephants, three stood sniffing, with their prosboces high up in the air, though the mobile movements of the sensitive, finger-like extremity seemed more like feeling the air. The wind, such as there was, came towards us. I had urged the men who were with me not to stir from the spot as they valued their lives; fortunately they saw, that our only safety lay in puzzling the elephants as to our whereabouts.

In the meanwhile some of the elephants clapped their huge

ears backwards, so as to meet with a thundering clap behind their head, scattering a cloud of dust. One elephant in his baffled rage tore up large lumps of grass and earth, and then threw them backward over his head in a paroxysm of blind fury. Others moved about, trampling down the tall grass in their search for the unseen foe. Curiously enough, whatever they did, they yet managed to maintain a sort of inner circle, and my men assured me that elephants often do so, when one

A LUCKY SHOT.

of their number has fallen, only leaving the spot when quite sure that their companion is dead. We thereupon crept away in the long grass and gave the herd a wide berth.

By-and-by a man was sent to reconnoitre and to report on the situation; and then we found, that the herd had disappeared, but that one elephant lay dead on the ground. A single shot had killed the animal; what had become of the second shot and the second elephant wounded by me we did not find out. The "kill" took place just half-an-hour's march from the camp. The illustration shows how the dead elephant lay, before the natives proceeded to cut him up. I claimed the head and the feet, and the natives, delighted to have such an unusual big feast of meat, gladly brought my share of the spoil into camp. The tusks were disappointing, but all in this herd had tusks of about the same size.

My men proceeded to roast a piece of the elephant's proboscis for my dinner. Luckily there was something else for me to eat, as the roasting, done according to native fashion, took all night. A large hole was dug in the ground, and a roaring wood-fire maintained in it and over it, till it resembled in very deed a fiery furnace. When sufficiently heated, and everything but the red-hot embers had been removed, the piece of trunk was thrown, with skin and bristles, just as it was excepting a preliminary wash, into this oven. A few faggots were now laid over the mouth of the hole, and then covered over with green leaves, using the leaves of the sweet-potato plant; finally, dry earth was placed over it all. The piece of meat, about a foot and a half of the proboscis, remained in this furnace all night, and next morning it was pronounced ready for use.

I had some of it, when re-crossing Lake Albert in a native dug-out. The meat was delicious, the best bit I had eaten for many a long day. It resembled the streaky hump of the African bullock, but had a peculiar, agreeable flavour of its own. Whether it was the fault of the second helping, or my gastric powers resented this new experiment, after the many severe trials they have been subjected to in Africa, whatever the cause may have been, the elephant "lay heavy on my chest," as ladies euphoniously describe dyspeptic suffering. I gave the elephant-roast one more trial in the evening at my frugal dinner, and this settled the matter finally. I was seized with such an irresistible fit of generosity, that I gave the meat away as a present, and refused to have anything further to do with it.

CHAPTER XV.

THE "MAN-EATER."

LIONS have occasionally been met with and shot at Mombasa, and I shot a lioness at Fajao, a thousand miles from the coast. Between these two extreme points there are, as might be expected, certain localities where the sportsman anxious to bag a lion has a better chance of finding one. As a general principle, lions follow the big game, and wherever zebras, antelopes, and gazelles abound, lions are not far off.

Some travellers never cross the game-stocked Athi plains without seeing lions; the late Mr. Dick once saw fourteen of them, and it is reported that a score of lions have been seen together at one and the same time. I have crossed the Athi plains six times without seeing a live lion; though once I picked up the fine skull of an aged lion at the Stony Athi, hyænas having just devoured the king of beasts. On another occasion, when the grass was about three feet high, I was stalking a waterbuck near the Athi river, when my gun-bearers declared they had seen a lion switching his tail and disappearing into the adjoining copse, and they persuaded me to keep from the gloomy thorn copse at a respectful distance.

On my fourth journey, I was warned by the missionaries at Kibwezi not to camp at Ngomeni, because a man-eating lion was haunting the neighbourhood. I had at the time amongst my porters a man who had camped at Ngomeni a few weeks before with another caravan. According to his story, he must have had a wonderful escape, for the lion pounced on him, and carried off his blanket and the tiny tent under which he lay sheltered. The porter however escaped unhurt. From Kinani to Ngomeni is twelve miles, but my caravan were in such a dread of spending the night at Ngomeni, that they begged me to push on to the next camp on the Tsavo river, nine miles farther. We therefore marched the twenty-one miles, crossed the Tsavo river, and camped.

It was a hot still night, and most of the porters slept in the open air by their camp-fires. No one dreamt there could be any danger; we all thought, that the man-eating lion had been left nine miles behind us at Ngomeni. I felt unaccountably restless, and kept tossing on my camp-bed. I could not sleep. I sauntered out of my tent, saw that the night-watchman was awake, looked at the sleeping figures around the glowing camp-fires, and then strolled into the silent darkness beyond the camp. It was providential that I was not seized by the man-eater, for he was close at hand at the very moment. He had followed us from Ngomeni, and had swum across the Tsavo river. My dog had followed me. He growled angrily at some bush, so near that I could see some of the leaves stirring. This was my fourth journey without ever meeting with a lion, and I was at the moment so completely unconscious of any danger, that I said to my dog: "You silly! to growl when the wind stirs a few leaves." Since this night I never like to venture outside the circle of camp-fires on a dark night, however safe others may consider the surrounding uninhabited country.

Leisurely returning to my tent, I lay down on my camp-bed, when I heard a horrid growling sound like "woohff" a few yards from my tent-door. The next moment there were shrieks and cries. In a second every man was awake, and shouting, "Simba! simba!" (lion, lion). Dashing out with a loaded rifle, I found that the man-eater had carried off one of my porters. Every one seized a firebrand, and we rushed in pursuit. It surprises me yet, that we rescued the man. About two hundred yards from the camp we found him lying on the ground severely lacerated; the lion had dropped him and fled. I carefully examined the spot next morning. A strong but withered branch stretched out horizontally a sharp-pointed arm; for some inches from the end, this was covered with the lion's short hairs. My belief is, that the lion, bounding away with his prey, accidentally struck his side against this sharp branch. He may have taken it for a spear-thrust from one of us pursuing him with shouts and blazing brands.

The wounded man was carried to my tent. He had dreadful

wounds in the upper part of the thigh, where the lion's jaws had seized him. As I had every surgical requisite at hand, he was soon bandaged up, and he remained that night under my tent. No one ventured to go to sleep, as we fully expected the baffled man-eater would make another attempt before dawn. The injured man was in great pain, and his moans were distressing. He told us a remarkable story—that, though the lion had seized him and was carrying him off, he was still asleep; that our shouts woke him up, and to his horror he found that he himself was the one being carried off by the lion, and then he clasped his arms round the lion's neck and screamed.

We were all wondering, why the lion did not pay us another visit; but it was explained next morning. A number of Wakamba natives on their way to Mombasa to barter their sheep and goats for cloth, beads, and brass-wire, had passed us. They camped for the night about half-an-hour farther on. The man-eater had visited them instead, and had carried off a native and devoured him. The others had fled. The road next day bore plain evidence of their headlong flight, being littered with beans, broken provision bags, and some leather garments.

With early dawn we left Tsavo; the injured porter we carried in a hammock. We saw the footprints of the lion along the dusty road apparently following the Wakamba. Two of my men declared that they saw the brute about mid-day, standing panting under a shady bush by the roadside, with the tongue hanging out of its mouth. I hurried up to them with a loaded rifle, but saw nothing except the footprints, which here did turn off the road. We made a double march, and reached the camp at Ndi in safety, and saw nothing further of the lion for the rest of the journey. The wounded man progressed favourably, and on our reaching Mombasa, he insisted on walking in the procession, supporting himself with a stick. He refused to be carried or to be assisted by others. The safe home-coming of a caravan to Mombasa is generally a day of rejoicing with the porters.

On my fifth journey—it was at Lake Nakuru—I had my first shot at a lion. I was returning to camp, and within sight of it, when I observed a jackal slinking round the base of a hillock. Intending to get a shot at him, I hurried up the hillock. As I reached the top, I heard shouts of "Simba! simba!" (lion, lion). I naturally turned round to see who were shouting, and then I heard some of my men call out, that the lions were in front of me. In fact, at the critical moment, when I would have seen them, I had turned round. A lion and a lioness, peacefully reposing in the grass, had been disturbed by my approach, and were now trotting off towards some high grass a few hundred yards away. I had barely time to fire three shots from the magazine rifle at their receding figures. The first two shots fell short, but my third shot, put at 300 yards, threw up the dust close to the left hind-leg of the lion. The shots did not apparently disturb their equanimity. After my third shot they stopped for a second to look at us. Before I could try a fourth shot, the pair had disappeared in the long grass, where it would have been foolhardy to follow them. The donkey-boy told me, that when he was bringing my riding-donkey to meet me, the donkey suddenly broke loose and galloped back to the camp. He had to return to fetch it, and leading it once more along, he and the others saw the lions which had terrified the donkey. That night we heard lions growling round the camp, but no one was attacked.

On my second visit to Fajao, our farthest military station towards the north, another lion incident fell to my lot. It was on the 25th November 1897. I had arrived in the early morning, and having attended to my medical duties, went in the afternoon unarmed for a walk to a narrow rocky gully which winds through the wood. Suddenly I observed the fresh footprints of a lion in the moist sandy patches between the rocks. The footprints of a young one by its side showed it must be a lioness with her cub. The tracks were so fresh, that it was evident the beasts had been disturbed by my approach, and had just passed ahead. I had never heard of any lions being in this immediate neighbourhood, and it was not pleasant to find myself unarmed and in such proximity to them. I retraced my steps pretty sharp, and beat a hurried retreat, thanking Providence for bringing me safely back to the station. I told the men what I had seen, and I inquired if they knew, that there were lions so near to us. I received the disturbing news, that a man-eating lion had harassed the neighbouring Wanyoro village for the past month, and that it had carried off four of the villagers. The inhabitants had deserted their homes *en masse*, and had fled for safety to another village; but hitherto the man-eater had not visited the Soudanese settlement.

Darkness sets in about 6 P.M.; and though I ventured by myself only sixty yards from my hut, I found next morning, that for the second time I must have been pretty close to the man-eater, as his track was but six inches from mine. I realised, how the merciful God had twice that day preserved me from death. Soon afterwards, news was brought me, that the man-eater had just attempted to carry off a woman at the nearest Wanyoro village, but was driven off, presumably with firebrands, by men who happened to sit near her. This alarming news was shortly followed by my cow stampeding. She was tied to a peg, close to the Soudanese watch-fire. Tearing herself loose, she bolted like mad. She never stopped until she reached a distant village, whence she was returned to me next day. The Soudanese on guard declared that he saw the lion crouching and trying to spring upon the cow, when, fortunately, she just tore herself loose in time and escaped. It was too dark for him to aim, or he would have fired his rifle.

The general excitement was increasing, when suddenly terrific screams of pain arose from the Soudanese village, followed by soldiers firing off their rifles in every direction, under the belief that they had seen the man-eater here, there, and everywhere. The brute certainly seemed ubiquitous. I felt uncomfortable at the thought that the bullets might knock some of us over, but, with the help of the native officers, we put a stop to this haphazard shooting, which was endangering our lives more than the man-eater's. On hurrying to the scene of the screams, I found that the man-eater had entered a hut, the door having foolishly been left open, and had tried to carry off one of our Soudanese soldiers. The huts are crowded together, and have a reed-fence round each, and narrow paths and winding entrances lead to each separate enclosure. It was therefore no easy matter, even for a lion, to carry off its prey. Owing to the general hubbub the lion had dropped the man. As in the Tsavo case, I was fortunately at hand to dress the wounds. There were ten of them. A scratch, about two inches long, had splintered the heel-bone. I removed a piece of bone about the size of a shilling. This was one of the minor wounds, the worst were in the thigh. The man ultimately made a good recovery, and so did the woman who was injured earlier.

To allay the excitement and to calm the people, I told them *I would kill the lion next day.* The natives were not surprised that this came true, for they are very superstitious, and with them "medicine-man" and wizard are synonymous terms. The native lieutenant reminded me of this fact. "You told us," he said, "that you would kill the lion next day, but then—you are a 'medicine-man.'"

I advised the men to retire to their huts, and to see that their doors were firmly secured. As regards my own hut, this was easier said than done, as the door was only a reed-screen leaning against the aperture, which it failed to close. But natives usually take the precaution of fixing two vertical poles inside the hut, so that the reed-screen slides between them, and is retained in position; the door is then firmly closed by some faggots placed transversely. Having dispersed the crowd, I determined to put out a bait for the man-eater, and to sit up and watch for him.

We tied a young goat to a tree a few feet from my door. The night was very dark, and I was obliged to kindle a fire to enable me to see the foresight of my rifle. Then the silent and dreary watch began. As the hours crept on, the stillness and the darkness told on me. I had had

THE CAGE FOR THE LION.

a fatiguing day. In the early morning I had marched from Wakibara to Fajao, afterwards I had attended to patients, and then came the lively doings of the evening. By-and-by I caught myself nodding. If the man-eater had chosen to pass my hut once more, it could have had me, notwithstanding the loaded rifle on my knees. At 3.30 A.M. I gave up the struggle to keep awake, and, resolving to set a trap for the lion, I went to bed.

At 8 A.M. next morning I began to build the lion-trap. Everybody helped willingly, although it was Friday, the

Sunday equivalent to the Soudanese who are Mohammedans and who have consequently had this day conceded to them as their day of rest. First of all we made a firm stockade of stout perpendicular poles; to these we lashed tree-stems laid horizontally one on top of the other; finally we planted an outer row of poles, perpendicular like the first row, firmly and deeply into the ground. This gave us the sides of the cage. The top we closed in with horizontally laid tree-trunks, on to which we piled large heavy stones, till we felt satisfied that the fiercest lion could not possibly break out of this cage. The trap-door consisted of seven heavy blocks of wood fastened together horizontally on top of each other, and held in position by short perpendicular pieces on both sides. So far all went smoothly. But never having constructed a wild-beast trap before, I was seriously puzzled, how to make the trap-door act.

There is something in this Robinson Crusoe life which stimulates the most uninventive intellect. It was an unpleasant predicament that, unless I found some means, the cage would very shortly be ready, and I placed in the ridiculous position of not knowing, how to make the trap work. Inspiration came at last. I had asked the native officers, the Soudanese soldiers, the Swahili porters, my Arab servant, and the Wanyoro onlookers, to find out, if any one could help me. They calmly assured me,

THE LION-TRAP COMPLETED.

that they had never built a trap; in vain I told them—nor had I. But I hit on the following plan. I constructed a sort of picture-frame, the trap-door resting in the forked ends of the two perpendicular pieces. Attaching a rope to the middle of the lower horizontal stick, even a slight tug withdrew the supporting framework, and caused the heavy trap-door to fall down into the required position, and thereby to shut the cage most effectively. The rope went to the farthest end of the cage, and there, passing over a horizontal pole and returning in the direction of the door, had its end securely tied to a goat placed as a bait inside the trap.

The goat had previously had its legs tied, so as to render it quite helpless. Of course the principle I went upon, was, that the lion would not stop to devour its prey, but would seize it and try to carry it off, and therefore would pull at the rope to which the goat was tied, and thus close the trap-door. As the lion had refused to accept the goat we had placed for it as a bait out in the open air on the previous night, we built a native hut over the trap, and the lion-trap was completed. Just before dark we baited the trap, and awaited the result. Everybody in the village was warned to be inside his own hut before dusk, and to see that his door was securely fastened. Though a tiger man-eater, having once tasted human flesh, is said ever after to prefer it to all other flesh, I do not know if the lion man-eater resembles it in this predilection; but it would seem it does, for this particular lion refused to take the goat twice offered him as a bait on two successive nights.

The Soudanese lieutenant, Said Jabara, was eating his evening meal at the door of his hut, when the man-eater suddenly entered his enclosure and bounded into the adjoining hut. With great presence of mind, the lieutenant at once flung burning brands in front of this hut, and thus promptly made a prisoner of the man-eater.

Soon a blazing fire was roaring, fed by many willing hands. Luckily the occupant of the hut was absent. When I arrived on the scene and heard how matters stood, I climbed on to the anterior shed, followed by my Arab servant with my rifle and a lantern. The Soudanese lieutenant also joined me. The lion had taken refuge in the inner hut. Cautiously the Soudanese officer removed some of the thatch. I pushed the rifle through the opening and peered into the dark interior of the hut, whilst my Arab endeavoured to throw the light of the lantern into it. It was very doubtful whether the weak framework of the roof would bear our united weight much longer; there were ominous crackings, and we were in danger of being precipitated into the hut right in front of the man-eater. There was also the possibility, that the lion, in endeavouring to escape by this new opening, might spring at us. We had some trouble too in pushing aside, with sticks, a mosquito-curtain intercepting our view of the interior.

It seemed a long while, though probably only a minute or two, before I succeeded in distinguishing the outline of the lion. I fired, but as I could not see very clearly the foresight of my rifle, I probably missed. The lion gave an ominous growl which was heard and received with mad shouts by the crowd surging around us at a safe distance. The brute bounded to the other end of the hut, but, as it left the hind part of its body exposed, I was able this time to take a better aim and to send the bullet crushing through its body. As it turned to escape by the door, I had time to re-load—I was using a Martini-Henri rifle—and to give it a good shoulder-shot. It staggered, and fell dead in the outer shed.

The men guarding the entrance, of course, did not know that it was all over with the man-eater, and they fired off their rifles. There was not much aiming, for one of these bad shots passed close to the Soudanese lieutenant and me. We slid off the roof, and got the men to stop the firing.

The man-eater turned out to be a lioness. It was gaunt and grim, old and emaciated. It had but five other wounds, in spite of the subsequent fusillade, besides the two inflicted by me; one of these five shots had carried off the little toe of the right fore-foot, the others were principally flesh-wounds. It required seven men to carry the lioness to where I camped. There was a feeling of joy and relief that the man-eater was slain. I had to remain close to the body to prevent its being torn to pieces by the frenzied mob. Even then one of the Wanyamwezi porters managed to dodge me and to deliver with a club a terrific blow at the dead lioness, smashing in her skull. The women joined in the uproar with their shrill tremulo-scream of "he-he-he-he-he" *ad infinitum*, only stopping when quite out of breath. This was meant as a sort of triumphal chant.

It was a strange scene: a pitch-dark night in the heart of Africa, scores of blazing torches lighting up the gloom of the tall forest trees around us, a surging crowd of black faces, half-naked women uttering their shrill cry, in the distance the incessant boom of the Victoria Nile where it foams down the Murchison Falls, the white race represented by one solitary being in this the most distant and remote outpost of civilisation and British authority, and the dead lioness! From tip of nose to tip of tail the lioness measured seven feet six inches, but the skin when stretched out to dry measured nine feet four inches. With man-eating tigers in India the skin is said to be mangy, but this skin was in beautiful condition.

I had left my hut at 7.30 P.M. and at 7.45 P.M. I was back with the dead man-eater, and yet so much was crowded into this quarter of an hour. It took a long time, before everybody

THE LIONESS AT FAJAO.

quieted down and went off to sleep. The goat was released from its unenviable position of serving as live bait for a lion, and then I too thought it high time to prepare for rest. Just then terrific screams from the Soudanese village once more caused me to hurry with loaded rifle to the rescue. Guided by the shrieks, we—the native lieutenant and others having joined me promptly on the way—reached a hut with the door fast closed. We burst the door open and rushed in. The torches lit up the interior, and showed us two women clinging to each other. One of them had had the nightmare, and had dreamt the dead lioness had come to life again and had entered her hut. Her shrieks had caused the other woman to scream in terror-stricken sympathy. This comical incident closed the evening. We calmed and reassured the women, and then returned to our respective huts.

On my sixth journey—we had pitched our tents at "Campi-ya-Simba," *i.e.* "the camp of lions"—we saw four animals in the distance, a mile or two off. No one could make out what they were. I came to the conclusion they must be wart-hogs, because the body seemed unusually long and the legs comparatively short. As far as the hills the treeless ground was covered with short grass, only here and there a patch of grass three feet high would dot the undulating surface. Accompanied by my gun-bearer, I tried to get as near as I could before attempting a shot. The place was too open to make stalking possible or practicable. Three of the animals trotted off to the left, one went off to the right in the direction of our camp. This one I followed. I felt more than ever convinced it was a wild boar, as it constantly placed its head near the ground and only occasionally raised it to look at us as we followed it. Our persistent pursuit seemed to annoy it, and it went to hide in a patch of high grass.

With my rifle ready, I cautiously approached the patch, but as I could not make out where the animal might be, I said to my gun-bearer: "I have lost it." The patch of grass extended perhaps for a quarter of a mile. Suddenly a long tail switched upward, and instantly a huge lion raised himself up and gave a fierce deep growl. Up went my rifle and I fired. The lion was fully two hundred yards off; the bullet almost grazed its head. The act was automatic; the shock of unexpectedly facing a lion must have paralysed volition, or I would most certainly not have risked at that distance my only shot, on which the life of the two of us might have depended.

This brings to my mind a passage in a medical lecture I once attended. The lecturer, to impress the medical students with the proximity of certain nerve-centres in the brain, used "Eve and the apple" as an illustration. "This is the centre for sight," he said, "Eve saw the apple"—"and this is the centre for movement of the arms—Eve stretched out her hand for it." In my case the sight of the lion prompted the defensive motion of my arms. Fortunately for me, the lion turned and bounded off. I reloaded my rifle, and hurried after it, eager to shoot it, and to secure such a splendid brute. But though it seemed to be merely trotting, and my gun-bearer and I were running, as if it were a racing match, the lion got steadily farther away and finally disappeared beyond the undulating ridges. When we reached camp, I was greeted by my companion with the remark, that a lion had passed in sight of the camp and had disappeared in the scrub near us: that he had gone to look for it, but had seen no trace of it.

The whole caravan were greatly excited, saying the lion was crouching in the long grass, and would wait till dusk, and then pay us an unpleasant visit. Having rested myself, I went once more after the lion; but I followed a different plan to what my companion had tried. As the lion had crossed the caravan road, I went to track him, instead of looking for him at haphazard. I found the footprints, and several of my men now systematically tracked them for me. The trail led downwards to a grassy dell. Just then a couple of partridges flew up and settled in a patch of grass on the higher ground. I exchanged my rifle for a gun, and thought I might as well bag a partridge for supper, whilst my men went tracking towards the dell. The boy who had carried the gun accompanied me, though the gun was now in my own hands.

As I skirted the edge of the grass-patch, I noticed a peculiar opening at one spot, as if a longish animal had entered there. I said to my boy: "I am sure the lion has passed here," but I never dreamt the lion my men were tracking down-hill could at that moment be so near to me near the summit of the hill. I had passed the spot half-a-dozen yards, when curiosity prompted me to go back and to have another look at it. Balancing myself on my left foot, with my fowling-piece held unconcernedly in my hands, I was leisurely turning the grass this way and that way with my right foot, when the same huge lion, just as it did on the former occasion, except that it was now only a few yards from me, sprang up, lashed its tail furiously, and growled or rather snarled at me. My boy was paralysed with fear. I could see how both his hands went up and his fingers curled inwards, and then he gave a yell of terror. As on the previous occasion, the sudden shock deprived me of the sensation of fear, but automatically my hands endeavoured to shoot back the safety-bolt of my gun and to get it ready for defence.

Before I could act, the lion had ample time to have killed both of us; but once more it turned and fled. As the black tip of the tail disappeared over the next undulation, I got at last my gun in position and sent some small No. 5 shot at it, though I might as well have tickled the tip of the tail with a feather-brush, as regards any harm I could have done with such tiny shot at that distance. But I was mad with myself at having lost such a splendid chance; only gradually better thoughts entered my head, and I felt thankful, that twice this day Providence had saved me, in spite of my folly, from painful mutilation and probable death.

My men, who were tracking down-hill, now hurried up to me, and we followed the fresh spoor of the lion for over an hour, but we never saw the brute again. We had at last to give up the pursuit and to return to the camp; but my caravan slept in peace that night, for the lion never ventured to come back to us.

CHAPTER XVI.

RHINOCEROS-SHOOTING.

THE rhinoceros met with in Uganda and British East Africa is the common black "rhinoceros bicornis," *i.e.* "the two-horned rhino." I have heard of "freaks" with three and even five horns, but I have never seen one of them. The Indian rhino has only one horn; it also differs in having huge massive folds of skin, which make it look as if clad in a coat-of-mail, like a battle-horse of the Middle Ages. Notwithstanding the absence of these folds, the skin of the African rhino is more than an inch thick along the back and sides; and over the abdomen, where it is comparatively thin, it is fully half an inch. An extinct two-horned species of rhino, discovered in the ice-fields of Siberia along with the extinct mammoth, had a shaggy coat of long wool; but the present African representatives of these antediluvian rhinos and elephants have practically a naked skin, with the exception of the tip of the tail, which is fringed with long bristles.

The Indian rhino is said to live in marshy jungles and to be fond of wallowing in the mud; but where I have encountered most frequently the African rhino, has been on treeless grassy plains, though sometimes I have met with it in bush-covered tracts.

Whereas hippos and elephants love to congregate together in herds, the rhinos prefer roaming singly or in pairs. Once only did I see three rhinos together; it was quite a model family, consisting of father, mother, and child. But generally the bull goes off by himself on his lonely travels, and leaves the cow to look after her calf. The cow has never more than one calf at a time. She takes care of her calf till it is almost full-grown. The cow has the domestic element largely developed, for I have always met her accompanied either by her young calf or by an adult bull.

RHINOCEROS-SHOOTING

The upper lip of the rhino overlaps the lower, and is pointed and prehensile. I watched a rhino browsing on the leaves of shrubs and bushes; it plucked off the single leaves as deftly as any experienced tea-gatherer stripping a tea-shrub of its leaves. It has very small eyes and a short range of vision; it does not seem to be able to distinguish a human being at a quarter of a mile, even when on a perfectly open plain.

Rhinos are greatly troubled by small crab-like ticks; these small red-brown parasites cluster under the tail, along the abdomen and thighs, and around the base of the eye-lashes. Though sight may be somewhat defective, hearing is fairly acute, and scent is extremely keen. I had occasion to notice this at Campi-ya-Simba. Only my gun-bearer, as we call the servant who carries one's gun or rifle, was with me, and I had but a single solid Lee-Metford bullet left, when we noticed a pair of rhinos, evidently a cow with her calf, on the open plain about a mile and a quarter from us. The calf was lying down, and the cow stood by it motionless with drooping head.

We had to pass them, as they were directly in our path; but we were not anxious to risk an encounter, having but one single solid bullet for our protection. We decided to give them a wide birth, and to outflank them at the same respectful distance of over a mile. As long as the wind was in our favour, the rhinos did not stir; but as we were bound to pass to windward of them, we kept a wary eye on their movements. Though there was but the faintest breath of wind, the very instant almost that we got to windward of them, the cow started and turned round and the young one jumped up. Both rhinos appeared greatly alarmed; and we could see that we were the cause, although invisible to them.

A RHINO HEAD.

The rhinos I have shot, amongst them two fine old bulls, were all smaller than my hippos. The rhino has three toes, the hippo four, and the elephant five. The foot of the elephant is the largest in size, the rhino foot comes next. The hippo has a comparatively small foot for so huge a body; this difference in size is explained by the fact, that the hippo spends the greater part of its existence in the water swimming. The horns of the rhinoceros are part and parcel of the skin, and merely a modification of it, like a nail. It follows that the horns can be stripped off the skull without injuring any bone. The anterior horn is usually longer than the posterior horn, but sometimes, as seen in the illustration of a rhino-head, the reverse is the case. The posterior horn rests between the eyes on the frontal bone, but the anterior horn is supported on the nose, the nasal bones being raised and strengthened to form a hard bony bump.

The horns are solid; the anterior curves backward, the posterior is straight and pyramidal. The anterior horn of the female is usually more elegant than the corresponding horn of the male, which is evidently a very terrible weapon for fighting with, being short, stumpy, sharply-pointed and very massive. The longest horn in my possession came from my first rhino, a female; it measures 25 inches along the outer curve from tip to base.

The rhino skull has a curious appearance, owing to the large nasal lump, and to the cranium curving upwards like a Pecksniffian tuft and terminating in a long horizontal ridge. The rhino has no front teeth. In the specimen I sent home for my collection, there are fourteen teeth in the upper jaw and twelve in the lower. I have generally found that the rhino, if left alone, tries to escape from the presence of man; and clumsy as its appearance is, it can gallop off at an astonishing rate, and would out-distance, I should say, even a horse. But if attacked or wounded, it shows fight and may charge; and therefore, according to some men, rhino-shooting is a dangerous sport; but till now I have only met with a single instance where the rhino tossed, gored, and trampled on its aggressor.

If a caravan walking in single file stretches a long threatening line across the path of the rhino, it probably will charge right through the line, under the impression that this is a hostile demonstration meant to encircle it; but once through the line it hurries away, only too eager to escape. It was at Nairobe, the Kikuyu end of the Athi plains, where I shot my first and my second rhino. I was in charge of a big caravan, as I was taking ex-king Mbogo with his family and followers back to Uganda. We were delayed at Fort Smith, and the food supply was running short. I therefore went to shoot game, and I had shot one hartebeest antelope and two Thomsonii gazelles, when a pair of rhinos appeared in the distance. The wind was blowing from the rhinos towards us, I was therefore able to approach to within 200 yards. I used the Lee-Speed rifle with solid bullet.

At the first shot, at the rhino with the longest horn, it sank into a sitting posture on its hind-legs, and at the second shot it rolled over. The other rhino raced furiously round and round in ever-increasing circles around the fallen one, and then went off at a tangent. On walking up to the fallen rhino, it staggered to its feet and attempted to charge, but it only gored the ground and fell down again. A bullet given as a *coup-de-grâce* in the head extinguished life. It was a huge old female.

Very few of the caravan porters had accompanied me, they could only carry therefore the rhino-head to Fort Smith, in addition to the game already shot. Early next morning a numerous crowd left the fort to supply themselves with meat off the rhino. I followed later on, but not feeling up to doing the six hours' march, required to get there and back, I decided to take with me my light network hammock. It is a very suitable one for travellers. I bought it at Zanzibar to meet any unforeseen emergency; it folds up and slips into a tiny satchel. I little thought how useful I should find it. On reaching Nairobe, I was met by my headman and the others who had gone with him. He told me that not a scrap of the dead rhino could be found. Lions and hyænas had devoured it during the night. In fact, if I had not brought already the rhino's head to Fort Smith, my story of having shot a rhino might have appeared a myth.

Just then a pair of old rhinos appeared in sight; there was a good deal of grass about, and I was able to stalk up to within a hundred yards. They were almost walking side by side, grazing as they went along. I aimed behind the right shoulder, using the same Lee-Speed rifle. On receiving the bullet, the rhino spun round towards me and gave a fierce snort of rage. I dropped flat on the ground to hide myself, fully expecting it would charge, and trusting it might not see me in the long grass. As it did not charge, I ventured to raise myself to find out what had become of it. Both rhinos had disappeared over the ridge of the hill. We followed with great caution, not knowing if the wounded rhino might not be playing a dangerous game of hide-and-seek with us in the long grass. I could see one rhino racing away in the plain beyond, already a mile or more beyond our reach. At last we discovered the other rhino; it was dead; killed by that one shot. It was an old bull with a short but very powerful horn. I was glad that the crowd, having come all this distance to get rhino-meat, would not be disappointed after all, and I left them chopping up the huge carcase.

In the meanwhile I tried to stalk an antelope I had seen about a mile off; for just beyond this patch of long grass the plain was covered with short grass barely six inches high. I had thus the advantage of seeing the game, but the disadvantage of being seen by it. As I drew nearer, I saw, still farther off, again a pair of rhinos. Trusting to their limited range of vision and to the wind being in my favour, I went straight towards the pair. At 200 yards they appeared to have noticed us, for they stood and looked towards us. Kneeling on the ground, I aimed at the one with the longer horn; but just as I pulled the trigger, the smaller rhino veered round and intercepted my bullet, receiving it somewhere high up in the back. Unfortunately, the wound was not a mortal one. With a snort of rage both animals came in a sharp trot towards us.

My two men would have started up and bolted, but I just managed to prevent it. All three of us now crawled off on our stomachs, endeavouring to get out of the way of the advancing rhinos. The two others got ahead of me, when suddenly my Martini rifle, which I was dragging along with my left hand, blazed off. The muzzle was pointing behind me and at the moment nearly touched my left foot. The bullet went clean through my foot. The trigger, I suppose, had got caught in some stubble. What made it worse, was that the loud report was accompanied by a cloud of smoke, though I am not sure now whether it was not this very smoke which hid us from the two approaching rhinos. My men jumped up and ran away, whereupon I too jumped up and ran; but within fifty yards or less I sank on to the ground overpowered by the pain in my wounded foot.

The rhinos fortunately galloped off without having seen us. I wore long, heavy leather shooting-boots reaching up to my knees. With some difficulty I got the boot and the blood-soaked sock off. The bullet had not smashed up the parts, but drilled a clean hole where the great toe joins the foot. The toe itself was cold, blue, and apparently dead. I tore off a long strip of cloth to serve as a tourniquet and bandage, and twisted it tightly over the injured part to staunch the flow of blood. My two men returned to me, with sincere regrets at not having noticed, in their panic, my accident. The sorrow and universal sympathy of my black servants and caravan porters was touching and gratifying, as I am in favour of upholding strict discipline in a caravan. I am certain, natives appreciate a white man's rule the more, if he is firm but at same time scrupulously just in his dealings with them.

My hammock now proved very welcome; and in it I was carried back to Fort Smith. What worried me on the way, was not so much the pain as the thought that, if the great toe was really done for, I should have to amputate my own toe, not a very pleasing prospect, or, as an alternative, something even more disagreeable to contemplate, I should have to ask one of the officials at the fort to cut the toe off, and not one of them had the necessary surgical knowledge. This brought vividly to my mind a scene once witnessed by my father in an Indian village. A blacksmith happened to be the accredited village surgeon. A man appeared at the forge with an injured great toe. The blacksmith requested him to put his foot on the anvil, and before either patient or onlookers had time to realise what was about to happen, with a stroke of his chisel and hammer the blacksmith had clean chopped off the toe.

The three-hours' return journey to the fort allowed time for the collateral circulation to establish itself in my injured foot, and when I dressed the wound at the fort, I was delighted to find that amputation was not necessary. Within a month, applying ordinary antiseptic treatment, the wound had thoroughly healed, leaving a linear scar on the dorsal surface and a round scar on the sole of the foot where the bullet had made its exit. Also the long tendon, upon which depends so much of the movement of the great toe, became reunited, though clean severed by the accident. In the course of months a good deal of the original movement was restored to the injured part.

My third rhino was again an old bull. I shot it near the Kiboko river, to the west side of the caravan route. There was a good deal of bush about, which made it easy to stalk to within twenty yards of the rhino. I used the Martini rifle. I preferred, owing to the position of the rhino, to try the shoulder-shot. At once it turned to charge, but it was evidently mortally wounded, for it staggered, as it gored at the nearest bush. A second bullet, fired at the head, entered the brain and rolled it over. One man went off to carry the welcome news to the caravan and to act as guide to those who were willing to fetch the meat-supply to the camp. In the meanwhile another of my men began to cut up the rhino.

The hide of rhinos and hippos is greatly valued in Africa because of the durable, one might say imperishable, whips and thongs which it provides. The hide is cut up into long narrow strips of suitable length. These are dried in the open air by being suspended vertically from the branch of a tree. The lower end of each strip is weighted with a very heavy stone. I sent some flaps of rhino-hide to London and had a tea-table made out of them, preserving the natural black and rough appearance of the skin. But there is a process by which the skin can be made more or less transparent, and shaped into bowls and similar fancy articles, which have the appearance of polished amber. Rhino feet and hippo feet, when set and mounted with the toe-nails polished, yield other interesting curios in the shape of door-stops, flower-pots, and boxes.

Some of my men made a fire and cooked pieces of the rhino-meat, whilst others were engaged in cutting up the body. My boy roasted on a green spit some of the liver for me; it was beautifully tender and very good indeed. When the heart was removed, it was found that the bullet had gone right through it, tearing a hole an inch in diameter. It is astonishing how, with such a mortal wound, the animal could have had the strength to gore at the bush. The right ear of this rhino was slit and torn in two places, but these were old wounds, probably got in some fight.

The last time I passed by the Kiboko river, I came, to the

east side of the caravan route, upon a fine old rhino bull; but I could not get sufficiently near, as a deep and wooded hollow intervened. I had three of my men with me, but the moment we sighted the rhino, they left me and swarmed up the nearest trees. Only some considerable time after the rhino had disappeared, crashing in headlong flight through the bushes, did my brave boys descend from their perch of safety.

My fourth rhino was a young solitary bull; I called it "the baby," though it was considerably larger than a donkey, and evidently old enough to have started on its solitary journey on its own responsibility. Owing to the drought, we had camped

TWO RHINOS.

where we could find water; and the porters called this camp "Campi-ya-daktari," — "the doctor's camp." It lies between Campi-ya-simba and Muani. The ground here was literally covered with large beetles and biggish scorpions.

My last two rhinos, an old female and a young male, I shot at Lanjora. I had to make a very wide circuit to get round them, so as to have the wind in my favour. The plain was perfectly open, and only quite short grass was on it, not a tree or shrub could be seen for miles around. When 100 yards off, the rhinos saw me and at once trotted towards us. I knelt down and fired, using the Lee-Speed rifle. The very first shot took effect, and caused the old cow to stagger, and rooted her to the spot. But the young bull was bent on doing mischief, and

I had to shoot him. I gave him two shots in rapid succession; he gave a scream and snort, staggered, and retreated to where the old one stood. As he got near to her, he rolled over with his feet in the air; but somehow he managed to scramble up once more, staggered a few yards farther, and rolled over finally on to his side. In the meanwhile I gave several shots to the old one, to put her out of pain, as blood was streaming from her nose and mouth. Then she too fell down and rolled over. Curiously enough, their backs were turned towards each other and their tails almost touching. The female had a remarkable pair of horns, the posterior being larger and longer than the anterior. I returned to our camp, and left the men to cut up the meat; but from what I heard afterwards, I was sorry that I had not remained.

The double supply of meat caused the cutting up to take the men longer than usual; and as it grew dark, a vast number of hyænas came, from no one knows where, and formed a sort of circle round the score or more of men who were busy with the meat. Some of the men told me that the old hyænas were patiently waiting till their turn of the feast should come; but in the meantime, the younger hyænas were frisking and gambolling about. The hyænas must have been rather disappointed at the short commons they found, as very little was left for them except tough hide.

CHAPTER XVII.

HIPPOPOTAMUS-SHOOTING.

SOUDANESE SOLDIER WITH THE FAJAO PADDLE.

THE hippo is a gregarious animal. In its native home, the rivers and lakes of Africa, the name of hippopotamus, i.e. "river-horse," given to it by ancient naturalists, is eminently suitable, as it usually shows only a narrow bit of its huge head. A line, drawn from the ears to the nostrils, would indicate the portion the hippo exposes above the surface of the water. In uninhabited regions the hippo is not only a perfectly harmless, but, according to science, a useful animal, designed by Nature to keep down the over-abundant river-vegetation. Where, however, the hippo crosses the path of civilisation, it becomes a nuisance and a menace, and it is sure to be exterminated.

My first acquaintance with hippos was on the Zambesi and Shiré rivers. As long as we travelled on the stern-wheel steamer, a sort of large-sized raft, the hippos caused us no trouble, but wisely allowed us to pass unmolested. On the Upper Shiré river we had to travel, two and two, in a boat with a sort of dog-kennel at the stern. In this kennel, the two adventurous travellers were expected to find during the day shelter from the broiling sun, and at night the solace of sweet refreshing sleep, in spite of the miasmatic emanations of the river and the countless swarms of mosquitoes. When to these attractions the hippo adds unexpectedly his appearance on the scene, and, as very nearly happened to one of our boats, threatens to capsize the boat and to throw the occupants into a river which simply swarms with crocodiles, the traveller can scarcely be expected to wish blessings on the head of the intruder, though the hippo probably rose in perfect innocence of heart to the surface of the river, merely to get a whiff of fresh air.

At Fajao, on the Victoria Nile, and in the Lur country on the west shore of Lake Albert, the natives complained to me of the depredations caused by hippos coming to their fields in the dead of night, devouring the crops of Indian and Kaffre corn, and trampling sweet-potato and similar crops to wreck and ruin under their heavy tread. At Fajao it became so serious, that scarcity of food began to grip the Soudanese garrison and the Wanyoro natives. The hippos apparently knew they were thieving, for they never showed themselves on moonlight nights. But if the night was particularly dark, some hippo would turn up and take a stroll, destroying the crops of perhaps two or three fields. The Soudanese captain went himself one night with a loaded rifle to watch for these marauders. According to his own account, it was too dark to aim, with the result that the hippo chased *him*, and he had a narrow escape. In such a struggle for existence, the hippo is locally exterminated, or the villagers must migrate to a region not favoured by these animals.

My first hippo I shot in the Athi river, where it forms a series of deep, broad pools to the east of the caravan route. Swahilies still call this river the "Mto Kiboko," which means "hippopotamus river." To shoot in absolute safety from the river-bank at a hippo in the water, partakes very much of the nature of killing pigeons at a shooting-match or bagging pheasants in well-stocked preserves. If one comes upon an unsuspecting hippo, one usually gets for the first shot sufficient time for a steady aim; afterwards it shows less and less of its head above water, at longer and longer intervals, and barely allows a second or two for taking aim. A successful shot is undoubtedly the one just below the eye, if the animal happens to offer this mark; but if it presents the back of its head, then midway between the ears. I have seen hippos sink dead to the bottom of the river with one successful shot, to rise only when the gases within the body produced by commencing decomposition have buoyed up the carcase and caused it to float. But more frequently death is not instantaneous, and the hippo rolls over and over in its dying convulsions, lashing and churning the water with its feet before it finally sinks. When the dead body floats, the head hangs deep under water, and the four feet with part of the light-coloured abdomen show above the surface. My first specimen was a bull, with fair-sized tusks.

These tusks are good commercial ivory, but, as a rule, out of the twelve ivory tusks the hippo carries, only the four large ones of the lower jaw are considered of sufficient weight and size to be purchased by ivory traders; two of these four tusks are curved, the two others lie between the curved ones and are straight. In addition to the twelve ivory tusks, the hippo has twenty-four ordinary teeth.

Hippo-meat is highly prized by every caravan. I gave my caravan therefore a day's rest to avail themselves of this fortunate supply of meat. Caravan porters get only vegetable rations allowed them, in the shape of beans, Indian-corn, rice or native flour. Meat rations are therefore a windfall to them. We had marched for the preceding ten days in daily drenching rains, the rest-day was therefore doubly welcome, and it turned out a lovely day with a blazing hot sun. An air of festivity and feasting spread like magic over the camp, and my first hippo gave a day of rejoicing and happiness to my weary and hungry caravan. The atmosphere was reeking with hippo-meat; some hung in long strips to dry in the scorching sun, some was placed on gridiron-shaped tressels of greenwood over a slow fire, some was grilling on spits stuck round the camp-fires, and some was broiling in cooking-pots. Neighbouring villagers came and visited us, and a brisk market was soon in full swing all over the camp. The skull of this hippo is now in my collection in England; I took the trouble to send it home, but to get it properly bleached in London cost alone £2.

My second hippo was a female; I shot it in the Victoria Nile at Fajao, where the river forms the northern boundary of the Uganda Protectorate. I was not very keen to go on the river which, here and there, is half a mile broad. It teems with crocodiles. The current, too, is very swift, and a native dug-out is not the most reassuring canoe to venture in. The Soudanese garrison, however, begged me to shoot one of the hippos in order to put a stop to the havoc caused to the fields. When I consented to try, they brought me the largest dug-out, named by them "Kabarega," because it was the royal canoe of King

Kabarega of Unyoro, from whom it had been captured in the last war. This canoe is nearly forty feet long and about three feet wide; it is simply the hollowed-out trunk of a good-sized tree.

The paddle used at Fajao is rather curious. Seen sideways, it has a slight spoon-shaped curve. The front surface of the paddle is hollowed so as to leave a strong overlapping lip all round; the back is like a broad leaf with a prominent midrib, terminating in a blunt knob which slightly projects to form the tip of the blade. The soldiers always embark fully armed, because the natives on the opposite bank of the river have not yet been subdued, are hostile, and would gladly seize any favourable opportunity to massacre a few of the hated Soudanese without running too great a risk of their own lives.

There was no need for the men with me in the "Kabarega" to paddle. The current swiftly and noiselessly carried the huge canoe like a bubble down the stream. We left at 6 A.M. Soon an inquisitive hippo raised his head out of the water. I fired and missed. After missing hippos five times in succession, I suspected there was something wrong with the fore-sight of my rifle, a sporting Martini-Henri. I borrowed the rifle of one of the soldiers. The longer and heavier military weapon felt cumbersome; but the sighting was excellent, and the very first bullet dropped into the very centre of the swirl caused by the head of another hippo disappearing below the surface of the water. My next bullet caught the hippo just below the eye, and we heard it crashing into the skull.

When it rose to the surface farther down-stream, it showed plainly that it was mortally wounded. The men paddled vigorously; and as we gained on it, I reserved my shot, because a severely wounded hippo has to rise very frequently to the surface to breathe. We manœuvred to drive it towards the British side of the Nile, so as to have nothing to do with the hostile Shuli bank of the river; and I gave the wounded hippo a second bullet at close quarters through the back of the head. It sank like a stone. We landed to await the rising of the body, when the decomposing gases would buoy it up. The canoe was moored three hundred yards lower down the stream as a further precaution. The hippo sank at 8.30 A.M.; exactly at 10 A.M. it rose with an explosive splash; but the time the body takes to rise I subsequently found to vary

HIPPOPOTAMUS-SHOOTING

considerably. The current carried the body beyond our dug-out; but it was ultimately secured and lashed to the side of the canoe.

Going down-stream with a swift current is one thing, but working up-stream against it in a heavy dug-out with a hippo in tow is preciously different. Expecting to be back at Fajao in a couple of hours, we had brought no food with us, and not even

LANDING-PLACE AT FAJAO.

matches. The hippo was dragged to the nearest papyrus sudd, and then and there cut up on the squashy surface, our feet sinking ankle-deep in the water.

The Soudanese have an ingenious method of getting a fire. Two dry sticks and a bit of tinder, represented by a scrap of bark-cloth in this instance; this was all that was required. It was interesting to watch the process, and one appreciates it the more, when about to share in the blessing of having a fire. One of the men selected two dry sticks. About the middle of one stick, placed horizontally on the ground and held down by the two feet, a small hole is scratched. The other stick is shaped into a long blunt-pointed pencil, held vertically, and made to fit the hole in the horizontal stick. The vertical stick is now twirled furiously between the two palms. Two men sit opposite each other, so that the instant one man stops exhausted, the other may keep up the twirling. In an incredibly short space of time a slight smoke arose from the stick on the ground. The bit of bark-cloth serving as tinder was now placed against the sticks, and the twirling continued vigorously. The bark-cloth caught fire. This was leisurely blown, with dry grass and dry twigs, into a bright flame. Soon a roaring fire, upheld by papyrus reeds, was crackling merrily on the surface of the sudd, with the Nile flowing but a few inches below it.

My boy now prepared some "imshikaki" for me. This is done by spitting small bits of meat, fat, and liver, the hippo supplying the ingredients, alternately on a green twig and propping it near the fire, without however letting it touch the fire. From time to time the spit has to be turned. I enjoyed my meal, "hippo à la imshikaki," washed down with Nile water. I became quite a connoisseur, and I began to pick out bits of fat in preference to the lean. Unfortunately it was very tough, and my jaws and teeth got soon tired. The Soudanese ate heartily and enjoyed this hippo picnic immensely. Not a scrap of the hippo was wasted. The very intestines, after being cleaned of contents, were carefully deposited in the canoe. The dug-out was heavily laden with the cut-up hippo piled into it.

The return journey to Fajao was decidedly unpleasant, and as we toiled slowly up-stream darkness overtook us. There was no moon, only the uncertain glimmer of the water in the starlight. Every now and then we would pass a spot, where the sickening odour of crocodiles would be overpoweringly strong on the sudd. Then again some inquisitive hippo would come to the surface unpleasantly near our canoe, and would remind us of the danger of being capsized.

A beacon had been lit to guide us to the landing-place We all felt thankful and relieved, on reaching our huts in safety. I was too tired to eat anything, but I had a little milk and brandy before tumbling into bed. Next day I had a grand distribution of hippo-meat to the whole of our Soudanese garrison and their families. This female hippo was enormously fat, a striking contrast to the lean male I had shot in the Athi river. Hippo-fat is greatly prized by natives, who attribute to it imaginary medicinal properties. For culinary purposes I can scarcely recommend it, but I do not wish to prejudice anybody who is anxious to try it. Unless hunger supplies the sauce and nature provides jaws and teeth like a negro's, hippo-meat is not likely to find favour in Europe.

A HIPPOPOTAMUS.

My third hippo was a bull; I shot it in Lake Albert. On a subsequent visit to Fajao I got my fourth hippo, a female, and exceedingly fat. I wasted a number of cartridges, missing time after time; but at last, one successful shot below the eye sent the huge animal splashing and struggling, with its feet in the air. The hippo sank mid-stream; after three hours the body rose from the bottom of the river and floated. The current carried it more than a mile beyond where we expected it. Owing to the serpentine curves the river makes at this spot, we should have lost our prize, had it not been for a friendly native who happened to be fishing lower down the river at the time. He saw the body float past and stopped it for us. There was a convenient inlet at hand, where we succeeded in rolling the huge body on to the grassy bank, as seen in the illustration.

On this occasion, we had a narrow shave of being upset in our dug-out. One of the hippos, either frightened by the shots or enraged, and either accidentally or intentionally, bumped up under us and partly tilted the canoe over. We could see him below the water doubling round and coming for us a second time. The second bump threatened to shatter the canoe. I fired at haphazard, as I could not possibly have hit, the part of the body visible to me being below the surface. Fortunately the hippo sheered off in one direction, and we hurriedly left in the opposite.

Some of the hippo-fat, melted down and strained, I filled into two large gourds, holding a gallon or two. This I kept for my private use. It came very handy later on, when I ran out of soap for washing my clothes. My little Wahima servant knew how to manufacture native soap; and as I promised him for his own private use one cake, or rather ball, of soap out of every ten he manufactured, he was keen to be entrusted with my soap-boiling venture. He certainly produced some excellent hippo-soap, but I should be afraid to recommend it for the complexion! He refused to try my suggestion of using wood-ashes, and preferred following his own method. It consisted in collecting the peelings of green bananas from all the refuse heaps in the village. He burnt these peelings, and used the ashes to form a lye in which he boiled the hippo-fat. This hippo-soap, kneaded into lumps about the size of cricket-balls, resembled the ordinary native soap in colour and consistency. It lasted me for some time, until a good supply of ordinary washing soap reached me from Kampala.

CHAPTER XVIII.

GAZELLES.

THE *Thomsonii* gazelle is found in smaller or larger herds between the Makindos river and Lake Nakuru. It is about the size of a goat, and provides the most exquisite roast for the hunter's table. It is not a bit shy, and often allows the hunter to walk up to within fifty yards of it. Of course, where it has been much shot at, as, for instance, in the immediate neighbourhood of the caravan road, it has learnt to distrust the approach of man, and to seek safety in flight already at 200 yards. Young Thomsonii gazelles are constantly being caught by the Masai, who bring them to Fort Smith and Naivasha station, and sell them for a mere trifle.

On my second journey I caught, with my hands, a young Thomsonii alive. It was at Lanjora. I had shot a zebra, and it was getting dusk, when, on my way back to the camp, I nearly trod on the little creature cosily curled up for sleep. I dropped at once on the top of it and seized it. Next morning we reached Machakos, and I bought a she-goat for eight rupees, equivalent at the time to ten shillings. The goat had a kid of about the same size as the young Thomsonii, and she made no difficulty in letting the stranger share with her own young one, provided we just held one of her legs. The young Thomsonii did not relish the first sip of goat-milk, but, being hungry, it came back for more, and after that took to it most naturally. On the march I had the Thomsonii carried; but before we started on the march, and immediately on arrival at camp, and whenever the caravan stopped to rest on the road, I saw to it myself that the Thomsonii was brought to the goat and fed. It had already become quite tame and a pet with my men, when, on a sudden, at Kibwezi it was seized with convulsions and died. Whether it had eaten some poisonous plant, or some one had hurt it, I do not know.

Such young ones, as are allowed to run about free in some of the up-country stations, thrive very well indeed, and have been successfully reared. They breed in captivity, and become very tame; in fact, they are apt to become too cheeky. "Billy," the pet Thomsonii at Fort Smith, has been an inmate for some years, and, as familiarity breeds contempt, he goes for natives without having received any provocation. I have seen brave Masai warriors edge sideways out of the fort in a hurry, when master "Billy" has been on the war-path. The captive Thomsonii appear to relish the leaves of the sweet-potato plant.

There is a great difference in the horns between the male and the female. The horns of the buck curve upward and backward, and then bend slightly forward, terminating in a very sharp and dangerous point. The last two inches near the tip are smooth, but the rest of the horn has the characteristic "rings." In some of the specimens I have shot, the horns diverge; in others they seem to run almost parallel. The horns of the female are tiny, compared with those of the male. They are short and slender, and lack the "rings." In two of the specimens I shot, one of the horns was deformed.

The skin of the Thomsonii, dressed and mounted, makes a very pretty mat. Owing to the abdomen being white, the mat has a white border. The back is a dark tan, which shades into a light brown at the flanks, where a characteristic dark brown stripe borders the white abdomen. A similar dark brown but short line fringes, at a little distance from the tail, each hind-quarter. I cannot remember having seen anywhere else so many Thomsonii gazelles as I saw on my third journey at Lake Naivasha, on the west side of the lake. The usual caravan route is along the east shore, but incessant rains had rendered the Morendat and Gilgil rivers, which flow into Lake Naivasha, impassable for our caravan, and we were compelled to try the west route. Both these rivers are now bridged, being part of the new caravan cart-road, on which so much money has been expended.

The *Grantii* gazelle is a handsome animal of a delicate fawn colour. In the Thomsonii the tan colour reaches right up to the tail; but in the Grantii the fawn colour stops some three or four inches from the tail and then changes into white. As in the Thomsonii, a dark brown but short line fringes, at a little distance from the tail, each hind-quarter. The horizontal dark brown stripe along the flank, which is a conspicuous characteristic of the Thomsonii, is absent in the Grantii.

Both sexes have horns. The horns of the buck usually measure about two feet, but may occasionally exceed three feet. They curve upward and backward, gradually diverging from each other; the direction then changes to upward and forward, and the last three inches bend gracefully forward and inward. The general shape of the horns belongs to the sort known as "lyrate." The last three inches are smooth and terminate in a sharp point, the rest is marked, as in the Thomsonii, with "rings." Grantii with the most symmetrical and typical horns are found in the Kilimanjaro region, to which the Kiboko river may be said to belong. It was at the Kiboko river, on my fourth journey, where I shot my finest specimen of a Grantii buck, as regards symmetry of horns. I kept the mask and had the head mounted in London. Subsequently the authorities at the South Kensington Natural History Museum asked me to let their artist take a drawing of it.

At Lake Nakuru I wounded a Grantii buck in the leg. This led to a tedious pursuit; for the wounded animal would frequently stop, but never let me get nearer than a quarter of a mile. Finally it went up a steep and rocky hill; I followed, when suddenly it descended again to the plain, leaving me exhausted and out of breath about half-way up the hill. I gazed down at the Grantii with a feeling of disappointment at losing it after all my energetic perseverance, when a novel and unexpected scene was enacted before my eyes. If I had been in the plain, I should not have seen this scene, but owing to my position half-way up the hill, I had a capital view of the plain and of what was taking place at the foot of the hill.

The Grantii had paused, and was so engrossed with looking up in my direction, that it did not observe the danger threatening it from quite a different quarter. I became aware of a large brown animal moving along the foot of the hill towards the Grantii. Neither animal suspected as yet the presence of the other, and neither could see the other, owing to the scattered boulders of rock. Of a sudden the new-comer stopped, raised its head, and sniffed the air. The next moment it rushed forward with astonishing speed. The wind blew towards it, and it must have scented, that a wounded animal was not far off. The attention of the Grantii was attracted by the noise; it gave but one look, and seemed to know that now indeed it was a race for life.

It made for the open plain, the pursuer after it. The pursuer gained steadily on it, when the Grantii doubled magnificently in the very nick of time to escape the fatal bite. I believe, if it had not been wounded and somewhat tired by my long pursuit, it could have escaped. But the pursuer again drew nigh, and though the Grantii staved off the fatal moment for a while by skilful doubling, it was seized at last by the flank. Both animals rolled over and over. The Grantii, having shaken itself free, once more dashed across the plain. But its minutes were numbered, and this exciting pursuit ended in the Grantii being torn down to the ground and lying helpless.

GRANT'S GAZELLE.

Three of my Swahilies, who had accompanied me, declared that only a lion could have captured the Grantii; and I felt inclined to think so too, as the scene took place in full, bright daylight between eleven and twelve in the morning. I now hastened down-hill to dispute with the lion, or whatever the animal might be, the Grantii which I considered mine. At the same time, there was the hope of bagging the other animal as well. As I drew near, I saw that it was not a lion, but a big brown hyæna which sneaked off when we advanced. As the hyæna had done me a good turn, I did not hurt it, but gave my attention to the Grantii which had its flank ripped open and the intestines protruding. The poor beast staggered up and tried to show fight. We seized its horns, threw it down, and saved it further suffering by cutting its throat.

The Grantii gazelles herd together in small numbers only. The horns of the female Grantii are different to those of the male. They are about a foot long and slender. They resemble somewhat the horns of the male Thomsonii, except that the "rings" are not so prominent, and the horns are more uniformly slender from the base upward. The illustration shows a specimen which I secured at Bondoni not far from Machakos.

CHAPTER XIX.

ANTELOPES.

THE broad distinction between antelopes and deer lies in the fact, that the horns of antelopes are hollow, and are set upon a solid bony core as in oxen. The horns are never shed, and have to last the animal through life; consequently, every now and then an antelope is shot, which has one of the horns broken off, just as an elephant may now and then be found with only one tusk, the other having been broken off or mal-formed. Antelopes vary considerably in size, from the eland, which almost approaches a rhinoceros in bulk, to the tiny pah, which is not much larger than a hare. Some, as, for instance, the striped koodoo and the spotted reed-buck, are very handsomely marked, but the majority of antelopes have a plain coat, either brown or grey. Some, like the hartebeest, have short hair; others, like the water-buck, are shaggy. The tail of the wildebeest resembles that of a horse; in the steinbok the tail is shorter than in a rabbit. Both sexes of some species, as the hartebeest, have horns; but only the buck of other species, as the impalla.

The horns do not branch, yet every species has its own characteristic and distinguishing variations in length and shape. The African antelopes have two horns; there are no four-horned species, as in India.

The Impalla or Pallah Antelope.—By the new game-laws all shooting is prohibited between the Athi river and the Kedong. But it happens that the impalla is most common just outside these limits. I have shot them as far south as Campi-ya-Simba and as far north as the Gilgil river.

The impalla frequents the bush. I have never seen it roam, like the Thomsonii gazelle, over extensive open grass-plains. The bush facilitates stalking, but it has its drawbacks. It screens the hunter from the game, but it also hides the game from the hunter; and as the game has the senses of smell, sight, and hearing more acute than man, it has time to escape before the hunter is aware of its proximity. The colour of the impalla is brown, and a dark brown vertical stripe fringes each hindquarter at a short distance from the tail. The doe impalla has no horns. The buck is usually accompanied by a small herd of six or more does.

On my fifth journey I had an exciting chase after a buck at Campi-ya-Simba. Time after time the watchful eyes of the does prevented my getting within range of the buck. I could have shot one of the does more than once, but I did not want to; and, as often

THE IMPALLA ANTELOPE.

happens in such a case, it seemed as if they knew it. At last I did succeed in giving the buck a bullet. It then left the herd, but it led me a fine chase over hill and dale, through bush and brake. More than once I got within range, and several times more it was hit. We followed it through a forest and up to a river. Owing to the reeds and bushes at the water's edge, we only got a glimpse of it, as it plunged into the river and tried to swim across. But the opposite bank was very steep; and as the buck swam along it, looking out for an open and convenient spot to land, we floundered through the reeds along our side of the river, trying to get a sight of the animal.

As it swam, it only exposed its head and horns; even the neck was immersed. I had two more shots. The first grazed one of the horns and struck off a splinter; the second went into the head. Instantly it sank, head downwards, as if trying to stand on its head, and the hind part of the body came for a second into view. It took some time before one of my men found a spot, where we could cross over to the other bank, and then we had the further trouble of fishing the body out. The horns reached England safely, and are in my collection; but when I look at them, the whole scene, as it happened in the solitude of the African wilderness, passes before me.

The horns of the buck impalla form a series of graceful curves; in their upward curve the direction is at first forward and outward, this changes to backward and outward, and then becomes backward and inward, and finally ends by being forward and inward. The last four inches near the tip are smooth and terminate in a sharp point, the rest of the horn is "ringed."

The buck shown in the illustration is not the one that gave us so much trouble. It is one that I secured at the Kedong with one bullet.

The Wildebeest.—The gnu or wildebeest is a singular creature. Its horns remind one of the ox, its tail and mane of the horse, its shaggy tuft of beard of the goat, and yet its trunk and limbs are those of an antelope. There are several species of gnu, but the one seen in these regions is the "blue wildebeest," so called from its bluish silver grey colour. The horns of an old male may be mistaken by the inexperienced as buffalo horns, because they form a similar broad band across the forehead, wide sweep to the side, and sharp terminal curve inwards. Both sexes have horns, but those of the female are more slender. In the young animal the horns take only a slight bend to the side and then run upwards.

The wildebeest is found either singly or in herds which may vary from a few individuals to many hundreds. The Athi plains and the open grass-lands by Campi-ya-Simba are some of its favourite spots. Where it has been much shot at, it has become shy and timid; but where shooting is prohibited, as on the Athi plains, it will calmly go on grazing within fifty yards of a passing caravan. It looks a formidable creature, but is really most inoffensive; even when wounded and pursued, it only seeks safety in flight and never attacks. A solitary animal, when chased, will sometimes go through singular antics, bobbing its head up and down and whisking the tail about. I have seen it tumble down as if shot, scramble up, career off to a distance, then suddenly turn round and stand still, staring at the pursuer, as if nothing had happened.

The flesh is not very palatable, but decidedly acceptable to the ever-hungry Swahili. On one occasion, on my fifth journey, I shot a female at Lanjora with my Lee-Speed rifle. The bullet broke both hind-legs and the poor brute dragged itself along on its fore-legs. I shall never forget the distressing bellowings of pain it uttered. For though, as a rule, game suffers death without a sound of pain, now and then some poor animal does moan or cry out. The herd of wildebeests remained standing near the one which I had wounded; but though my men urged me to shoot some more, I would not, as I considered one animal sufficient for the caravan. Meat can only be kept for a very few days; sometimes it goes bad already on the following day. It would, therefore, be wasteful to shoot more than is absolutely required. The herd moved off, as I advanced towards them, and I speedily ended the sufferings of the wounded one. A good many wildebeest must fall a prey to lions, judging by the skulls which litter the grassy plains. Hartebeest skulls are also fairly common; but skulls of gazelles are rarely seen, and perhaps are devoured by wild beasts, owing to the bones being smaller.

A PAH ANTELOPE.

The Pah.—From Mombasa right up to Singo this tiny antelope is more or less common. Near the Tsavo river used to be its favourite haunt. It prefers grassy jungles, where it can hide among the thorny shrubs and undergrowth, impassable to larger animals. It is easier to bag a specimen with a shot-gun than with a rifle.

On the march through Singo, happening to be a little ahead of my caravan, and tramping along with a walking-stick in my hand, one of these little creatures suddenly jumped up out of the grass at my feet. Before it could dash away, up went my stick and caught it a whack on the neck, stretching it dead. The Soudanese soldier walking behind me then carried it for me, slung from the stick, till the caravan overtook us.

Natives have a clever way of making a sort of pouch or hand-bag out of the skin of small animals, such as kids, pahs, weasels, or wild-cats. One cut or stab through the throat sideways furnishes an opening large enough to enable the operator to withdraw the whole of the body of the animal, peeling the skin off as if it were a tight-fitting glove. The skin is then turned inside out, dried in the sun, and manipulated until it is soft and pliant. The pouch is carried suspended from the wrist or arm, by slipping the hand through the hole at the neck. I have in my collection one of these curious hand-bags, which I got on my journey through the Magwangwara country in German East Africa. It is the skin of a weasel, and has the jawbones and teeth left *in situ*. The native to whom it belonged carried in it his most cherished possession, which happened to be a snuff-box. He sold me the handbag, but he would not hear of parting with his snuff-box.

THE KOBUS THOMASI ANTELOPE.

The Kobus thomasi Antelope.—I have shot only one specimen of this fine antelope. I secured it on the march through Singo, one of the Uganda provinces. Shortly before reaching our camp at Busibika, we were crossing a grassy plain with a few shrubs and scattered trees, when I caught sight of a large herd of antelopes; but curiously enough there was only one amongst them which had horns. I decided to stalk it, a comparatively easy matter, owing to the scattered shrubs. I got to within 120 yards of it; but as the animal stood facing me, I was compelled to give it the chest-shot, though I dislike this shot as it rarely bowls the animal over. We found afterwards, on examining the body, that my first shot did enter the chest, but was deflected to the left by the breast-bone; it penetrated sufficiently far to disable the left fore-leg. I fired two more shots at the animal as it galloped off, but missed both times. Fortunately, owing to the wound, it had soon to stop; and I was able to stalk up to eighty yards and give it the shoulder-shot. It managed, however, to leap away and disappeared behind some ant-hills. When we got to the ant-hills, not a trace of the antelope could we see far or near; but a diligent search in the grass showed us the animal lying dead. On cutting it up, we found that the second bullet had gone clean through the heart; and yet the animal was able to give a dozen or more bounds before it fell dead. This may perhaps be accounted for by its being hit when in full gallop.

It is of the size of a large stag. The two white patches round the eyes and the white patches on the upper lip are very distinctive. The abdomen is also white; the rest of the body is a tan, with the exception of a black patch at the knees, and a black line running from the knees down the front of the leg. The Waganda call it the Sunu or Nsunu. The horns start close together upward, then they diverge outwards and backwards; curving round, they converge inwards and backwards, then a second bend occurs and the horns terminate curving forwards. The horns are "ringed," with the exception of the last three or four inches, which are smooth and terminate in a sharp point.

The Nswallah.—This is a favourite word with the Swahilies to designate any antelope or gazelle larger than a pah or smaller than a kongoni. It is a very convenient word wherewith to cloak ignorance; and as I am not certain to which particular species the antelope shown in the illustration belongs, I cannot do better than give it the Swahili name. It was a female without horns, and this makes it doubly difficult to classify it. A shot through the back at two hundred yards laid it low, practically in sight of the camp, and two Soudanese soldiers at once hurried off to fetch it. I came across several more of the same sort in Ingo, where I shot this one. It frequents grassy plains dotted with shrubs or bush. It is found either solitary or with a companion, probably a young one. I have never seen it in herds; and I unfortunately failed to come across one with horns. It had a white abdomen and a bushy tuft to its tail, which was also white on the under surface. The general colour is a soft dark brown with a darker patch on the forehead.

THE NSWALLAH ANTELOPE. ♀

The Hartebeest Antelope. — There are two species of hartebeest met with on the journey to Uganda, though there are several more in other parts of Africa. The species found along the caravan route through British East Africa is the Cokei, which also reaches for some distance into the Uganda Protectorate, and is then replaced by the Jacksoni, which stretches right up to the north of Unyoro. It is sometimes seen alone, but, as a rule, it is found in small herds. Near the Mto-ya-Mawe (or Stony River), between Muani and Campi-ya-Simba, I saw, on my last journey, a huge herd which must have numbered several hundreds. The hunter soon finds out, that it is easier to shoot a solitary individual than one in a herd.

The hartebeest has rather an ungainly appearance, as the hind part of the body droops. When it gallops, it looks as if it were limping, especially as the head bobs up and down with the motion. It misleads the inexperienced who imagine they have wounded the animal. In spite of this halting movement it gallops very swiftly, and soon out-distances pursuit. Generally, one sentinel looks after the safety of the herd, but the others are not indifferent as to their common security, and their keen senses soon apprise them of approaching danger. They often fall a victim to their curiosity. After the animal has galloped a certain distance, it will stop and climb the highest white-ant hillock in order to satisfy this craving to know the actual whereabouts of the pursuer. I have found it a good plan, when stalking hartebeest, to run after it whilst it is running, and to drop flat on the ground the moment it stops to reconnoitre. If there is sufficient cover, I then proceed to stalk it by crawling nearer to it under cover of the grass and shrubs. If there is absolutely no cover, I remain motionless, and then it is a struggle of patience between hunter and game. As a rule, the hunter has not sufficient time or patience, and the moment he moves the hartebeest bolts.

Young ones are occasionally run down by natives, and brought to the station alive and sold for a trifle; but hitherto the hartebeest has proved very different to the Thomsonii in captivity. Thomsonii can be reared with, comparatively speaking, no trouble at all; but the hartebeests until now, in spite of the utmost care and attention, have not proved in up-country stations successful in captivity—they have always died young. The last time I passed the Eldoma Ravine Station, a young hartebeest was running about in the inner court. It was being fed on cow's milk from a bottle. A piece of calico, punctured with a number of holes, was tied so as to form an elongated and soft mouthpiece, which the young one could take into its mouth. The allowance was a bottle in the morning and another towards dusk. The young one seemed to appreciate its food; for if the boy who fed it was not up to time, it would impatiently follow him about. On one occasion, when we experimented, it followed, though with evident reluctance and hesitation, right up the steps and into a private sitting-room.

A young water-buck was at the Ravine Station at the same time, and its graceful form, notwithstanding its shaggy coat, formed a striking contrast to the ungainly and inelegant young hartebeest. Both young antelopes were exceedingly tame. The young water-buck would coolly walk up to my tent, which had been pitched in the inner court, and help itself to water out of the pail or basin. But when it began to consider that my tent-ropes were meant for the purpose that some one is said to have blessed the Duke of Argyle for in the case of the new milestones, namely, to scratch the back against, I began to consider the water-buck's affection for my tent as rather a nuisance.

The head of the Jacksoni is anything but handsome. It is elongated, and narrows to almost a blunt point at the muzzle. From the forehead rises a bony protuberance, covered for two or three inches by the skin. Upon this bony elevation are perched the two horns. Their direction is at first outward and backward, then comes a rather sharp bend, and they proceed forward and almost parallel with each other; then occurs another sharp bend, and the horns point backwards and slightly outwards. The first portion of the horn is stumpy, thick, and somewhat rugose; the middle portion, between the two bends, is "ringed"; the terminal backward portion is smooth for the last six or seven inches, and ends in a sharp point.

My first specimen of Jacksoni I shot at the Eldoma Ravine on the first journey. I saw a small herd of about four or five, and I fired at 150 to 200 yards. I was using my Martini-Henri rifle, and there was such a cloud of smoke that it was impossible at the moment to see what had happened. As the smoke cleared, I noticed that the herd had not disappeared as I had expected, but were in evident hesitation. I fired hurriedly a couple more shots, which missed. Walking leisurely up to the spot, I was pleasantly surprised to find that my first bullet had hit, for a kongoni, as hartebeest are called by the Swahili, lay expiring. I sent the horns to the coast to be forwarded to England, but, like many of my other shooting specimens, they never reached home. It does happen, that specimens arrive at the coast without any vestige of address remaining, and after some time such are sold as unclaimed goods; but it is annoying, when they miscarry after every precaution has been taken to ensure their reaching safely their destination. After a while the traveller ceases to look upon these mishaps as annoyances, and he rather congratulates himself when things he has sent do reach safely his home or his friends.

My second Jacksoni gave me a deal of trouble. It was in the uninhabited region between the Ravine and the Kavirondo. My first shot wounded the animal badly, but when we went to look for it on the brow of the hill, we saw it galloping off in the distance, leaving a broad blood-spoor on the grass. This incited us to follow, as from time to time the animal lay down; but for a long time I never could get within half a mile of it. During the pursuit we suddenly came upon a splendid buffalo, the first and only one I have ever come across. I used my Lee-Speed, as it was rather far off, and I presume I missed, for my subsequent shots only accelerated its flight. I had always heard, that a buffalo invariably attacks its aggressor, but this is evidently not the case. I confess I hesitated at first to risk an attack from the huge creature, but I trusted to having my magazine-rifle, which enables me to have eleven shots running without re-loading, since by a simple movement the empty cartridge is automatically extracted and replaced by a loaded one from the attached magazine. I speculated that, as the attacking animal came closer, my chances of hitting it would be increased. But with further experience I am not so sure, that I should like to trust to a Lee-Metford bullet having sufficient stopping power to arrest the rush of an enemy, man or beast, though mortally wounded. The buffalo might still have had enough life left to toss and gore me, even though its minutes were numbered, and it should sink down dead afterwards.

When I succeeded in coming up with the exhausted hartebeest, I gave it a bullet from my Lee-Speed rifle at close quarters. It jumped over a grassy elevation, and when we had climbed this, we saw a hartebeest slowly galloping off at a distance. Thinking this was the wounded one, as it had already shown such marvellous powers of endurance, we were following for a while, when I felt convinced that it must be another hartebeest, and that consequently the wounded one must be lying dead somewhere. The only way to ascertain this, was for us to retrace our steps to the last spot, where we had seen the wounded one, and from there to track it. This we did, and thus we came upon it, lying dead in the grass, and completely hidden from us even within five feet of it.

My third Jacksoni I got to the south of the Ravine. The fourth Jacksoni I shot in Singo. Whilst the alarmed animals were rushing across a swamp, I ran in pursuit, and I dropped on my knees, when the herd paused on the other side of the swamp to look round. I was obliged to give the chest-shot, as the nearest animal was one which faced me. I found afterwards, that the Martini bullet had hit, and had been deflected to one side under the skin, where we felt it and cut it out. Owing to the scattered bush, it was difficult to follow the animal, but in the end we succeeded in securing it, though it required several more bullets.

The Cokei Hartebeest.—It has quite different horns to the Jacksoni. This is due to a slight difference in direction where the two bends occur. Instead of curving, as in the Jacksoni, almost straight forward at the first bend, the curve in the Cokei is to the side. This gives a wider stretch between the horns. Then again at the second bend, instead of pointing straight behind, the horns of the Cokei point almost straight up. In other respects, even including the perch on the bony skin-covered protuberance, the Jacksoni and Cokei horns resemble each other. There are slight but interesting variations among the Cokei horns themselves; in some the terminal points are directed backward, in others inward, instead of the more common direction of upward.

The first antelope I ever shot was a Cokei hartebeest, and I am not likely to forget the danger I unconsciously exposed myself to on that day. We had got to that part of the Kiboko river, which lies on the old route. I was near the head of the caravan with another European. The caravan stopped, and I was told we were going to pitch the camp there. My companion had already gone off to stalk some hartebeest seen in the distance. I thought I might as well do the same, and I took a slightly different direction. My companion returned to the camp without firing a shot. I fired at 400 yards. I did not know whether I had hit, but on going to examine the place, my boy pointed out to me some drops of blood.

We two, my boy and I, went in pursuit, and, after a fatiguing chase, we came, more by good luck than skill, upon the wounded animal which had not been able to keep up with the herd. I succeeded in rolling it over. My boy cut its throat; for though it was quite dead, no devout Mahommedan will eat the flesh of an animal which has not had its throat cut, nor will he eat it unless it is cut by a Mahommedan. According to Koran teaching, the Mahommedan should not eat the flesh, unless the throat was cut when the animal was still alive; but this part he discreetly ignores, especially when on caravan journeys, as it would make his limited chances of getting meat practically nil. Having cut the animal's throat and satisfied his conscience, my boy divested himself of his water-bottle, which we had emptied, and we followed a zebra which I had also wounded. Though we got very near the zebra, in fact within fifty yards of it, I found that my remaining five cartridges were useless, as they would not fit the rifle. As neither of us felt inclined to attack the zebra with a knife, for it can give quite as bad a bite as any horse, we retraced our steps.

Hitherto I had placed the utmost reliance on a native finding his way about by a sort of instinct. I was therefore taken aback, when my boy could not discover, where the dead hartebeest lay. I began to be anxious about our finding our way back to camp, when I noticed some birds at a distance alighting on the grass. My boy promptly pronounced them to be guineafowls, but I felt convinced they must be gigantic guineafowls, to be seen at that distance. Then the thought flashed through my brain, that they might be vultures at my hartebeest. This proved to be the case, and they had already pecked out one of the eyes, devoured half the tongue, ripped open the abdomen, and polished off most of the entrails. The empty water-bottle however assured us that it was the hartebeest which I had shot.

My confidence in the native topographical instinct was restored, by seeing that we were after all so near the dead antelope, though we had discovered it by an accident. As we were both under the impression, that the camp was pretty near, perhaps at the utmost half-an-hour off, we held a short consultation, and decided that he should hurry back to the camp with the hartebeest's head and horns, in order to guide a sufficient number of men to carry the meat to the camp. I was to remain on guard, lest vultures or hyaenas should quite devour the carcass. As my rifle was useless, except that in an emergency I could use it as a club, I told the boy to leave me the kitchen-knife which, in the hurry of starting from camp, he had taken with him instead of my huntingknife. The boy went, and I was left alone.

The broiling sun drove me to seek the shelter of the meagre shadow cast by a thorn-tree, while the vultures, a score or more, perched patiently a few yards off. At last the amount of shade barely sufficed to cover my head, while I lay stretched at full length on the ground. The vultures seemed to know to a nicety, how long I remained awake. Not one of them ventured near, to my knowledge. Then the heat and fatigue overpowered me. I fell fast asleep.

Some sense of approaching danger, curiously enough, must have entered into my dreams. I awoke with a start, looking for the enemy. So sure was I, that I was not surprised to see some naked savages approaching swiftly and silently in the distance. They had not noticed me, being attracted by the dead hartebeest which was being devoured by scores of vultures. The savages were well armed; they carried bows and arrows and long knives. I certainly thought my fate was sealed. It seemed the best thing to play up bravely, if the worst was to happen. I jumped up and shouted, attracting at once their attention. I waved my rifle, slapped the barrel, pointed triumphantly to the dead hartebeest, and beckoned to them to hurry up. I could see they hesitated. This made me more friendly and pressing in my invitation to them to join me.

When they had grasped the fact, that I did not intend to harm them, they cautiously drew nearer. After a long parley, carried on in gesture-dialogue, I got them to cut up the meat and to load themselves with it. The vultures, while I slept, had devoured heart, lungs, and liver, and picked the bones of one hind-quarter perfectly clean. I am sure, they would have polished off the whole hartebeest at one sitting, if left undisturbed. I never saw again such a variety of vultures and other carnivorous birds. While the savages were cutting up the meat, I kept reminding them of the presence of my rifle. I could not divest my mind entirely of all fear of foul play on their part. This made me display my handful of five useless cartridges, and flourish the kitchen-knife in my right hand. Fear of losing my life and determination to sell it dearly were struggling for mastery.

When they had shouldered the meat, I insisted on their walking in single file in front of me. They evidently disliked this arrangement, being as much afraid of me, as I was of them. But, when I urged them to take notice of rifle and kitchen-knife, they reluctantly complied. Unfortunately I had not the least idea in what direction my camp lay. I saw that they wanted to take a direction almost opposite to the one my boy had taken. Of course I protested in dumb-show, and pointed out what I imagined to be the right one. They jabbered noisily, shook their heads, and pointed in the direction they wanted to take. I let them finally have their own choice. We walked for fully an hour. Then we steered for a large tree, where a crowd of similarly armed savages awaited us.

Here my first set of savages threw down their burdens of meat, squatted down, and entered into a noisy palaver with their comrades. I waited patiently for a while. Then, as no one seemed willing to make a move to accompany me a step farther, I decided to take the initiative by renewing our pantomime gesture-dialogue, which had proved successful so far. I confess I was not at all sure but that the savages had already taken me miles and miles away from the caravan route. They might, for all I knew, be waiting to take me to one of their distant villages, and to disarm me whenever I fell asleep. How I blamed my stupidity in permitting my servant to leave me! What solemn resolutions I formed, as we probably all do when we realise the feebleness of our unaided intellect, if it should please Providence to help me safely out of this scrape! I felt convinced, that any sign of fear might end in my ruin. I approached the savage who was evidently the leader.

He remained sitting. Silent and sullen he only stared at me. I slapped him patronisingly on the shoulder. I professed to be most anxious to explain to him the mysteries of the deadly rifle. I even showed him how I took aim. This manoeuvre led to the younger savages making a precipitate movement to the side to get out of the line of aim. But the old sullen rascal remained unmoved. When I had done enough of this dumb-crambo business, slapping his shoulder and occasionally shaking him up, I assumed an authoritative tone, and hoisted one of the loads of meat on to his shoulders. This made him budge; and as he pointed out a younger man sitting near to him, I soon had all the meat shouldered again. Then we moved off in single file, leaving the other savages squatting under the tree.

In about two hours we came upon my hartebeest's head. I heard afterwards that my boy, having lost his way, became tired and nervous, and then chucked away the trophy. My friendlies, for at last I felt convinced that my savages were dealing honestly with me, lifted up the hartebeest head and carried it along. The sun was getting low, when we entered the caravan road. Then my boy met us. He was accompanied by two or three of our caravan porters, and he brought my riding-donkey. My friendlies carried the meat right into camp for me, where I shared it with them, they grinning with pleasure and satisfaction.

Though this little adventure had ended happily and now looked rather comic, I took the lesson to heart not to risk losing myself again in a wild jungle, with neither water nor fire within available distance, without a companion, and practically unarmed. Our caravan leader assured me I was lucky in falling in with friendly Wakamba, and that I should never have returned, if I had met a band of Masai on the war-path. That he was in the right, and that these adventures do not always have a happy ending, was proved within a few months on this very spot. Dr. Chartres, the Mission doctor at Kibwezi, went with a friend, Mr. Colquhoun, for a day's shooting to this very neighbourhood.

These two men were never seen again. According to the servants who accompanied them, as soon as the tents were pitched, the two white men, followed by a gun-bearer, stalked some antelopes, wounded one and followed it. The gun-bearer returned to the camp and said, that he had lost sight of the "musungu" (the white men). As he had not succeeded in finding them, he had decided to go back to the camp. Hour after hour passed, and neither of the white men turned up. The camp got alarmed. Everybody went to search the bush, calling and shouting. Not a trace could be found. Night rendered further search useless. Next morning the search was resumed and kept up for some days. Not the slightest clue was forthcoming. The servants returned to the Mission Station and reported the disaster.

It is not likely that these two unfortunate white men were killed by lions. The lions would have devoured them on the spot, and the rifles would have been found. Dr. Chartres knew the neighbourhood thoroughly, it is therefore improbable that they lost themselves. It is believed, that they were met by hostile savages, probably Masai on the warpath, and were captured and killed.

On my first journey to Uganda, we had a major as caravan leader. On my subsequent five journeys I was in charge of the caravan. In the event of my not turning up before dusk, our caravan leader had already decided to leave one European with some porters at the camp to wait a day or two and to search for me. The bulk of the caravan, some four hundred men, could not of course be delayed, as the food question is a serious one in a wilderness. It turned out, that the caravan, instead of camping where we had halted in the morning and were supposed to camp, had moved off two hours farther on. When I arrived at our camp, I got of course a wigging for having left, as I was supposed to have done, a caravan on the march ; but I was able to explain, that I should not have

NEUMANN'S STEINBOK.

left but for the misleading assurance of the headman, that we had reached our destination. In fact, the caravan would have camped, where I had started from, but that owing to the drought there was no water to be had till the Kiboko river was reached.

Neumann's Steinbok.—On my sixth journey I shot two small antelopes, one at the Molo river, the other at the Kiboko river, the first in the Uganda Protectorate, the second in the British East Africa Protectorate. Both were males. The females of this species have no horns. I was puzzled to know to which of the small species of antelopes my specimens belonged. I submitted them to Mr. Oldfield Thomas, the authority on antelopes at the South Kensington Natural History Museum. He was interested, because the Museum had not yet one specimen of the sort in its vast collection. Mr. Thomas considered mine to belong to a new species quite recently added to science by the German traveller and naturalist in whose honour it has been named Neumanni. But there appears to be a slight difference which places my two specimens as a sort of connecting-link between the South African steinbok and Neumann's. The South African species has a black patch on the nose and a black horse-shoe patch on the forehead. Neumann's has neither the one nor the other. My two specimens do not have the black horse-shoe patch, but they both have the black patch on the nose. Mr. Thomas places, therefore, my specimens amongst the Neumanni, as they are nearest to the specimen described as Neumanni. This antelope has tiny horns, somewhat rugose. The general colour is a rich brown. It frequents bush-covered districts in the neighbourhood of water. It is either solitary or in companionship with one or two others. It is a pretty and graceful animal; and it can run apparently as fast on three legs as on four. One specimen I bowled over with a single shot; the other, in spite of a broken hind-leg, gave me some trouble before I could secure it.

CHAPTER XX

SMALL MAMMALS.

LOPHUROMYS ANSORGEI.
(Half life-size.)

MY interest in small mammals was aroused by my capturing one new species of rodent at Mumia's in Kavirondo in 1895.

I am indebted to Mr. E. de Winton, F.Z.S., for the list of names of the specimens collected by me in Uganda and in British East Africa, and to the Zoological Society of London for permission to use their description of the new Lophuromys.

Two specimens (♂ and ♀) of the dwarf mungoose (*Helogale undulata*) I presented to the British Museum (Natural History); they were got with one shot, as they crossed the caravan road at Masongoleni in British East Africa.

The large ground-squirrel (*Xerus erythropus*) was caught with a noose in a maize-field at Masindi in Unyoro. It is covered with short stiff hairs, some of which are as hard and bristly as the small quills of a porcupine. When running along the ground, the animal holds its tail horizontal.

The small ground-squirrel (*Xerus rutilus*) can frequently be seen on the march, racing ahead along the dusty caravan road on a hot sunny day. From time to time the animal pauses to sit up in a pretty begging attitude to look around and listen, and finally it scampers off into the bush.

Emin's striped-squirrel (*Funisciurus boehmi*) is very common at Fajao in Unyoro. It is a small green animal, with three horizontal black stripes along the body from the neck to the tail. Where the trees were close together, I have seen it jump from tree to tree; but if the branches happened to be rather far apart, it ran down the trunk of the tree as easily as if it were on level ground, and hurrying on to the next tree, it ran up with equal ease and rapidity, however vertical and high the tree might be.

The ochre-footed scrub-squirrel (*Funisciurus genana*) is pretty often met with, rustling in the foliage of the shrubs and bushes along the caravan road between Kinani and Kibwezi in British East Africa.

The bats were captured with the butterfly net, some in the open air on bright moonlight nights, some in my hut, and some in banana plantations.

The musk-shrews were caught with a steel-trap in my hut. Other troublesome visitors the steel-trap has rid me of, viz., the *Mus hildebrandti*, the *Mus gentilis*, and the *Mus Ugandæ*.

The harsh-furred field-mouse (*Lophuromys flavopunctatus*) was caught with the hand in a field of sweet-potatoes at Masindi in Unyoro. The *Lophuromys ansorgei* and the *Tachyoryctes splendens* were collected in clearing the jungle, where formerly had stood a Kavirondo village.

The tree-rat was caught with the hand, when a tall forest tree was felled at Fajao. This rat has a reddish patch near the nose, and a similar mark near the root of the tail.

The two species of small grass-mice differ in colour. The reddish one I got from a bird's nest hanging from a bush; the young of this species, however, are dark grey, for I saw four such in a nest cleverly constructed between the bananas of a green banana-bunch.

The striped field-rat (*Arvicanthus pulchella*) is a pretty animal with its zebra markings. It is very common in the sweet-potato fields at Masindi in Unyoro. I once came across three young ones in a nest built in the fork of a small tree. The tiny size of the markings gave them the appearance of having spots instead of stripes.

The curious *Heterocephalus glaber*, or hairless rodent mole, I shot in 1896 at Kinani in British East Africa. I found it in a small sandy patch, surrounded by scattered bush and thorn-trees, near the caravan route. Whereas the *Tachyoryctes splendens*, or bamboo-rat, was observed by me in Kavirondo to throw up the earth like a giant mole, and to live in rich, cultivated soil overgrown with vegetation, this *Heterocephalus* threw out the earth with its hind-legs from a small tunnel, like a rat-hole, in a sandy, bare, and barren patch. The hairless, yellowish skin of the *Heterocephalus* felt to the touch something like a frog's naked skin. The eyes are so small, that I thought at first this animal had none, but they can be seen by using a magnifying glass. The animal is not absolutely hairless, for it has a few scattered hairs on its head and feet. To secure the specimen I had to shoot it. On presenting it to the British Museum (Natural History), Mr. Oldfield Thomas told me, that the first of this species came from Abyssinia, but as nearly half a century passed before another was obtained, it was thought to be rather a freak of Nature than a distinct genus. In course of time, however, a similar animal, but belonging to a different species, was brought from Somaliland. My specimen, Mr. Thomas tells me, is interesting because it is the first from British territory.

Bats

1. Epomophorus minor (fruit bat)   From Masindi in Unyoro.
2. Hipposiderus caffer .   Do.   do.
3. Vesperugo nanus . .   Do.   do.
4. Taphozous mauritianus .   Do.   do.
5. Nycteris thebaica .   From Kampala in Uganda.

Musk-Shrews.

6. Crocidura doriana   From Masindi in Unyoro, and Kampala in Uganda.

Squirrels.

7. Funisciurus genana (ochre-footed scrub-squirrel)   From Kibwezi and Kinani, in British East Africa.
8. Funisciurus boehmi (Emin's striped-squirrel) . . . From Fajao in Unyoro.
9. Xerus erythropus (ground-squirrel) . . . . . .   From Masindi in Unyoro.
10. Xerus rutilus (ground-squirrel)   From Mtoto Ndei, British East Africa.

Gerbil.

11. Gerbillus (Tatera) afer .   From Masindi in Unyoro, and Mumia's in Kavirondo.

Reed-Mouse.

12. Dendromys mesomelas .   From Masindi in Unyoro.

Field-Rats.

13. Arvicanthus abyssinicus   From Mumia's in Kavirondo; Masindi in Unyoro; Kibero, on east shore of Lake Albert; Mahaji, on west shore of Lake Albert.

Striped Field-Rat.

14. Arvicanthus pulchella   From Masindi in Unyoro.

Tree-Rat.

15. Mus hypoxanthus   From Fajao in Unyoro.

Tree-Mouse.

16. Mus dolichurus   From Fajao in Unyoro.

House-Rats and Mice.

17. Mus hildebrandti .   From Masindi in Unyoro.
18. Mus gentilis .   Do. do.
19. Mus ugandæ .   From Kampala in Uganda.

Small Grass-Mice.

20. Mus (Leggada) musculoides .   From Masindi in Unyoro.
21. Mus (Leggada) minutoides   Do. do.

Harsh-Furred Field-Mouse.

22. Lophuromys flavopunctatus .   From Masindi in Unyoro.
23. Lophuromys ansorgei   From Mumia's in Kavirondo.

ON A NEW RODENT OF THE GENUS LOPHUROMYS FROM BRITISH EAST AFRICA.

By W. E. DE WINTON, F.Z.S.

(From Proceedings of the Zoological Society of London, 19th May 1896.)

In a small series of mammals presented to the national collection by Dr. W. J. Ansorge, Medical Officer to Her Majesty's Government in Uganda, who is now home on leave,

I find two specimens of a very handsome mouse of the genus *Lophuromys* new to science, which I propose to name in honour of the collector.

Lophuromys Ansorgei, sp.n.

The whole of the upper parts of the head and body smooth dark chocolate colour, with no markings whatever, the underparts uniform pale cinnamon, the feet dark above and below, the tail black-brown, slightly greyer beneath, especially basally, rather short and thick, covered with hair, but not densely enough to conceal the scales, ears moderate, rounded, covered with close short hairs.

On parting the fur of the upper parts, it will be found that the tips only of the hairs are dark, shading gradually into bright tan at the bases; there is no under-fur, all the hairs are perfectly straight, of a uniform length, and of very much the consistency of a stiff camel's-hair brush.

Measurements taken from dried skin: head and body 135 mm., tail 49 mm., pes 22 mm., forearm and hand 33 mm.

Skull: greatest length 33.5 mm., greatest breadth 17 mm., basifacial length 20 mm., basicranial length 10 mm., incisive foramina—length 6.5 mm., breadth 2.8 mm., nasals—length 15 mm., breadth 3.5 mm., upper molar series 5.5 mm., lower molar series 5 mm., mandibles, from condyle to incisor tips, 24 mm.

Hab. Mumia's, Kavirondo, N.E. of Lake Victoria.

Type No. 96. V. 8. 1, in Brit. Mus.

The nearest ally of this species is most likely *L. sikapusi* from West Africa, but it is easily distinguished by its rather larger size and much darker and handsomer colouring.

Seen through a lens, each hair is flattened like a blade of grass, tapering abruptly to a sharp point at either end; some of the hairs are flat, others have the edges turned over so that the cross section forms the segment of a circle. The claws are long and straight; these and the hairy nose and other peculiarities of the genus are well described by Mr. F. W. True (Proc. Nat. Mus. Washington, 1892, vol. xv. p. 460) in his description of *Mus aquilus*, which no doubt should be referred to this genus. I may mention that there is in the British Museum a specimen which seems to agree with the description of *Mus aquilus*; this is a smaller animal, freckled with light tips to the hairs, and is otherwise very distinct from the animal now under notice, but shows that

Mr. True's specimen was about full grown, and that the tail was not materially shortened by the injury mentioned.

Dr. Ansorge has been hitherto known in connection with zoology as a collector of insects, but he gives me an interesting account of the accident which put him in possession of this collection of mammals in 1895. The site of a long-disused village had been purchased for the purpose of building the new Government Hospital, and in clearing the long grass and scrub towards the centre, as the circle narrowed it was discovered that there was a large number of small mammals enclosed. It being observed that there were "rats of all colours," a selection of pairs of different sorts was made, with the result that some ten or a dozen specimens were obtained. Dr. Ansorge describes the *Rhizomys* heaving up the ground like giant moles; many of the new *Lophuromys*, quite twenty, were left on the ground.

The two specimens agree in every particular, and are said to be male and female, but are not labelled.

Bamboo-Rat.

24. Tachyoryctes splendens   From Mumia's in Kavirondo.

Hairless Rodent Mole.

25. Heterocephalus glaber .   In 1896 from Kinani in British East Africa.

CHAPTER XXI.

REPTILES.

Frogs.—There can be little doubt that an interesting collection of frogs could be obtained in Uganda and on the march up-country. The difficulty of making such a collection lies in the necessity of having to provide oneself with a good supply of the indispensable methylated spirits and pure alcohol, and suitable stoppered glass jars. Once only, it was on my third journey, did I take some methylated spirits with me. I was promptly relieved of it, on the third day's march from Mombasa, by the professional thief who, having enlisted as a caravan porter, absconded with his load. On my first journey—we were camped at the famous water-holes in the Taru desert—I caught a greyish white frog in one of the small water-holes, and I was tempted to bottle it, sacrificing some of my brandy to preserve it in. This specimen has since found its way to the Natural History Collection at South Kensington. On my fifth journey I was tempted once more to secure the specimen I saw. This time it was a bright-red frog, noticed by me in the slushy caravan road near Masongoleni, when incessant and depressing daily rains kept my eyes directed to the ground. The following day I found with regret, that the brilliant red colour had disappeared under the action of the spirits, and had been replaced by a dingy grey, whereupon in disgust I threw the specimen away. I am sorry for it now, as I have not found anything like it in the South Kensington Museum. I may have thrown away a very interesting novelty.

My third and last attempt was to bring to the coast a very tiny little grass-frog from Kavirondo. This little creature was sitting snugly on some tall blades of grass. In colour it was almost white, in size about half an inch. Owing to the white, purple, and yellow flowers scattered among the grass, it might be easily overlooked. Swahilies say this little frog poisons cattle. It is quite possible that cattle out grazing may swallow some of them. As Nature did not intend that cows should devour frogs, it is not at all improbable that gastric irritation may be set up by the unnatural food, and in severe cases may produce death. These little frogs are very numerous in certain localities; hundreds could have been collected easily. A few days later I happened to look at the pickle-jar which contained my specimen. I found the spirits had been upset, and the specimen, dried up and spoiled, had to be thrown away. But the remarkable differences which exist among frogs in colour, size, shape, and habits, and which I, with an uninterested eye, have noticed, convinces me that any one, willing to devote some spare moments to this particular subject, would find it well worth his while.

Chameleons.—Among the many interesting objects the traveller meets with, the chameleon deserves mention. If for nothing else, the ludicrous mobility of its eyes must arrest one's attention. The chameleon has a perpetual stiff neck, the apoplectic shortness of which prevents the head being turned. Kindly Nature has, however, provided abundant compensation, by enabling the chameleon to look behind without having the trouble of turning round, and to look straight up without having to move the head.

To watch the eye of the chameleon gaze upward, then straight behind, now downwards, now forwards, is sufficiently amusing; but when the two eyes are seen to have the power of moving perfectly independently of each other, one eye staring stonily backward, and the other eye fixed in heavenly rapture upward, and after various other squinting gymnastics, both eyes suddenly shoot back and assume a normal position; then the effect is decidedly laughable. In squinting human eyes, only one eye does really the work of seeing, the other eye, for the matter of that, might be closed or non-existent; the brain taking cognizance of what the one eye reports to it, and ignoring all impressions on the other eye. But in the squinting exercises of the chameleon, both eyes, whether working in unison or independently, have what they communicate to the brain impartially attended to.

The fore-foot of the chameleon has two of the four toes

forward, and the other two backward. This gives to it somewhat the appearance of a crab's pincers, and imparts to it, at the same time, the grasping power of the hand. There is an awkward stilted movement in the limbs of the chameleon, as it unclasps its hold, extends the limbs, and fastens on to some object. The tail is long and prehensile.

Everybody knows that the chameleon has the power, apparently depending on its volition, of changing its colour; but judging from the African specimens I have observed, there seems to be a very limited choice of colour and of pattern. The most common colours are green and yellow, and the usual patterns are a yellow mottling on a green ground, or dark green vertical patches or stripes with a yellow base line. With the lantern light thrown on them on a dark night, chameleons appear as plain whitish-yellow bodies among the dark foliage.

Natives have a superstitious dread of chameleons, and believe their bite to be poisonous. It required a good deal of persuasion to get any one to carry for me a small branch on which a chameleon perched motionless; but if the chameleon, disturbed by the movement, began to walk towards the hand, the man would drop the branch in fear and horror. When irritated or frightened, the chameleon opens wide its jaws and utters a hissing sound like "shah." If greatly annoyed, it will snap and bite at the object held out to it; but it is really very timid and inoffensive, and all it desires, is to be left alone, to fulfil its mission of clearing the world of flies and other insect pests.

Lizards.—Judging from what I have seen, apparently a great variety of species exist of the useful and harmless lizard. It is a pleasure to watch the alert movements of their head, their diligence in hunting down troublesome insects, their nimbleness in darting on their prey, and the rapidity with which they race up the perpendicular surface of a tree, rock, or wall. They have to keep a sharp look-out for their own safety, for they are evidently considered delicate morsels by more than one enemy. I have often seen a hen catch a lizard, kill it by dashing it repeatedly against the ground, and then swallow it whole. Some of the lizards in these Protectorates are brilliantly coloured in blue, orange, and red; but many of the smaller, decked in inconspicuous colours of grey and brown, are admirable in the beauty of the patterns traced on them.

There is a very large water-lizard, known by Swahilies as the "kengé," which may grow to an enormous length, and is appreciated by them as food. I was startled once by nearly treading on one of these big lizards at Fajao near the bank of the Nile. At first I took it for a small crocodile, but as it swiftly clambered up a steep sandy bank I saw my mistake. On the overland journey from Lake Nyassa through the Magwangwara country in German East Africa, one of our Swahilies shot a water-lizard six feet in length. It was the largest I have seen, the one at Fajao could not have been much over three feet. The skin of the "kengé" is used to ornament various fancy articles. In Usoga it is used instead of the conventional drum-skin of leather for small drums; it also serves to form the sound-board in typical Usoga harps.

One night the cold, wriggling body of a lizard rushing down my leg made me jump out of bed pretty sharp, under the impression that it was a snake.

The larger lizards will catch and devour the smaller species. I have watched a lizard going through a curious sort of muscular exercise, consisting in raising the head and the fore-part of the body up and down. Occasionally this was the prelude to attacking and pursuing another lizard. In these fights one of the lizards may lose its tail, which seems to drop off easily and then lies for a considerable time wriggling about. In a short time a new tail has grown and replaced the one that was lost.

Eggs of lizards have more than once been brought to me by natives as eggs of birds, because they happened to be unusually large; but lizard eggs are more elliptical in form, and even a gentle touch will often indent their white, leathery surface.

Tortoises.—One comes across tortoises pretty often in these Protectorates, but, as a rule, they are small and worthless. Some species are found in the grass, others frequent rivers and lakes. From Ndi to Muani they are constantly met with. The largest specimen I saw, was in one of the pools of the Athi river; as it rose to the surface of the water, we thought at first that it was the head of a hippo appearing. The smallest specimens I found in pools and puddles in Kavirondo. I have seen Wanyamwezi eat a tortoise, but none of the other natives. A good many tortoises must perish in the annual grass-fires, for one comes not unfrequently upon their calcined remains.

REPTILES

Two curious specimens of the "leathery" variety I saw caught at Kibero by two Soudanese children fishing with line and rod in Lake Albert. Instead of the usual hard carapace, these tortoises had a soft flexible shell, hence the name "leathery." They were brownish-black in colour, dotted all over with green specks. They had a curious, pointed snout. When placed flat on the back, they had the power to wriggle themselves right again. I kept them alive for many months in an earthen bowl filled with water. I hoped to have brought them with me to London, but owing to unforeseen circumstances they had to be left at Kampala.

Snakes.—When I first visited Central Africa and Lake Nyassa, I used to carry some capsules containing ammonia in my pocket, in anticipation of a snake-bite. I was agreeably surprised to find how rarely one sees a snake, and I never heard of any one being killed or even bitten by one.

But, though far from common, one is forcibly reminded every now and again in British East Africa and Uganda that there are snakes about, and that they can and do kill human beings.

Most travellers have met the deadly puff-adder, the big python, and the green, slender grass-snake. At least a dozen other species have come at one time or another under my notice. There was a conspicuously coloured yellow and red snake which I killed near Kilungu on my third journey. A tiny black snake with white spots, which I tried to intercept on the caravan road at Kasokwa in Unyoro, turned and sprang at me; it was not much over a foot in length, and a blow with my stick knocked it over dead. At Masindi we despatched two long grey snakes which had taken up their quarters in the hospital dispensary. When we cleared the ground for a new road leading from the foot of Kampala hill in September 1894, several bluish-grey and brown snakes were brought to light and destroyed, and also a long black one which was discovered inside a white-ant hill that was being levelled. I once saw a very long python lying dead near the Nzoia river in Kavirondo.

On my fourth journey, near Lake Nakuru, one of my porters warned me just in time, as I approached a shrub on which lay curled a young python four to five feet long. I blew its head off with my shot-gun. On the west shore of Lake Albert I fired from a dug-out canoe at some baboons, and a long green snake, which I had not observed, was accidentally killed by the shot and dropped from the overhanging branches into the water.

What strange tent companions one may have, I experienced at Mtiabua on the east shore of Lake Albert. We had camped on a sandy tongue of land, sparsely dotted with bush and shrub; I was dressing, and my Arab servant was removing something or other from the tent, preparatory to our striking tent for the day's march, when a snake sprung and struck at his hand, but fortunately only hit his sleeve. We soon killed it. It was three feet long, and had a lovely geometrical pattern in red-brown along its back.

When visiting the Murchison Falls of the Victoria Nile, some one just called out in time, as we were about to pass underneath a branch on which lay extended a silver-grey tree-snake. The way this creature slid swiftly and noiselessly along the branches, and from one bush to another, was simply marvellous. Twice at Fovira did I see water-snakes in the Nile; the one was close to the shore, where Soudanese women went to bathe and to fetch water; the other started boldly from our side of the bank, and, though the river is here over half a mile broad, attempted to swim across to the other side, but meeting one of the small floating islands of papyrus sudd, it cleverly wriggled up a papyrus-stem, and thus secured for itself a free passage on it down the Nile.

At the Makindo river, on my fifth journey, I was on the point of entering one of the many small, scattered clumps of bushes, when I fortunately noticed, and had just time to jump back, a snake, part of it standing erect, three feet high. Its head was slightly drawn back, and it was ready to strike. I had a narrow escape. On my sixth journey, I watched at Kiwalogoma, in Uganda, a small brownish tree-snake climbing the perpendicular trunk of a big tree with comparative ease and rapidity. It was much too small to encircle the tree trunk, but its writhing body took advantage of minute inequalities in the bark, found support thereon, and used them as a sort of ladder.

The most dreaded snake is the deadly puff-adder; I have shot two specimens. The first one was on my third journey, at the Kedong. It had been raining incessantly for days, and the camp looked like a swamp. Walking along in single file, I was passing a large boulder, when I saw one of these hateful reptiles coiled on the top of it just out of reach of the water. As I had the gun in my hand I fired, and owing to my being so near, the shot cut the snake right in two and blew both parts off the stone into the water. The second specimen I got at the Kiboko river on my fourth journey. It lay right in the middle of the caravan road through the wood, extended at full length, and leisurely moving along. I had only a small-shot cartridge with me; the shot therefore did not injure the skin perceptibly, though it killed the puff-adder on the spot.

On the 10th of February 1898, in Singo, a province of Uganda, I had three narrow escapes from snake-bite. In the morning a snake was disturbed under the awning of my tent, but fortunately it was killed before it could get at me. On the march, another crossed the narrow footpath right under our feet. It suddenly emerged from the tangled weeds on our right and disappeared in the long grass on our left. Luckily it was not trodden on, so no one was bitten. The third was to cloud the day with a sad event. I was riding at the time on my donkey, and my Wahima servant, "Ferhani," was by my side. Two Soudanese soldiers were walking in front of us. With a start they sprang to one side, calling out "snake"; but we were so immediately behind them, that my donkey, my boy, and I were already over the spot, and had no time to avoid it. The snake could have struck at me as easily as at the boy, because on donkey-back one's legs are not very many inches from the ground.

With a scream of fear, and his face distorted with terror, Ferhani jumped from my side. Too late! The snake struck him; my donkey and I escaped unhurt. I jumped down to attend at once to the poor fellow. He had sunk on the ground, clasping his leg. He exclaimed: "Master, I shall die." Then he kept reciting his Mohammedan prayers, "There is but one God and Mohammed is his prophet, and is with God," up to almost the moment of his death. The wound consisted of four tiny punctures, mere pin-pricks; and while one man was vigorously sucking the wound, I twisted my handkerchief round the limb to arrest circulation. The Soudanese soldiers were most sympathetic and attentive. Taking Ferhani of their own accord on their back, they carried him to my tent, running the whole distance. I used ammonia and stimulants, the remedies at hand, but nothing could save him.

He died within two hours and a half, and I lost a most faithful and attached servant. It brought the uncertainty of life very forcibly before me, to think how near I had been to falling myself a victim to this horrid snake, the third one that endangered my life in the course of one day. My Arab servant expressed surprise, that the bite did not kill Ferhani more quickly. If what he says is correct, the puff-adder's bite may prove fatal in a very few minutes. He told me, that on one occasion, when some Arabs were together in a hut, one of them left the company and went to a cocoa-nut palm close by; the others heard a scream and saw the man sink down at the foot of the palm, but by the time they had hurried up to him, he was *in extremis*, and died. A puff-adder had bitten him.

Ferhani had been only ten months in my service. Before he came to me, he had tried various callings, including that of a small pedlar, but had failed to earn enough to provide the bare necessaries of life. In a starving condition he applied at Fort Masindi for work, and was sent on to me, as I was willing to add another to the number of my servants. He did not know a word of Swahili, and knew absolutely nothing of the duties of a servant. Yet very soon he had learnt enough Swahili to make himself understood, and had mastered all the details of his duties to render himself indispensable to the household. He was a Mohammedan, and a strict observer of the Mohammedan ritual. He was frugal and thrifty, and a sum exceeding £2 was left by him in cloth and rupees, and taken over by the Government for any heirs that might turn up. He was devotedly attached to me, and a plucky little fellow, standing by my side and carrying my rifle for me on more than one occasion, when I was in imminent danger of death. To me his death was a great loss. He was willing and hard-working, tidy, sober, and scrupulously honest.

As he was being carried into my tent, he asked for his "kitabo," or book; this contained certain passages of the Koran. When it was brought to him, he was already too drowsy to remember it.

The bite of the snake was almost instantly followed by a racking pain which travelled up the poor fellow's leg, and then passed on successively to the abdomen, both arms, and the other leg. Severe vomiting set in within a quarter of an hour, and continued to within half-an-hour of his death. He frequently pressed both his sides in pain and clutched at my arm. A spasm seized his throat, as if he were suffocating. The whole body rapidly became icy-cold, in spite of friction and other artificial means of keeping it warm. A cold sweat covered head and chest. The power of speech was then lost, but consciousness and hearing remained almost to the end. The sense of drowsiness increased; he seemed unable to resist an overpowering desire to sleep. All our attempts to keep him awake proved vain; and the instant he yielded to sleep, he was dead.

He died in my tent. I had the body removed to a grass-hut to be buried in the morning by his co-religionists according to their burial rites. The grave was dug the same night by torchlight. The body was wrapped up in a clean white cotton cloth, so that it looked like a mummy. In the morning it was buried, a large white cloth being held as a cover over the mouth of the grave, on the floor of which a sort of deep gutter had been prepared to receive the body facing towards Mecca. A number of short sticks, placed slantingly against one side of the pit, formed a sort of inclined roof over the body, this was covered with grass, and, finally, some wet earth was spread over the grass. The pit was then filled up, a mound raised over it, and four sticks stuck at the four corners. The mourners repeated some verses of the Koran, probably a burial formula, holding up their hands as if reading from some imaginary book. Some water was sprinkled over the grave, and the mourners went through gestures suggestive of washing their hands and faces.

Then the signal was given to march. We left Ferhani in his lonely grave, and the busy duties of another day claimed our attention. Yesterday he marched by my side in perfect health, to-day he had dropped out of the ranks. He lay cold and still, and another had taken his place. Four tiny punctures, mere pin-pricks, and yet in a few hours he was snatched from among the living! What an emphatic illustration of the saying, that we are "fearfully and wonderfully made"!

Crocodiles.—Ascending the Shiré river in 1893, our sternwheeler stuck on a sand-bank. In anticipation of such an event, apparently of common occurrence, extra natives had been shipped aboard. It was their duty to jump into the river and pull the vessel into deep water again. Only a few yards from us the water was deep enough. The river teems with crocodiles, but there is a general belief, that the splashing and the shouting frightens the crocs away. The men toiled all day; but, if anything, we got more firmly fixed than ever on the sand. In the evening the captain told me, that one of the natives was supposed to have been drowned, as he had disappeared in the water. It seems to me, however, just as possible that he was quietly "annexed" by a crocodile, in whose "sphere of influence" he happened to be. As the steamer could not be got off, boats came from higher up the river to our assistance and took us to the landing-station.

On our way we saw numbers of crocs basking on the sandbanks and plunging into the water as our boat drew near to them. One huge monster refused to budge. My boat-companion got greatly excited, and begged the loan of my revolver, the only weapon we had.

When thirty yards off, he fired at the eye of the croc. A furious switch of the tail followed and the monster lay still. I knew my companion was a good shot, but I was amazed at this marvellous exhibition of skill, and at the astounding accuracy of his aim from a moving boat; but there, apparently, lay the proof before my eyes. My companion was naturally doubly sure, and he decided to land and secure the croc. I agreed to follow, but not a native would stir from the boat. I do not wonder now, since I have had a little more experience of crocs. Once on the same sand-bank with our motionless croc, I suggested that my companion should fire another shot to make quite sure that the reptile was dead. This shot was followed by such a furious lashing of the tail and such an unpleasant opening and clapping together of the huge jaws, that we thought it advisable to retreat backwards, scramble into the boat, and push off, especially as the croc was trying to screw himself round on its fore-legs in our direction. We should probably not have troubled ourselves further about it, if one of the other boats had not appeared on the scene. My companion borrowed a rifle from one of the new-comers. Once more we ventured on the sand-bank, and my companion sent the bullet crashing into the head of the reptile. Instantly the croc began rolling over and over, but fortunately towards the distant end of the sandbank. We had not a spare cartridge, and were on the point of losing the croc, when my companion produced a knife.

REPTILES

Digging at the throat of the reptile with the knife, whenever the under surface came into view, and jumping aside at each snap, we succeeded in cutting the jugular, and the croc succumbed to its many wounds, within a few inches of the edge of the water. Our boatmen even then would not venture near for some time. The carcass was drawn into the boat, and we proceeded on our journey, whilst I made my first—and I take care it shall be the last—autopsy on a croc. It was interesting to dissect the reptile, examine its internal organs, and ascertain that the stomach con-

CROCODILE-POOL AT FAJAO.

tained apparently a bushel of pebbles, but absolutely no vestige of food; but—the odour on my hands afterwards and for days! No amount of soaping and scrubbing seemed to get it off, and it almost nauseated me, when I raised food to my mouth.

Some natives do eat croc, but very few. The gall-bladder, with the contained gall, was in great request. According to some natives, it is highly prized by their "medicine-men" for supposed medicinal virtues; according to others, it is used in the manufacture of some very deadly poison. On rejoining the travellers in the other boats, the miraculous revolver shot which disabled the monster croc at thirty yards, was explained by the fact, that some one in the first boat had already hit it with a rifle bullet, and had left it for dead on the sand-bank.

At the south end of Lake Nyassa, I have seen scores of crocs floating lazily on the water, whilst natives would bathe with the greatest unconcern in the lake. They explained this to me, on the strength of their possessing from their "medicine-man" some special charm which gave them immunity from crocs. If occasionally the crocs caught and devoured some one, it was attributed to neglecting to purchase the necessary charm.

Visiting the hospital at Kilwa in January 1894, I saw among the patients a man who had lost both his hands quite recently; a croc had snapped them off, when the man was washing clothes. At Kibero, on Lake Albert, I shot a young croc, but the bullet shattered the upper half of the head.

I shot several crocs at Fajao. The river is simply alive with them at this place, especially at "Crocodile-Pool." The Nile dashing down the Murchison Falls, indents the southern bank with a sequence of curves separated by rocky hills. A series of pools is thus formed, owing to the fierce current of the stream, by the back-wash of the water. Crocodile-Pool is the one most handy for the villagers; and here, any day, scores of women and children may be seen bathing, in spite of the crocs which bask open-mouthed on some of the rocks in the stream or congregate in scores on the opposite northern bank of the Nile.

No doubt the Soudanese settlement, which is comparatively recent, has driven most of the reptiles to the Shuli side, but there are still a good many on the British bank of the river. Even though the croc may not be visible, it may be quite close. One day I shot a small bird on a branch overhanging the river. The bird dropped into the water, perhaps six or seven feet from the bank. As it touched the water, the open jaws of a croc rose above the surface, snapped up the bird and disappeared. To my horror one of the boys plunged into the water. As if he could possibly have recovered the bird! I yelled out to him to come back, fearing every second to see a dreadful tragedy; the boy himself was much surprised at my excitement. But I took care never again to shoot a bird which might fall into the river.

On another occasion I heard a loud snap and splash. Looking in that direction, I saw the head of a croc above the water with a big fish in its jaws; the posterior half of the fish was flapping violently from side to side. A second and a third snap

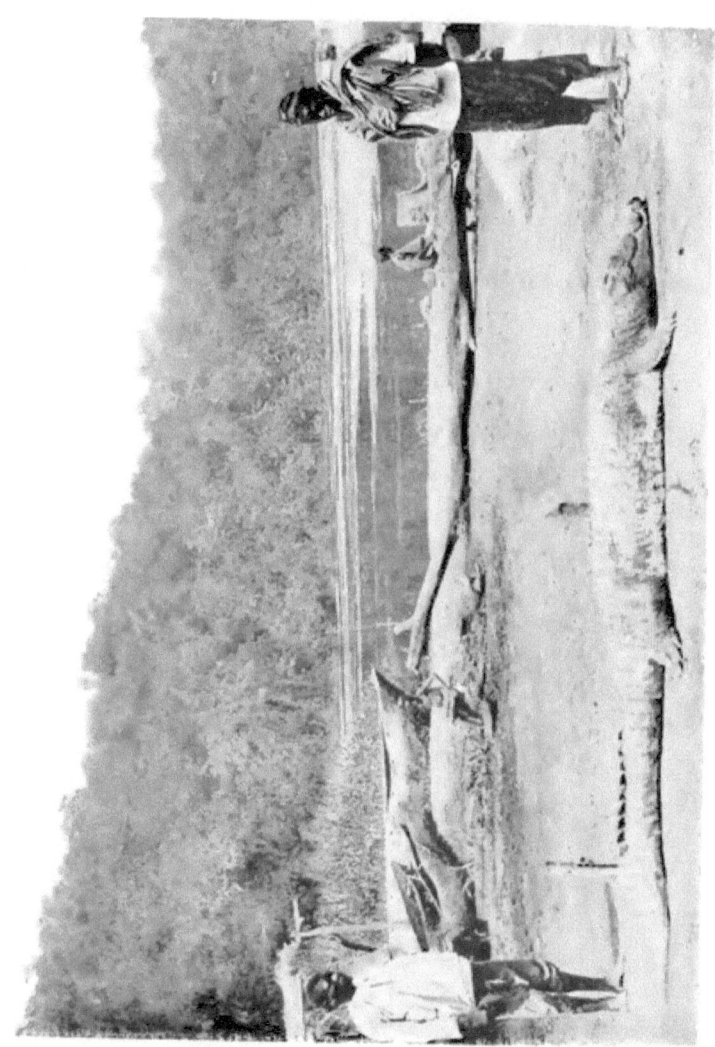

A CROCODILE OF THE VICTORIA NILE.

succeeded, and the fish disappeared inside the croc, and the croc vanished in the stream. It all happened in a few seconds.

When I have been hippo-shooting on this river, I have had an uncomfortable feeling of the danger of the dug-out canoe upsetting. Between my first and second visit to Fajao such an accident did occur to two men in a canoe. I was told, that the moment the canoe was upset, the spot seemed alive with crocs. One of the men got safely into another dug-out close by; but when the rescuers were trying to pull in the other man, who was one of our Soudanese soldiers, it was found that it was a tug-of-war against crocs. Thereupon the unfortunate soldier called out: "What's the good? they have got hold of me; you had better let go." According to the English officer who told me the particulars of this accident, the would-be rescuers thereupon *did* let go, and of course the next moment it was all over. The Soudanese take mishaps and misfortunes with stoicism; their Mohammedan religion bids them to accept everything as "kismet," *i.e.* fate.

I lost several crocs, before I managed to secure a specimen. The convulsive start given by the dying reptile used to send it into the stream, and then I was sure never to see it again. Determined to get a specimen, I went in a dug-out, rounding as noiselessly as possible a tongue of land, where I knew there were lots of crocs. I used my Martini-Henry sporting rifle. I aimed at the reptile farthest from the water; it was apparently shot dead, and I had time to shoot another. In the meantime the first one gradually recovered and began crawling towards the water, leaving a blood streak in its path. But though I plugged three more bullets into it, and could see the blood spurting out, the reptile managed to tumble into the water, and, as on former occasions, I never saw it again. I hurriedly returned to my second croc, and as it opened and snapped its jaws, though apparently too badly wounded to be able to move, I advanced to within a few yards and sent a bullet crashing into its head. This killed it outright.

We fastened the body to the side of our dug-out and towed it to the landing-place, where it was dragged ashore and cut up; the native officer annexing a sort of musk-gland in the armpit, which some appear to value highly. I kept the paws, which are partly webbed. Some of the Soudanese belonging to the Makraka tribe eat crocodile. Among those who wanted the croc flesh there was a leper with some of his fingers gone. I heard that some natives believe, that eating the reptile cures leprosy, whilst they also believe this fell disease is caused by eating however tiny a bit of crocodile flesh.

These diametrically opposite views have their European representatives in so-called homœopathic treatment of disease, and in the queer notion of curing rabies by applying "a hair of the dog that bit you."

In the stomach of the croc we found, besides the usual quantity of stones, a huge fish; but it was too decomposed even for native insensibility to eat. The fore-paws of the croc have five toes and resemble hands; they are small, and only the three inner toes have nails. The hind-paws are huge, but have only four toes, three of which have nails. From tip of snout to tip of tail this croc measured 13 feet 11 inches.

These reptiles have not the narrow-pointed jaws of the Indian "gavial," and they differ from New World alligators in the teeth of the lower jaw fitting into notches in the upper jaw, and not into specially provided sockets.

On a subsequent visit I secured a second specimen of croc. This one I also shot with a Martini bullet. It was much smaller, it measured only 12 feet 1½ inches. I removed the teeth, and kept over fifty of them, not counting small ones. The large teeth are curios worth keeping. In both crocs I cut off the flap of skin over the abdomen; this is the softest part of the skin, and when tanned it constitutes the valuable crocodile leather of commerce.

As soon as the Uganda railway is completed, and the Cairo-to-Cape line realised, some enterprising individual may succeed in establishing a brisk and lucrative trade with Europe in crocodile skins from Fajao and the upper reaches of the Nile.

CHAPTER XXII.

BUTTERFLIES, MOTHS, AND BEETLES.

MISSIONARIES, doctors, and military officers are amongst the principal collectors of butterflies, moths, and beetles. Now and then some one engaged in the construction of a new road or railway has his attention arrested by a beautiful or curious insect, and suddenly he too falls under the collecting spell. But there are comparatively few professional collectors; it is next to impossible for such to find enough purchasers to make the business pay. The public is not interested in this sort of achievement, though willing to spend money on the latest sensational improbabilities from the fertile brain of an untruthful adventurer.

It would cost the professional a small fortune to reach the best collecting areas which the amateur visits at the expense of some Mission society or the Government. To the amateur it does not matter whether the locality or the season are favourable or not, whether the specimens are common or rare, whether he catches few or many; to him it is merely a pleasant recreation to employ his leisure-time. It often means life and health to a man, leading a lonely existence in some out-of-the-way station, to have some object which will divert his thoughts pleasantly and cause him to take the needful outdoor exercise. "All work and no play makes Jack a dull boy," whether he be fifteen or fifty; and there are healthier ways of spending one's leisure than "killing time" with the assistance of a French novel and whisky.

There is a popular prejudice, that collecting butterflies is "childish," because we unconsciously associate it with boyhood's happy days of sailor-suit and Etons, and imagine that it is summed up in the capture of a "Garden White." With a deeper insight into the subject, we are astonished at the vast number of new species added every year to science.

To the dull eye of ignorance, the starry firmament conveys no more than the presence of certain specks of light, and similarly the universe of myriad forms of life is to the many nothing more than the existence of animated particles of dust. Two years ago I was the guest of a gentleman, a Scotchman, who called the collector's pursuit "womanish"! Yet it was in his house, that I captured two *new* species of choice moths, one of them being the "*Eucrostes impunctata*," of a beautiful apple-green colour with a lovely crimson marginal line.

I became interested in butterflies, moths, and beetles, rather late in life; and yet I have succeeded in adding more than fifty new species to science. How I wish I could recall the wasted opportunities of earlier years!

The traveller to distant or rarely visited regions of the earth is almost sure to come across new forms of insect life, and, with comparatively little trouble, he could bring thence valuable information. Of course he must go properly equipped. As I am a self-taught collector, my present *modus operandi* is the result of experience gained by passing through the preliminary stages of loss and failure. The collector's outfit should comprise butterfly nets, paper pockets, collecting box, killing-bottle, biscuit tins, and naphthaline.

Butterfly Net.—This must not be a toy, but the best form of net to be obtained in London, sufficiently large to capture the largest butterfly or moth without injury to its wings; soft and pliant, with the starch taken out of the stiff new net. It should hang limp and close, so as to enfold the tiniest specimens. At least half-a-dozen spare nets should be kept in reserve, owing to the impossibility of replacing a torn or ruined net in these remote regions. It should always be ready for use, and on the march it should be carried by a servant who should be at hand at a moment's call.

Paper Pockets.—The paper used for making paper pockets should not be too thin. Ordinary curl paper is not suitable, the specimens get injured in it. A number of these pockets, of different sizes, should be carried ready folded for immediate use on the march. The best sort of paper is provided by the various illustrated papers edited for transmission abroad. To prepare paper pockets, use a rectangular piece of paper, and fold thus:—

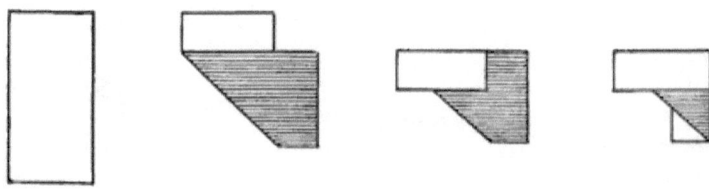

Butterflies can, as a rule, be killed instantaneously by a moderate pressure on their thorax. Having killed the specimen, drop it head first into the paper pocket, taking care not to damage the antennæ or any other part of the body. Let the body slide down along the diagonal line of the pocket, turn down the flap, and the specimen is safely enclosed. Never place more than one specimen in one and the same paper pocket.

Collecting Box.—This should be filled, but not too tightly, with cotton-wool. I have found the botanical form of box the most useful on the march. I carry in it the empty paper pockets ready for immediate use, as well as those filled with the captured specimens. I keep the empty ones at one end of the box and the filled at the other. The cotton-wool prevents the specimens from being shaken about and from getting injured, should the box fall to the ground.

Killing-Bottle.—This is absolutely necessary for killing beetles and such of the thick-bodied lepidoptera as would get spoiled, if killed by pressure on the thorax.

Biscuit Tins.—An empty biscuit tin is the most convenient receptacle for packing away the captured specimens for transmission to Europe. Beetles should never be placed in the same box with butterflies and moths; they should have a separate box for themselves. The biscuit tins should be neither too small nor too large. A good pad of cotton-wool, placed on top of the paper pockets, will prevent them from shifting their position, and as more and more specimens are added, the pad of cotton-wool should be reduced in size. The pad should always just suffice to fill up the tin.

Naphthaline.—Without this drug, the collector may find all his specimens spoiled by ants. On my first visit to Zanzibar, a gentleman arriving from Uganda presented me with his "whole" collection. I am glad I insisted, that he should open the box himself, and hand me each specimen in turn; he found that barely half-a-dozen of the specimens were uninjured, the rest were a mass of fragments of wings and bodies, for ants had been at work on them. He himself had no idea of the condition of his so-called collection, till he opened the box. The naphthaline should be crushed into fine powder, and a little sprinkled into the empty biscuit tin, and then a little more on the top of the last layer of specimens. It should never be placed inside the paper pocket, where it might injure the specimen. A little sprinkled on the top pad of cotton-wool will often suffice to keep ants and other insects away. The beetle collection should be treated in the same way.

I shall now enumerate the different *new* species which I have had the good fortune to capture.

(A) Two butterflies (described by Miss Emily Mary Sharpe). *Vide* "Annals and Magazine of Natural History," Ser. 6, vol. xviii. August 1896.

Amauris ansorgei, sp. nov. (Plate I. fig. 6).

It belongs to the family Danaidæ, and is allied to Amauris Ellioti Butler, but differs in having the spots on the forewing white instead of yellow.

Forewing: ground-colour brownish-black with white spots. Expanse: 3.1 inches.

It was caught at Chagwe in Uganda on December 1894 near a stream.

Mycalesis ansorgei, sp. nov. (Plate I. fig. 7).

It belongs to the family Satyridæ, and is allied to Mycalesis rhanidostroma Karsch and Mycalesis saga Butler on the underside.

Forewing: basal area dark velvet-brown; a round dark spot or brand close to the cell is marked between the first and the third median nervules. Expanse: 2.1 inches.

It was caught at Mtebe (Port Alice) in Uganda on July 12, 1894, in the little wood which fringes Lake Victoria Nyanza, near the Commissioner's residence. It frequents the shady depths of the wood. Some more were caught at the same place in January 1897.

(B) One butterfly (described by the Hon. Walter Rothschild). *Vide* "Novitates Zoologicæ," vol. iii. September 1896.

Papilio phorcas ansorgei, subsp. nov.

It belongs to the family Papilionidæ, and differs from Papilio phorcas F., by the spots on the forewing, situate along the stem of veins 7 and 8, being smaller and separated from the spot at the base of the fork by a black interspace; the tails are broader than in phorcas. It is, as its name indicates, a green swallow-tail.

It was caught on the bleak and cold Mau, in the Uganda Protectorate, on May 1895. It flies high, and settles on the flowers of certain shrubs which bloom in May.

(C) Fifteen moths (described by Mr. F. Kirby, Assistant in Zoological Department, British Museum, Natural History). *Vide* "Annals and Magazine of Natural History," Ser. 6, vol. xviii. November 1896.

Ægocera triplagiata, var. (?) nov. dispar.

It belongs to the family Agaristidæ. Four specimens of this insect were taken at the same time and place as three specimens of Ægocera triplagiata Rothschild, which it resembles greatly, except in the colour of the three transverse white bands on the forewing. It is in all probability a dimorphic form of Ægocera triplagiata Rothschild.

It was caught in the Magwangwara country, German East Africa, on January 11, 1894, in a tract thickly covered with brushwood.

Protocerœa geraldi, sp. nov.

It belongs to the family Agaristidæ, and is allied to Protocerœa albigutta Karsch from Lower Guinea (?), but in that species the forewings are described as black, apart from other differences. Expanse: 33 millim.

Forewings are deep red, with five white spots; hindwings, orange.

It was caught near the Narogare River, Kavirondo, in the Uganda Protectorate, along the old caravan route, on May 19, 1894, on an open grass plain.

Zygæna Semihyalina, sp. nov.

It belongs to the family Zygænidæ, sub-family Zygæninæ, and is allied to Zygæna marina Butler, but has much larger vitreous spots. Expanse: 29-30 millim.

It is a lovely little moth. The head is green; the antennæ are reddish-brown, white towards the tips; thorax reddish-brown, scaled with bluish-green above; abdomen coppery-green. Wings are cupreous.

The forewing has 5 large transparent spots and the hind-wing has 2 such spots.

It was caught at Port Alice in Uganda on June 30, 1894, on flowering weeds, on the edge of the wood which borders Lake Victoria Nyanza.

Aletis ethelinda, sp. nov.

It belongs to the family Nyctemeridæ; and is allied to Aletis monteironis Butler from Delagoa Bay, except in colour.

The wings are deep orange-red with broad black border. Forewings have a large oblique subapical white band and 3 spots; hindwings have a rather small oval spot. Expanse: 52-64 millim.

It was caught at Parumbira at the north-east end of Lake Nyassa on November 8 to 10, 1893.

Aletis erici, sp. nov.

It belongs to the family Nyctemeridæ.

The wings are rather pale orange-tawny (perhaps faded); forewings with a broad oblique subapical white band and 3 white spots below it; hindwings with 7 or 8 white spots on the nervures. Expanse: 65 lin.

It was caught at Port Alice in Uganda near Lake Victoria Nyanza on July 19, 1894.

Neuroxena ansorgei, sp. nov.

This very rare moth had to be classed as a new genus (Neuroxena).

It belongs to the family Nyctemeridæ.

The forewing is light brown, with a uniformly broad oblique pale yellow bar running across it. Hindwing is pale orange. Abdomen red. Expanse: 46 millim.

Only one specimen, caught at Mtebe (Port Alice) in Uganda on July 12, 1894.

Redoa maria, sp. nov.

It belongs to the family Liparidæ, and is allied to the Indian species Redoa clara Walk. and Redoa rinaria Moore. Expanse: 43 millim.

It is iridescent white, thinly scaled, subhyaline, with 2 silvery-white bands on the forewings.

It was caught at Mtebe (Port Alice) in Uganda on July 12, 1894.

Cropera pallida, sp. nov.

It belongs to the family Liparidæ. At the Natural History Museum, South Kensington, there are specimens from Natal and Delagoa Bay. Expanse: 24–34 millim.

Forewings pale yellow with slight orange tint, with 3 or 4 irregular and indistinct transverse whitish bands; an orange spot in the middle of the wing. Hindwings pale yellow, unspotted.

It is noted as abundant on the coast of Mozambique in 1893.

Lasioptila ansorgei, sp. nov.

It belongs to the family Saturniidæ.

This very rare moth had to be classed as a new genus (Lasioptila).

It is of a rich fawn colour, slightly varied with rosy grey. The forewings have a slight transverse black dash towards the base, and a narrow vitreous lunule bordered with black on both sides, and with the horns turned outwards, at the end of the cell. Hindwings with a narrow black lunule opening outwards, and most distinct on the underside, at the end of the cell.

Only one specimen, a female, was caught in Uganda on December 12, 1894.

Hibrildes ansorgei, sp. nov.

It belongs to the family Lasiocampidæ.

Body is reddish-brown, antennæ strongly bipectinated. Forewings smoky hyaline with black cilia; a blackish mark at the end of the cell, beyond which is a broad white band; a row of submarginal white spots between the nervures. Hindwings tawny yellow, with a broad lunule at the end of the cell; a rather narrow black border marked with 6 large white spots between the nervures. Expanse: 60 millim.

Only two specimens, both females, were caught in the Magwangwara country, German East Africa, on January 19, 1894.

Hibrildes venosa, sp. nov.

It belongs to the family Lasiocampidæ, and is allied to Hibrildes norax Druce, the type of the genus; but in that species the thorax is white, and the wings are also much whiter than in Hibrildes venosa. It may be the male of Hibrildes ansorgei.

It is creamy white and subhyaline. Forewings have costal area yellowish, tips brownish. Antennæ black, head orange, thorax clothed with yellow hairs, abdomen reddish. Expanse: 57 millim.

Three specimens, all of them male, were caught in the Magwangwara country, German East Africa, on January 16 and 19, 1894.

Lichenopteryx conspersa, sp. nov.

It belongs to the family Lasiocampidæ.

Antennæ very long, brown, very deeply bipectinated. Wings buff and very densely clothed with scales and hair. Forewings with many scattered brown and black spots. Hindwings nearly as long and broad as the forewings. Expanse: 53 millim.

Two specimens, a male and a female, were caught near the Kesokon River in the Uganda Protectorate, along the old caravan route.

Pyramarista rufescens, sp. nov.

It is a very rare moth, and has been classed as a new genus (Pyramarista). It belongs to the family Hypopyridæ, and is allied to Hypopyra bosei Saalmüller from Madagascar.

Fawn colour; tinged with rosy on the costa. Antennæ with a row of short triangular teeth on each side, terminating in a slender curved bristle. Forewings with a triangular black spot on the middle of the costa. Abdomen with small anal tuft. Expanse: 81 millim.

Only one specimen, a male, was captured at Parumbira at the north-east end of Lake Nyassa on November 15, 1893.

Maxula africana, sp. nov.

It belongs to the family Hypopyridæ, and is allied to the common and variable East Indian Maxula unistriata Guen., but without the zigzag lines and rows of black dots on the disc which we meet with in that species.

The male has the wings grey, dusted with black, with a submarginal white stripe. Forewings have 4 black costal spots. Underside orange-tawny. The female is much lighter. Expanse: 45-53 millim.

It was caught in the Magwangwara country, German East Africa, on January 11 and 13, 1894.

Paracumelea conspersata, sp. nov.

It belongs to the family Geometræ; and is allied to Paraeumelea perlimbata Guenée, but that species has orange markings, and a row of long sub-marginal streaks in place of the brown sub-marginal lines of Paraeumelea conspersata.

It is pale yellow, thickly speckled with brown, with black discoidal cell. Underside whitish. Expanse: 45 millim.

It was caught at Port Alice in Uganda on June 24, 1898.

(D) One butterfly (described by the Hon. Walter Rothschild). *Vide* "Novitates Zoologicæ," vol. iv. April 1897.

Charaxes ansorgei, sp. nov.

It belongs to the family Nymphalidæ, and is allied to Charaxes pollux, but the white band of the upperside of the hindwing distinguishes this species at a glance from pollux.

Forewing rufous chestnut, with marginal ochreous spots rounded. Hindwing with a complete series of dark ochraceous sub-marginal spots; a milky white median; wing outside the band black, inside the band brownish-black.

It was caught at Patsho, in the Nandi country of the Uganda Protectorate, on December 11, 1896.

(E) Two moths (described by the Hon. Walter Rothschild). *Vide* "Novitates Zoologicæ," vol. iv. August 1897.

Ceranchia ansorgei, sp. nov.

It belongs to the family Saturniidæ. Differs from Ceranchia mollis Butler, its nearest ally, especially in the presence of the sub-marginal white band on both wings.

Forewing hair-brown; just before middle of wing there is an almost straight transverse white band; a second band runs in a slight curve from the costal margin; upon the discocellulars there is a small eye-spot, 2 mm. in diameter, consisting of a yellow, a black, and a white ring surrounding a black centre. Hindwing white from base to apex of cell, gradually becoming dark-greyish drab, a sub-marginal white band edged outwardly with pale yellow; a small black spot at end of cell. Length: forewing 40 mm., hindwing 29 mm.

Only one specimen, a male, of this rare moth has been caught, at the Kiboko river, British East Africa, on November 5, 1896.

Ægocera ansorgei, sp. nov.

It belongs to the family Agaristidæ, and is closely allied to Ægocera menete Cram., but has a narrower and differently marked forewing. The hindwing as in Ægocera rubida Feld., but the border and the central spot deeper in colour.

Costal and inner margins are dusted over with creamy buff scales; nervules close to the fringe with metallic scales.

It was caught at Muani in British East Africa on November 11, 1896.

(F) Nine moths (described by Mr. W. Warren, M.A., F.E.S.) *Vide* "Novitates Zoologicæ," vol. iv. August 1897.

Agraptochlora nigricornis, sp. nov.

It belongs to the sub-family Geometrinæ.

Forewings: deep grass-green without markings; costa deep ochreous. Hindwings: wholly green. Face, palpi, and forelegs deep red; antennæ with the shaft reddish, pectinations blackish; thorax and base of abdomen deep green. Expanse: 24 millim.

It was caught on Mombasa Island in October 1896.

Eucrostes impunctata, sp. nov.

It belongs to the sub-family Geometrinæ.

Forewings: apple-green, marginal line crimson, fringe snow-white. Face and palpi red, thorax green, abdomen ochreous with snow-white red-edged dorsal spots. Expanse: 15 millim.

Caught several on Mombasa Island in October 1896.

It is distinguished by the entire absence of the dark cell-spot.

Craspedia sagittilinea, sp. nov.

It belongs to the sub-family Sterrhinæ.

Forewings: ochreous with an olive tinge; a row of distinct black marginal spots; fringe greyish-ochreous; cell-spot black. Hindwings: the same, but the dark cell-spot is surmounted by a round spot of snow-white raised scales. Expanse: 26 millim.

It was caught on Mombasa Island in October 1896.

It is remarkable for the dense and rough scaling.

Chloroclystis grisea, sp. nov.

It belongs to the sub-family Tephroclystiinæ.

Forewings: ochreous, suffused with grey and tinged with rufous; basal patch with traces of waved grey lines through them; fringe chequered light and dark grey. Underside pale grey. Expanse: 16 millim.

It was caught on Mombasa Island in October 1896.

Eulype (?) *disparata*, sp. nov.

It belongs to the sub-family Hydriomeninæ.

Forewings: glossy, leaden grey; three transverse broadish lines white; minute dark cell-spot. Hindwings: white, fringe ochreous-grey. Expanse: 28 millim.

The antennæ of the male are lamellate and subserrate.

One male and one female were caught at Nandi in the Uganda Protectorate in December 1896.

Plerocymia nigrocellata, sp. nov.

It belongs to the sub-family Hydriomeninæ.

Forewings: uniform glossy grey; cell-spot oblique, velvety black. Hindwings: hardly paler, without markings of any kind. Expanse: 32 millim.

Two males and one female were caught at Nandi in the Uganda Protectorate in December 1896.

Hyostomodes nubilata, sp. nov.

This very rare moth has been classed as a new genus (Hyostomodes).

It belongs to the sub-family Semiothisinæ.

Forewings: whitish, thickly dusted and striated with dark grey, lines starting from dark costal spots. Hindwing with black cell-spot. Expanse 26 millim.

One male and one female were caught at Muani in British East Africa in December 1896.

Trysindeta subspersa, sp. nov.

This very rare moth has been classed as a new genus (Trysindeta).

It belongs to the sub-family Ennominæ.

Forewings: pale straw colour, marginal dots brown, cell-spot dark brown. Expanse: 32 millim.

It was caught at Nandi in the Uganda Protectorate in December 1896.

Zamarada ansorgei, sp. nov. (Plate I. fig. 5).

It belongs to the sub-family Ennominæ. This species is certainly related to Guenée's secutaria (Stegania) from Abyssinia, but does not in all points agree with his description; that, however, was made from a single female.

Forewings: pale yellowish-ochreous; cell-spot brown; a row of dark marginal dashes. Head, thorax, and abdomen ochreous. Expanse: 20 millim.

It was caught at the Kiboko river in British East Africa in November 1896.

(G) Two moths (described by the Hon. Walter Rothschild). *Vide* "Novitates Zoologicæ," vol. v. March 1898.

Nudaurelia ansorgei, sp. nov. (Plate I. fig. 4).

It belongs to the family Saturniidæ; distinguished from the allied species, especially by the post-discal bands of the forewing being curved anteriorly, the ante-median band being angulate, and the black outer band of the hindwing being $2\frac{1}{2}$ millim. wide.

Upperside: forewings chestnut-brown, speckled all over with black scales. About one-fourth from the base the wing is crossed by a black line. At the apex of cell is a round eye, consisting of a vitreous dot surrounded by a broad ring of tawny ochraceous and enclosed by a narrow line of dull whitish-pink. Half-way between this eye and the outer margin the wings are crossed by a black transverse line. Hindwings: basal two-thirds brownish-pink, crossed between middle and base by an indistinct black band. In the centre of the wing is a large eye, having a vitreous centre, outside this a dark yellow broad ring, then a narrower black one, followed by a dark red one, the whole enclosed by an outside whitish-pink ring. A little beyond the eye the wings are crossed by a broad black sinuous band, edged on the inner side with a narrow grey line. Outer third of wings chestnut, freckled with black like forewing.

Underside: ante-median bands absent; eye-spot of forewing as large as above, but with a black ring between the tawny ochraceous central ring and outer whitish-pink one. Hindwing from post-discal black line towards base pinkish-grey; eye-spot reduced to a vitreous dot surrounded by a broad tawny ochraceous ring.

Antennæ dark brown; basal part of stalk yellow. Head, thorax, and abdomen tawny ochraceous.

Size as Nudaurelia nictitans Fabricius.

Of this rare moth only one specimen, a male, has been caught, at Masindi, in Unyoro, in the Uganda Protectorate, on April 30, 1897.

Pseudaphelia ansorgei, sp. nov. (Plate I. fig. 8).

It belongs to the family Saturniidæ.

The two spots at the end of the cell of both wings of apollinaris are absent in ansorgei, being replaced on both wings by a black dot just behind the origin of vein 5, which has, however, on the underside a yellow centre; fringe fuscous. Post-discal line of hindwing closer to cell than to outer margin of wing.

It was caught at Masindi, in Unyoro, in the Uganda Protectorate, on April 15, 1897.

(H) Two moths (described by Mr. W. Warren, M.A., F.E.S.). *Vide* "Novitates Zoologicæ," vol. v. March 1898.

Xanthorhoë conchata, sp. nov.

It belongs to the sub-family Hydriomeninæ.

Forewings: with the ground-colour yellowish-white, suffused and dusted with fulvous, and crossed by numerous darker tremulous lines; cell-spot black; pairs of small black dashes along the margin at the ends of the veins.

Hindwings: whitish, with dark cell-spot and exceedingly faint traces of a dark post-median line; fringe yellowish, with the marginal spots as in forewings.

Palpi long, thick, and roughly haired. Thorax and abdomen greyish-ochreous; the face and palpi brownish. Expanse: 26 millim.

Two males were caught in Nandi, in the Uganda Protectorate, in December 1896.

Eurythecodes impunctata, sp. nov.

It belongs to the sub-family Ennominæ. It appears to be quite distinct from any of the forms of Eurythecodes flavidinaria.

Forewings: pale yellow with faint brownish freckling; the lines grey-brown; cell-spot blackish.

Hindwings: with a curved and sinuous post-median line. Expanse: 28 millim.

Two males were caught at Kampala in Uganda in January 1897.

(I) One butterfly (described by Mr. Guy Marshall). *Vide* "Proceedings of the Zoological Society of London, 1897," p. 13.

Teracolus ansorgei, sp. nov.

It belongs to the family Pieridæ.

Upperside: light ochreous with black markings. Forewing: pattern and colouring similar to that of Teracolus aurigineus Butler, except in the following points:—

- (*a*) There is no trace of the whitish-grey patch at base, it being replaced by slight blackish clouding;
- (*b*) The discal zigzag black band is narrower, and ends abruptly on inner nervure.

Hindwing: ground-colour as in forewing, base with very slight fuscous clouding.

Underside: pattern exactly like that of Teracolus vesta Reiche, but the ground-colour of the forewing is somewhat lighter. Hindwing: pale yellow; a longitudinal ray from base in cell, and a shorter one above it deep pink. A thin black line runs along extreme hind margin of both wings, which is present in Teracolus vesta but absent in Teracolus aurigineus.

This is a most interesting species, combining as it does the upperside colouring of Teracolus aurigineus with the underside colouring of Teracolus vesta, being at the same time quite distinct from either species.

It was caught on January 5, 1894, in German East Africa.

(J) Eleven butterflies (described by Mr. H. Grose Smith, B.A., F.E.S., F.Z.S. &c.). *Vide* "Novitates Zoologicæ," vol. v. August 1898.

Pinacopteryx helena, sp. nov.

It belongs to the family Pieridæ.

Upperside: both wings slightly greenish-white. Anterior wings with an outer-marginal rather broad black band, broadest at the apex; costal margin narrowly black, and a small black dot at the end of the cell.

Underside: anterior wings white, with the apical area broadly and outer margin more narrowly pale yellowish-green; a small black dot at the end of the cell. Posterior wings pale yellowish-green, with a curved row of dusky lunular markings crossing the wings in the middle of the disc. Expanse: 1½ inches.

It was caught at Kabras, in Kavirondo, in the Uganda Protectorate, in December 1896.

Acræa dissociata, sp. nov.

It belongs to the family Acræidæ.

Upperside: anterior wings ashy grey, semi-hyaline; a narrow pink streak in the middle of the inner margin. Posterior wings pink, except at the base, which is rather broadly dusky grey; an irregular row of black spots surrounds the cell; a rather large spot in the cell, and a cluster of spots near the inner margin towards the base, some of which merge in the dusky basal area.

Underside: anterior wings pinkish dull brown, posterior wings pale tawny; the disc is traversed by a very broad chestnut-brown band. Expanse: 2¼ inches.

It was caught at Patsho, in the Nandi country, in the Uganda Protectorate, in December 1896.

Acræa unimaculata, sp. nov.

It belongs to the family Acræidæ.

Differs from Acræa quirina Fabr. in the absence of spots on both sides of both wings, except on the underside of the posterior wings, where there is one spot in the cell near the base. On the upperside the basal tawny area is rather more extended, thus resembling Acræa cerasa Hew., and on the posterior wings it extends lower towards the anal angle; both wings are dusky grey at the base. Expanse: 2 inches.

It was caught at Kabras, in Kavirondo, in the Uganda Protectorate, in December 1896.

Acræa disjuncta, sp. nov.

It belongs to the family Acræidæ. Nearest to Acræa cydonia Ward and Acræa flava Dewitz, but smaller than either of those species.

Upperside: dark brown. Anterior wings with a pale tawny band crossing the wings, as in Acræa cydonia Ward, but divided between the two upper median nervules by a blackish-brown irregular band, which partially covers the interspace between the two upper median nervules, but is narrower than in Acræa cydonia Ward and Acræa flava Dewitz. Posterior wings with the basal three-fourths light brown and outer fourth dark brown. Expanse: 1½ inches.

It was caught in the Nandi country in the Uganda Protectorate in December 1896.

Acræa ansorgei, sp. nov.

It belongs to the family Acræidæ.

Upperside: anterior wings dark brown, with a rather bright tawny band from the costa crossing the end of the cell, thence becoming wider to the inner margin; towards the apex is a bright tawny spot near the costa, divided into three by the veins, and a quadrate spot above the upper median nervule nearer the outer margin. Posterior wings bright tawny, becoming dusky at the base.

Underside: dusky pale brown with the transverse tawny band indistinct. Posterior wings with the disc crossed by an indistinct irregularly undulated dusky brown band, inside which, but outside the cell, are two small black spots, a similar spot in the middle of the cell, two in the interspace above the subcostal nervure, one on the shoulder, and six or seven others near the inner margin below the base of the cell. Expanse: 1¾ inches.

It was caught at Nandi Station, in the Nandi country, in the Uganda Protectorate, in December 1896.

Acraea conjuncta, sp. nov.

It belongs to the family Acraeidæ.

Upperside: both wings dull brown. Anterior wings with a transverse tawny band resembling the band of Acraea nandina, but not extending to the costal margin; the subapical spots as in A. nandina, but smaller. Posterior wings crossed in the middle by a suboval tawny band; in this band are a black spot near the costa and two smaller spots, one above and the other below the discoidal nervule.

Underside: both wings resemble A. nandina, but on the posterior wings the space beyond the undulated band is much darker; the spots are arranged as in A. nandina. Expanse: $1\frac{1}{2}$ inches.

It was caught at Nandi Station, in the Nandi country, in the Uganda Protectorate, in December 1896.

Acraea anacreontica, sp. nov.

It belongs to the family Acraeidæ.

It differs from Acraea anacreon Trim. in several respects. On the upperside of the anterior wings the black discal and cellular spots are larger. On the underside of the posterior wings the spots in the discal row and those nearer the base are respectively more confluent, forming two irregular bands, the space between which is uninterruptedly pink, which colour forms an irregular band extending from the costal to the inner margins; the outer marginal row of pale fulvous spots is narrower and bordered inwardly by very narrow black lunules. Expanse: ♂ $1\frac{7}{8}$ inches, ♀ 2 inches.

The male specimen was caught at Patsho and the female at Rau, both in the Nandi country, in the Uganda Protectorate, in December 1896.

Junonia rauana, sp. nov.

It belongs to the family Nymphalidæ; it is closely allied to Junonia Kowara (Ward), Junonia Sinuata (Plötz), and Junonia aurosina (Butler), but it has the outer margins of anterior wings less falcate, and the bands on the upperside considerably broader.

Upperside: both wings dark brown, crossed by a common

pale brown band, three minute dots in the band between the median nervules and a white subapical spot; the basal dark area is not interrupted by paler markings. Posterior wings with a row of six small dots in the pale band.

Underside: with dark bands and markings closely resembling Junonia Kowara (Ward). Expanse: 1¾ inches.

It was caught at Rau, in the Nandi country, in the Uganda Protectorate, in December 1896.

Mycalesis nandina, nom. nov.

[I would suggest the name *Mycalesis nandina* for the Mycalesis ansorgei Grose Smith, to prevent any possible confusion with Mycalesis ansorgei Sharpe.—W. J. ANSORGE, *September* 1898.]

It belongs to the family Satyridæ; in shape it resembles Mycalesis elionas Hew.

Upperside: both wings velvety dark brown, slightly paler towards the outer margins.

Underside: both wings with the basal three-fourths dark velvety brown, the outer fourth paler brown with a row of spots crossing the disc of both wings, the spots being surrounded by slightly greyish-brown rings. On the anterior wings the spots are five in number. On the posterior wings is a row of seven spots, of which the four uppermost are the smallest, centred with white dots. The posterior wings are more acute at the anal angle than is usual in the African section of this genus. Expanse: 1½ inches.

It was caught at Patsho, in the Nandi country, in the Uganda Protectorate, in December 1896.

Mycalesis fluviatilis, sp. nov.

It belongs to the family Satyridæ, and is near to Mycalesis dubia Auriv.

Upperside: dark brown, with an indication of a paler submarginal line on the posterior wings.

Underside: both wings with the basal half darker brown than the outer half; towards the apex, in a paler area, are two contiguous ocelli, of which the upper is the larger, and is surrounded by a fulvous ring; one large ocellus is situate between the two lowest median nervules, surrounded by a pale ring. On the posterior wings a row of seven ocelli crosses the disc; the ocelli are surrounded by pale brown rings. The outer margins of both wings are rather deeply indented. Expanse: 1¾ inches.

It was caught in the Subugo Forest, in the Uganda Protectorate, in December 1896.

Everes kedonga, sp. nov.

It belongs to the family Lycaenidae.

Upperside: anterior wings bluish-grey, with silvery-white veins. Posterior wings pale silvery-blue, with a submarginal row of round black spots of uniform size, except at the anal angle, where there are two small dots; the outer edge of the spot is narrowly white, and the outer margin is narrowly dark grey; one slender black tail.

Underside: grey. Anterior wings, with discal and sub-basal spots, arranged almost as in Everes fischeri Eversm. and Everes filicaudis Pryer. Posterior wings with sub-basal and discal spots surrounding the cell, closely resembling those species. Cilia of both wings greyish-white. Expanse: 1 inch.

It was caught at the second Kedong, in the Uganda Protectorate, in November 1896.

(K) Two Longicorn beetles (described by Mr. C. J. Gahan, M.A., of the British Museum, Natural History). *Vide* "Annals and Magazine of Natural History," Ser. 7, vol. ii. July 1898.

Xystrocera ansorgei, sp. nov. (Plate I. fig. 2).

Head, prothorax, and underside of body reddish-brown in colour. Elytra bone-white in colour, but marked with a large number of small rounded fuscous spots; the surface of the elytra presents a number of minute granules, each of which bears a short seta, while close to each granule is a small shallow puncture.

This species of Xystrocera may be easily recognised by the peculiar and unusual colour of the elytra.

Long. 25, lat. 5½ millim.

Only one specimen, a female, caught in Uganda.

Compsomera ansorgei, sp. nov. (Plate I. fig. 3).

This species is very closely allied to Compsomera nigricollis Gah., which it resembles exactly in the markings of the elytra, with the exception that the metallic-blue colour in the type of Compsomera nigricollis is here replaced by metallic-green. It differs chiefly from Compsomera nigricollis in having the head, legs, and antennæ quite black in colour.

Long. 26, lat. 7 millim.

Only one specimen, caught in Uganda.

(L) One butterfly (described by the Hon. Walter Rothschild). *Vide* "The Entomologist," June 1897.

Papilio mimeticus, sp. nov.

It belongs to the family Papilionidæ. This most remarkable butterfly is closely allied to Papilio rex Oberth.; but while that species is almost the exact mimic of Melinda formosa Salv. and God., Papilio mimeticus mimics Melinda morgeni mercedonia Karsch.

♂ Forewings: differ from Papilio rex in having the basal area deep chestnut instead of orange-rufous; in this chestnut area is a longitudinal pale streak behind cell, not present in typical Papilio rex.

Hindwings: One of the most striking differences, however, between Papilio rex and Papilio mimeticus is that while in Papilio rex the ground-colour of the hindwings is uniform black, in Papilio mimeticus the disc of the wing is dull chestnut, this colour extending along the abdominal margin to near apex of vein.

Underside: The two anterior white marginal spots of Papilio rex are absent in Papilio mimeticus.

Oberthür, in his original description of Papilio rex (Bull. Soc. Ent. Fr. 1886, p. 114), says "Abdomen black above, white on sides and below;" but in the specimen of Papilio rex from Uganda Protectorate the underside is black, with a narrow but distinct median white line, and in this agrees entirely with Papilio mimeticus.

It was caught at a streamlet which crosses the caravan route not far from Msarosaro in Uganda on December 28, 1896.

(M) The Hon. Walter Rothschild has very kindly sent me, October 1898, the description of two new species of lepidoptera (a butterfly and a moth), which I captured in Unyoro and at the Eldoma Ravine respectively :—

Kallima ansorgei Rothsch., sp. nov. (Plate I. fig. 1).

Forewing more produced at apex than in *rumina*, hindwing with a long tail, slightly curved inwards.

Upperside: forewing, basal two-thirds plumbeous blue-green, metallic, this area evenly and slightly convex outwardly; a narrow indistinct band from costal margin to vein 3, where it approaches the metallic area, pale brown covered with metallic blue-green scaling; interspace between this band and metallic area black, rest of marginal region dark brown, a series of indistinct dots, the uppermost of which has a white dot at its discal side, and a submarginal, indistinct, narrow band blackish-brown. Hindwing, basal two-thirds as on forewing; marginal area brown, with a blackish-brown submarginal band; between veins 2 and 3 there is an oblong eye-spot of 2 and 3 mm. width, consisting of an outer ochraceous ring that encircles an outwardly black, discally brown-red space with a minute blue centre; a smaller eye-spot behind vein 2.

Underside: blackish broccoli-brown, powdered over with single white scales. Forewing, 4 undulate lines in cell, a fifth upon disco-cellulars, another beyond, 2 lines behind cell, and a zigzag line from costal to inner margin, 14 mm. distant from apex of wing and 10 mm. from tip of vein 1b; a series of small post-discal black dots with white centres, the one between veins 2 and 3 forming nearly an eye-spot; a series of thin, small, more or less curved, black submarginal spots. Hindwing, an indistinct undulate line from costal margin across middle of cell to vein 1b; a distinct narrow band straight across the disc from costal margin (9 mm. from the tip of vein 8) to tail, consisting of a black line thinly bordered with pale blue and green proximally, shaded at both sides with dark brown; post-discal spots as on forewing, surrounded with paler scaling, nearly forming eye-spots, the spot behind vein 3 as large as above, much paler, with a pale ochraceous centre; submarginal spots linear, the one behind vein 2 extending to tip of tail obviously bordered grey outwardly.

Length of forewing 40 mm. Length of hindwing from base of cell to tip of tail 41 mm.

Hab. Kasokwa, Unyoro, 1 caught on the 2nd of November 1897.

Bunæa ansorgei Rothsch., sp. nov.

♀ Allied to *B. acetes*, Wester., from West Africa. Wings above grey, without sprinkling of black scales. Forewing with a small vitreous spot at the end of the cell, barely 2 mm. in width; an irregular, indistinct, blackish-grey band across middle of cell to inner margin, the cellular portion lunate, bordered greyish-white outwardly; a greyish-black line from apex of wing to inner margin as in *acetes*, but much thinner, bordered outwardly by a broad band of greyish-white scaling which is convex between the veins. Hindwing without band in basal half; the eye as in *acetes*, but the outer ring greyish-white, without pinkish tint; black band beyond eye thinner than in *acetes*, contiguous with the eye from second discoidal to first median nervule; costal area from base to band and eye brighter red than in acetes, the red not extending beyond middle of cell and upper discoidal vein respectively. Underside whitish-grey, with a slight buffish tint. Forewing red beyond cell from base to near post-discal blackish-brown line, the latter much thinner than in *acetes*; no black irregular mark at basal side of vitreous spot, but a very obscure, rather broad, brownish band from costal margin straight across the vitreous spot to inner margin. Hindwing, a tiny black dot between costal and subcostal nervures near base, as in *acetes*, the obscure median band of forewing continued across hindwing, here situated at the basal side of the small vitreous spot; outer discal line much narrower than in *acetes*.

Head and legs as in *acetes*; thorax above and below concolorous with base of wings; abdomen with a yellowish tint at the edges, below slightly darker grey than breast; first joint of antennæ white as in *acetes*; apical processes of joints shorter than in *acetes*.

Hab. Eldoma Ravine, 22nd March 1898; 1 ♀.

Dr. K. Jordan, the eminent entomologist, wrote to me, October 1898, about my collections which are deposited at Tring, as follows:—

"Your collections are of great scientific interest for two reasons. Firstly, the number of species which are new, or of which only a few specimens are known to exist in other collections, is remarkably large. Your list of novelties will certainly be trebled when the whole of the material you have collected has been worked out. Unfortunately there was too little time at our disposal to supply you with a complete list, as you suggested, of the whole of your collection. Such new forms as have been described by Mr. Rothschild, Mr. Grose Smith, and Mr. Warren, were limited to certain families of the lepidoptera; but your other specimens will be carefully examined and made known to science in due time. Where you have collected, the countries have been comparatively little explored as regards butterflies and moths; and lepidopterists must be gratified at your important contributions to our knowledge of the lepidoptera of those regions.

"Uganda and the Nandi country have yielded the greater proportion of your novelties and rare species; here we have the true East African fauna with a small mingling of the West African, but mostly somewhat modified, species; whereas, in the more remote Unyoro, the number of West African forms is already very large. Many species which appeared to you very rare, because you found them only in Unyoro, are, as a matter of fact, rather common West Coast and Congo insects. The discrepancy between the fauna of Unyoro and Uganda is, for example, very strikingly illustrated by the *Pieridæ*, there being in your collection very few species of *Teracolus* from Unyoro, while there are splendid series of a great number of species of this pretty genus from the countries farther east.

"The following are some of the choice captures you made, to mention but a few of them:—Both sexes of *Kallima jacksoni*, a good series of *Melinda mercedonia* and *Melinda formosa*, inclusive of their rare females; a series of *Papilio jacksoni* and *Papilio mackinnoni*; some specimens of *Papilio pelodurus*, also *Papilio pringlei* (♂ and ♀); *Acræa poggei*; *Pseudacræa kuinowi*; *Charaxes pithoiorus*, &c., &c.

"A most interesting and noteworthy specimen is undoubtedly the female of *Papilio rex*, which you captured in the spring of this year at the Eldoma Ravine, where, on a former journey, you secured the male *Papilio rex*. Entomologists will be interested to know that this female of *Papilio rex* does not differ essentially in pattern from the male, except in some details which do not affect very much the general appearance.

"Among the Heterocera your *Saturniidæ* are interesting. There is also a fine show of the day-flying moths belonging to *Xanthospilopteryx*, including some undescribed forms. Your discovery in those regions of a West African Hawkmoth of peculiar appearance, *Lephosthethus dumoulini*, or a close ally of it, equally deserves to be noticed.

"Yet, however rich in rare forms your collection is, its greater scientific value, in my opinion, consists, secondly, in your having given the exact date and locality of capture of every specimen, and in your having marked all the individuals you caught in *copula*. With such material to work with, the entomologist is able to investigate questions of geographical distribution and to study seasonal variation and individual variability; whereas, unfortunately, many collectors confine themselves merely to recording the country where their specimens were caught."

APPENDIX.

BIRDS.

APPENDIX.

BIRDS.

ON THE BIRDS COLLECTED BY DR. ANSORGE DURING HIS RECENT STAY IN AFRICA.

By ERNST HARTERT.

HAVING been asked by Dr. Ansorge to name the birds he collected in Africa, I herewith give a list of the two hundred and sixteen species he obtained.

This collection is scientifically of much interest, not only because it contains some species which hitherto have not been described, but because he has found a number of birds of which formerly only one or two specimens were known, some of them having been unique in the Berlin Museum. By recording the localities where he found them, he has extended considerably our knowledge of the distribution of certain species, and in other cases he has added valuable confirmation of facts which hitherto were open to doubt. Very interesting forms, among others, are the *Francolins*, of which Dr. Ansorge collected some very rare ones; the new Guinea-fowl, which I have called *Numida ansorgei*; the rare Woodpecker, *Campothera tæniolæma*; the Swift (No. 73), a tropical ally of our common swift of Europe; several of the Flycatchers and Shrikes; the new *Pyromelana* and some of the other Weaver-birds; the Larks; a number of Sun-birds; some of the *Timeliidæ*, and others. During his former stay in Uganda Dr. Ansorge discovered a new Barbet, described as *Tricholæma ansorgii* by Shelley in Bull. B. O. Club. vol. v. p. 3 (1895).

TRING, *September* 1898.

(TERNS.)

1. *Hydrochelidon leucoptera* (Schinz)

Pongo and Kibero on Lake Albert, August and October 1897.

(GEESE.)

2. *Chenalopex ægyptiacus* (L.)

♀ Campi-ya-Simba (the camp of lions), British East Africa. "Iris red-brown. Bill pinkish with brown edges, feet rosy flesh-colour."

(DUCKS.)

3. *Nettion punctatum* (Burch.)

Lake Naivasha, Uganda Protectorate, April and November. "Feet slate-blue with a more or less distinct green streak along the middle." In the female the upper tail-coverts are *not* undulated with narrow black lines. The abdomen is paler, less rufous than in the male, and hardly differs from the breast in colour. The wing is about 15 mm. shorter (♂ 150–156 mm., ♀ 143–145 mm.). The adult male agrees perfectly with Salvadori's description.

4. *Nettion capense* (Gm.)

♀ ad. Lake Nakuru, Uganda Protectorate, 30/11/1896. "Iris red. Feet yellow-brown with black web. Bill pink with black base."

(WADERS.)

5. *Œdicnemus vermiculatus* Cab.

Kibero, on the east shore of Lake Albert in Unyoro, ♂ ♀ 21/8/97. "Iris lemon-yellow. Feet pale green, yellow towards the thigh. Bill blackish, soft parts on sides from nostrils to base and basal half of mandible greenish-yellow."

6. *Hoplopterus spinosus* (L.)

Kibero, Unyoro, 29/10/97. ♂ "Iris purple-red, bill and feet black."

7. *Ægialitis hiaticola* (L.)

Kibero (Unyoro, 12/10/97. Migrant from Europe.

BIRDS

8. *Tringa subarquata* (Güld.)

Kibero (Unyoro), 12/10/97. Migrant from the North.

9. *Glottis nebularius* (Gunn.)

Kibero (Unyoro), 13/10/97. Migrant from the North.

10. *Tringoides hypoleucus* (L.)

Kibero (August, October), Fajao, and Masindi in Unyoro; also Mombasa, British East Africa. Migrant.

11. *Totanus ochropus* (L.)

Kampala (Uganda), February. Migrant from Europe.

12. *Totanus glareola* (L.)

Masindi (Unyoro), April. Migrant.

13. *Totanus stagnatilis* (Bechst.)

Lake Naivasha, Uganda Protectorate. November.

14. *Pavoncella pugnax* (L.)

Lake Naivasha, Uganda Protectorate. November.

15. *Tringa minuta* Leisl.

Lakes Nakuru and Naivasha, Uganda Protectorate. November.

(BUSTARDS.)

16. *Otis melanogaster* Rüpp.

♂ ad. Kiboko river, British East Africa, 7/11/96. "Iris orange, feet yellowish-white, bill white with black stripe along the culmen. Length from tip of beak to tip of toe $31\frac{1}{2}$ inches."

17. *Eupodotis kori* (Burch.)

Bondoni in Ukamba, 15/4/97. British East Africa.

(RAILS.)

18. *Limnocorax niger* (Gm.)

Four specimens, two males and two females, from Masindi, Unyoro, May and June 1897. "Iris bright red, a narrow flesh-red circle round the eye (eyelid), feet copper-red, bill light green." The wing of the female is about 1 cm. shorter than that of the male.

19. *Phyllopezus africanus* (Gm.)

♂ ad. Fajao, Unyoro. "Iris chocolate-brown. Feet light slate-blue. Bill light slate-blue. Bare forehead, slate-blue."

(SAND-GROUSE.)

20. *Pterocles gutturalis* A. Smith.

♂ April 1898. Campi-ya-Simba (the lion camp), in Ukamba, British East Africa. "Iris dark brown, feet blackish-grey, bill bluish-grey."

(STORKS AND HERONS.)

21. *Hagedashia hagedash* (Lath.)

Fajao, Unyoro, 10/12/97. "Iris light straw-yellow." Wing 360-365 mm., bill 150 (♀), 180 (♂) mm.

22. *Ibis æthiopica* (Lath.)

ad. Lake Nakuru, Uganda Protectorate, 23/3/98. "Iris dark brown."

23. *Bubulcus ibis* (L.)

♂ Pongo, Lur country, north-west shore of Lake Albert, 24/10/97.

24. *Ardetta payesi* (Verr.)

♀ Kibero, on east shore of Lake Albert, Unyoro, 15/8/97.

I believe there is no doubt that this specimen must be called *A. payesi* (Verr.). It agrees with *A. pusilla* (V.) in most characters, *but the sides of the head and neck are bright cinnamon*. It is certainly not *A. podiceps* (Bp.), of which I have a large series. *A. payesi* is as yet, according to Neumann (J. F. O. 1898, p. 284) only on record from South and West Africa, and specimens from there, and most likely other parts, have hitherto been mixed up with *A. pusilla* or *A. podiceps*.

BIRDS

(FLAMINGOES.)

25. *Phœnicopterus roseus* Pall.

Common on Lake Nakuru (Uganda Protectorate) in March. The small *Phœn. minor* was not to be found in March. (See No. 26.)

26. *Phœniconaias minor* (Geoffr.)

Lake Nakuru (Uganda Protectorate) in November, in large numbers. Only this species was then noticed, instead of *P. roseus*.

(PIGEONS.)

27. *Vinago calva nudirostris* Sws.

♀ ad. Fajao, on the Victoria Nile, Unyoro. "Iris: innermost rim bright light blue, shading into dark grey towards the outside." Salvadori unites the forms from West, Equatorial, and East Africa. Neumann separates *V. calva calva* and *V. calva nudirostris*, making *V. salvadorii* a synonym of the latter. *Nudirostris* would be the northern form.

28. *Turtur senegalensis* (L.)

This common African pigeon is represented from Ndi (British East Africa), 28 10 96; and from Kampala (Uganda), various dates.

29. *Turtur damarensis* Finsch & Hartl. (? an subsp.)

♀ Kampala (Uganda), 10 1 97. ♂ ♀ Masindi (Unyoro), 16 6 97. "Iris dark brown, a narrow yellow edge round eyelid, feet pink, bill black." I am in doubt about the correctness of the above nomination. Specimens in Mus. Tring from Lake Nyassa, as well as from Western Somaliland, agree *inter se*, but are much paler on abdomen and belly. I fancy that these birds belong to a new sub-species, but more material is necessary to decide about this. Count Salvadori has also enumerated birds from Ndi, Pangani, Ugogo, Dar-es-Salaam, Mombas, as *damarensis*; O. Neumann records it from Zanzibar, Kibaya, Kavirondo.

30. *Chalcopelia afra* (L.)

One skin without label, with green wing-spots.

31. *Oena capensis* (L.)

♂ Mto-ya-mkuyuni (Ukamba), British East Africa, 13.11.96. "Feet red. Bill orange, red at base." This little pigeon, so common in most parts of Africa, was only met this one time. It is rare on the East African coast, but very common in the interior (Neumann).

(GAME-BIRDS.)

32. *Francolinus granti* Hartl.

♀ Mtoto Ndei, British East Africa, 1.11.96. "Iris red, feet red-brown, bill black."

33. *Francolinus kirki* Hartl.

♀ Maharagwe-fundi, in the Taru desert, British East Africa, 23.10.96. "Iris dark red-brown, feet red, bill black." Is this really a distinct species? I share Mr. Neumann's doubts in this respect.

34. *Francolinus uluensis* Grant.

This species, only quite recently described by Mr. O. Grant, was found, in April 1898, on the Kiboko river and at Muani in Ukamba, British East Africa. "Iris dark brown, feet lemon-yellow, bill greenish-black, yellow at base." Only three females were sent.

35. *Francolinus gedgei* Grant.

Two males, one from Mondo in Uganda, and one from Hoima in Unyoro. The latter seems to be younger, its iris is described as dark brown, feet orange-yellow; while of the former the feet were copper-red, black in front, and its iris red. Maxilla black, mandible orange.

Only a single specimen was obtained by Mr. Gedge on the Elgon Plains (Kavirondo), where it is common. (Grant, Ibis, 1891, p. 124, id. Handbook Game-birds, i. p. 127.)

36. *Francolinus hubbardi* Grant.

One male, River Molo, twelve miles south of the equator, Uganda Protectorate, Ravine district. "Iris sepia-brown, feet lemon-yellow, bill black at the tip, yellow at base."

Grant (Bull. B. O. Club. vol. iv. p. 27, id. Handbook Game-birds, i. p. 112) described it in 1895 from the Nassa district.

37. *Pternistes infuscatus* Cab.

This common species was shot at Makindos, Ukamba, British East Africa. (See Neumann, J. F. O. 1898, p. 302.)

38. *Numida reichenowi* Grant.

♂ ♀ shot on the Kiboko river in Ukamba, British East Africa, 26/4/98. "Iris red-brown, bill and feet black." The wattle at the gape seems to be almost quite red.

39. *Numida ptylorhyncha* Less.

A female and a young male from Kitanwa, 2½ hours' march from the east shore of Lake Albert, Unyoro.

Lesson, who was evidently a very poor Greek and Latin scholar, spelt the name *ptylorhyncha*.

40. *Numida ansorgei*, sp. nov.

An adult male of a guinea-fowl, shot at Lake Nakuru (Uganda Protectorate), on March 28, 1898, cannot be united with one of the described forms. It stands probably somewhat between *N. reichenowi* and the form named *N. intermedia* by Oscar Neumann. It differs from *N. reichenowi* in the form of the helmet, the high ridge of caruncles at the base of the bill, the broad, not narrow and not hair-like feathers on the back of the neck, and the colour of the wattle at the gape, but it agrees with this species in the form of the wattle at the gape and the barred neck-feathers. It differs from *N. intermedia* Neum. in the beak being blackish-green, not red, the larger wattles at the gape, and their colour, and probably also the more spotted chest. The type-specimen has on the hind-neck, just below the head, a bunch of broad pointed black feathers, which seem to point upwards; the feathers below this bunch are very finely, but regularly barred with numerous white bars. The red naked skin on the nape is divided by a narrow black line in the middle; the wattle at the gape is broad and largely extended in front and behind, but not very pendant; and there is a red spot in front as well as on the hind-tip. "Iris red-brown."

Wing 282 mm., tarsus 75, middle toe without claw 55, helmet in a straight line from the bottom 34, bill 24.

From *N. coronata*, which is not yet known to occur north of the Zambesi, it presents many points of difference, notably the bunch of feathers on the hind-neck, the deep black ground-colour, the form and colour of the wattles.

(BIRDS OF PREY.)

41. *Lophoaëtus occipitalis* (Daud.)

♀ ad. Masindi, Unyoro, 6 8 97. "Iris golden-yellow, feet lemon-yellow. Bill slate-blue, black towards the tip. Cere greenish-yellow."

42. *Circus macrurus* (Gm.)

♀ juv. Fovira, Unyoro, 2 1 08. "Iris orange-red, feet lemon-yellow."

(PARROTS.)

43. *Pœocephalus rufiventris* (Rüpp.)

Voi river and Mtoto Ndei in British East Africa. "Iris bright orange-red in both sexes, bill and feet blackish."

(ROLLERS.)

44. *Eurystomus afer* (Lath.)

Kampala (Uganda) and Kibwezi (British East Africa).

(PLANTAIN-EATERS.)

45. *Turacus hartlaubi* (Fisch. & Rchw.)

♂ ♀ Subugo Forest, Uganda Protectorate, 6/12/96. "Iris chocolate-brown, feet black, bill red."

46. *Schizorhis leucogaster* Rüpp.

♀ ad. Muani, British East Africa, 11/11 96. "Iris greenish-brown; feet black. Bill greenish-black."

(COLIES.)

47. *Colius leucotis affinis* Shelley.

In 1885, in the Ibis, p. 312, Shelley separated from "*Colius leucotis typicus*," of which he says that it inhabits "N.E. Africa, southward to Kitui in Ukamba," a form which he called *Colius leucotis affinis*, and of which he says that it is found on the "Upper White Nile to Dar-es-Salaam," and that it differs from *C. leucotis typicus* in being smaller, and in having the neck and back generally less distinctly barred, the white on the throat and sides of the head clearer, the tail-feathers generally slightly narrower. He adds that "these sub-species appear to run into each other." In 1892, in the catalogue of Birds, vol. xvii. p. 342, Dr. Sharpe separates "*Colius affinis*" as a sub-species from *C. leucotis*. Of the latter he says that it occurs in "Abyssinia and Bogosland, south to Shoa," and of the former that it is found from the "White Nile district to Central Africa, and thence to Eastern Africa." In 1898 (Nov. Zool., vol. v. p. 76) I was able to quote what I called *C. affinis* as far south as New Heligoland in German East Africa. According to Reichenow it occurs all over German East Africa. After carefully reviewing the available material, I find that there are two forms now mixed under "*C. affinis*," i.e. a smaller form from the drier parts of East Africa, and a larger one from the interior. Shelley (l. c.) had already noticed that his *C. leucotis affinis* were not all alike. Both forms have been found by Dr. Ansorge. One from Mombasa Island (13. X. 1896) and another from Maharagwe-fundi in the Taru desert, British East Africa (24. X. 1896) are true *affinis*. "Iris dark brown."

The three forms might be separated as follows:—

1. Throat and neck distinctly and strongly barred, some bars indicated on the whole back, wing longer (100 mm.), ear-coverts silvery grey :

C. leucotis leucotis Rüpp.

(Abyssinia, south to the elevated parts of Somaliland.)

2. Throat and neck less strongly barred, back without indications of bars, wing as long and ear-coverts of the same colour as in *leucotis* :

C. leucotis berlepschi, subsp. nov.

(Central Africa, from the White Nile to German East Africa.)

3. Throat and neck less strongly barred (as in *berlepschi*), back without bars, wing much shorter, 90–94 mm., ear-coverts of a less silvery-grey, more buffy shade, upper and under surface generally slightly more rufous :

C. leucotis affinis Shelley.

(Drier eastern districts of East Africa—Bagamoyo, Dar-es-Salaam, Zanzibar, Witu.)

48. *Colius leucotis berlepschi* Hart.

This form is characterised above, the type being from New Heligoland, German East Africa. Dr. Ansorge sent specimens from Masindi in Unyoro, Hoima in Unyoro, and Kampala in Uganda. "Iris: upper brim yellow (or yellowish-green), lower half greenish-yellow (or greenish-grey)." This is rather different from *C. leucotis affinis*.

This form is named in honour of my friend Count Berlepsch, who has lent and given me valuable material for comparison.

(HORNBILLS.)

49. *Lophoceros erythrorhynchus* (Tem.)

♂ Kinani, British East Africa, 2/5/98. "Iris light yellow, feet black, bill red, mandible black towards base, base yellow."

50. *Lophoceros melanoleucus* (Licht. sen.)

♂ ad. Kibwezi, Ukamba, British East Africa, 28/4/98. "Iris whitish-yellow, feet black, bill red."

(CUCKOOS.)

51. *Centropus superciliosus* H. & E.

Kampala, Uganda, January.

(HONEY-GUIDES.)

52. *Indicator indicator* (Gm.)

A male in moult and very abraded; Mondo, Uganda, 25/12/96.

(BARBETS.)

53. *Melanobucco (Pogonorhynchus) irroratus* (Cab.)

Mwachi, two days' march from Mombasa, and Taru (British East Africa), October 1896. "Iris red-brown, feet and bill black."

54. *Trachyphonus boehmi* Fischer & Rchw.

♀ Ndi, British East Africa, 27/10/96. "Iris chocolate-brown, feet slate-green, bill slate-green."

The bird figured as *T. boehmi* in Reichenow's "Vögel Deutsch-Ost-Afrika's," seems to be *T. margaritatus*.

55. *Tricholæma lacrymosum* Cab.

? Masongoleni, British East Africa, 2/11/96.

56. *Barbatula affinis* Rchw.

? Taru, British East Africa, 22/10/96.

57. *Barbatula leucolæma* Verr.

Mondo, in Uganda, 25/12/96. "Iris chocolate-brown."

(WOODPECKERS.)

58. *Mesopicus gartan* (P. L. S. Müll.)

An adult male and a young one from Masindi and Fajao in Unyoro, 13/11/97. Has no sign of red on the abdomen or breast, and resembles entirely a male shot by the writer on the Benue. I should have expected *M. rhodeogaster*, which is probably *not* the same as *M. spodocephalus*, at Unyoro.

59. *Dendropicus zanzibari* Malh.

♂ ad. (marked ♀ erroneously). Between Maungu mountain and Voi river, British East Africa. "Iris chocolate-brown, feet greenish-grey, bill dark slate-grey." Probably sub-species of *D. guineensis* (Scop.) = *D. cardinalis* (Gm.) = *D. hartlaubi* Malh.

60. *Campothera tæniolæma* Rchw. & Neum.

Subugo Forest, in the Uganda Protectorate. "Iris red, feet green, bill slate-bluish."

(KINGFISHERS.)

61. *Halcyon semicærulea* (Forsk.)

Kibero (Unyoro), 12/10/97, ♀. "Iris dark brown. Bill and feet red." Kibwezi, Ukamba, British East Africa, 29/4/98.

62. *Halcyon senegalensis* (L.)

♂ Pongo, Lur country, north-west shore of Lake Albert. There are apparently several sub-species of this species, but *H. cyanoleuca* cannot possibly be a sub-species (= geographical race) of it, for it occurs in many parts together with *H. senegalensis*. It is either a species or a stage of plumage of the latter.

63. *Halcyon chelicuti* (Stanley.)

Mahaji in the Lur country; Masindi in Unyoro; Kitanwa in Unyoro; Mwachi, two days' march from Mombasa, in British East Africa. "Upper bill (maxilla) slaty-brown or dark reddish-brown; under (mandible) red. Iris brown."

64. *Corythornis cyanostigma* (Rüpp.)

Kibero on the shore of Lake Albert and Mruli on the Kafu river in Unyoro.

65. *Ceryle rudis* (L.)

Kibero and Mruli (Unyoro).

(BEE-EATERS.)

66. *Merops bullockoides* A. Smith.

Lake Naivasha, Second Kedong, and First Kedong.

67. *Merops apiaster* L.

♂ Muani (British East Africa), 11/11/96. In much faded and worn plumage.

68. *Merops albicollis* Vieill.

Kampala (Uganda) and Masindi (Unyoro).

(HOOPOES.)

69. *Upupa africana* Bechst.

Mau and Kariandus in the Uganda Protectorate.

70. *Irrisor viridis* (Licht.)

Kibwezi, Ukamba, British East Africa, 29/4/98.

71. *Irrisor jacksoni* Sharpe.

♂ ad. Eldoma Ravine, Uganda Protectorate, 23/3/98. "Iris dark brown, feet brick-red, bill blood-red." (Salvin, Cat. B., Brit. Mus. XVI., Pl. 3, f. 1). Wing 130 mm.

72. *Rhinopomastes cyanomelas* (Vieill.)

♂ ad. Samburu, fourth camp on road from Mombasa to Uganda.

(SWIFTS.)

73. *Apus shelleyi* (Salvad.)

One male of a swift, shot at Kakamaga's on March 12, 1898 (Kavirondo), belongs to *A. shelleyi*. It closely resembles *A. apus*, but is smaller; the secondaries are decidedly paler, but the difference in the shape of the rectrices is very slight. Wing 145 mm., tail 70. "Iris chocolate-brown, feet light brown, bill black."

Very little is known about this swift, which must be resident in some parts of North-Eastern Africa.

74. *Tachornis parvus* (Lcht.)

Fovira in Unyoro, January 12, 1898.

(SWALLOWS.)

75. *Hirundo senegalensis* L.

Masindi, Unyoro, 27/6/97.

76. *Hirundo rustica* L.

Kibero (Unyoro) in October; Kampala (Uganda) in February.

77. *Hirundo gordoni* Jard.

Road between Kampala and Port Alice, Uganda, 11/2/97. This species does not seem to be recorded so far east.

78. *Hirundo puella* Temm & Schleg.

Mombasa (British East Africa).

79. *Cotile riparia* (L.)

Kibero in Unyoro, October.

Y

80. *Psalidoprocne albiceps* Scl.
First Kedong, British East Africa, 6/4/98.

(FLY CATCHERS.)

81. *Platystira cyanea* (S. Müll.)
Masindi, Unyoro. "Wattle above eye bright red. Iris light blue-grey, with white inner margin. Bill and feet black."

82. *Batis orientalis* (Heugl.)
Fajao on the Victoria Nile, Unyoro. "Iris bright yellow."

83. *Batis senegalensis* (L.)
Mombasa Island, Maji Chumvi (three days' march from Mombasa), British East Africa.

84. *Bradyornis pallidus* (v. Müll.)
Taru desert, British East Africa.

85. *Bradyornis murinus* F. & H.
Kibwezi in Ukamba, British East Africa.

86. *Dioptrornis fischeri* Rchw.
Eldoma Ravine; Pashto in Nandi (Uganda Protectorate); March 1898. "Iris dark brown, bill and feet slate colour." The sexes are fully alike.

87. *Terpsiphone perspicillata* (Sw.)
Taru desert and First Kedong, British East Africa.

88. *Tarsiger stellatus orientalis* Fisch. & Rchw.
I believe *T. orientalis* to be a poor sub-species of *T. stellatus*. The difference in the colour of the upper tail-coverts stated in J. F. O., 1884, p. 57, does not exist, but the black tip to the tail is a little wider, and the yellow breast and abdomen somewhat paler. Mau (Uganda Protectorate) 8/12/96.

BIRDS

89. *Muscicapa murina* (Fisch. & Rchw.)

Eldoma Ravine; Subugo Forest; Pashto in the Nandi country; Fajao, and Mruli on the Kafu River, in Unyoro. Uganda Protectorate. (Perhaps better called *Alseonax murina*.)

90. *Muscicapa grisola* L.

Mtoto Ndei and Makindos River, British East Africa. November and May 1st.

91. *Campophaga nigra* Vieill.

Mwachi, two days' march from Mombasa (British East Africa), and Nandi (Uganda Protectorate).

92. *Elminia teresita* Antin.

Masindi (Unyoro) and Kampala (Uganda). "Iris chocolate-brown, bill and feet black." A nestling was found on August 2, 1897, which is very pale-bluish, with pale-brown tips to the wing-coverts and feathers of the head.

93. *Melænornis ater* Sundev.

Kibwezi in Ukamba, British East Africa, 29/4/98.

94. *Melænornis edolioides* (Swains.)

Masindi, Hoima, and Kaligire in Unyoro; and Kampala in Uganda.

(SHRIKES.)

95. *Sigmodus tricolor* (Gray.)

? Mazera's (nine miles from Mombasa), British East Africa, 17/10/96. "Iris orange, feet red, bill orange-red."

96. *Prionops talacoma* A. Smith.

Maji Chumvi (three days' march from Mombasa), Ndi, and Kibwezi (British East Africa); Fajao (Unyoro). "Iris yellow in the old birds, greenish-brown in the young, feet orange, bill black."

97. *Nilaus minor* Sharpe.

Taru, British East Africa.

98. *Eurocephalus rüppelli* Bp.

Taru desert, 22/10/96. "Iris chocolate-brown."

99. *Dryoscopus major* (Hartl.)

Masindi in Unyoro, April and June. "Iris red-brown."

100. *Lanius caudatus* Cab.

Kiboko River, British East Africa, November. "Iris dark brown."

101. *Lanius collaris humeralis* (Stanl.)

Masindi in Unyoro, April and May. "Iris chocolate-brown."

102. *Lanius excubitorius* Des Murs.

Kamunina in Unyoro, June. "Iris chocolate-brown."

103. *Dryoscopus gambensis* (Licht.)

Fajao on the Victoria Nile, below the Murchison Falls, Unyoro.

♂ ad. "Iris bright orange, feet slate-blue, bill black."

104. *Lanius dorsalis* Cab.

♂ ad. Voi River, in British East Africa, 25/10/96.

This species, although described long before 1883, is left out of vol. viii. of the Cat. B. Brit. Mus.

The peculiar pattern of the under-wing seems to be undescribed. The lesser under wing-coverts as well as the under primary-coverts are black, while the remainder of the under wing-coverts are white.

105. *Laniarius nigrifrons* Rchw.

♂ ad. Fort Smith, Kikuyu, British East Africa.

106. *Lanius collurio* L.

Kiboko River and Kibwezi in Ukamba, British East Africa, April 26th and 28th, 1898, both adult males, bills and wings rather small.

107. *Telephonus minutus* Hartl.

♂ Kiwalogoma, Uganda, 26/12/96. "Iris red, feet and bill black."

108. *Telephonus senegalus* (L.)

Taru and Mwachi (two days from Mombasa) British East Africa.

109. *Laniarius erythrogaster* Cretschm.

Saridzi, Unyoro, April. "Iris light yellow."

110. *Dryoscopus rufinuchalis* Sharpe.

A ♂ from Kinani, British East Africa, belongs to this species, described from Somaliland. I doubt its distinctness from *D. ruficeps*, also described from Somaliland. "Iris chocolate-brown, feet dark greenish-brown, bill black."

(ORIOLES.)

111. *Oriolus rolleti* Salvad.

Ndi, British East Africa, 27/10/96. "Iris red, feet slate-green, bill reddish-brown."

(DRONGOS.)

112. *Dicrurus afer* (Licht.)

Mazera's, nine miles from Mombasa, British East Africa.

(STARLINGS.)

113. *Lamprotornis purpuropterus* (Rüpp.)

Hoima in Unyoro; Pongo in the Lur country, on west shore of Lake Albert. "Iris whitish-yellow."

114. *Lamprocolius sycobius* Hartl.

Samburu, British East Africa, 20/10/96. "Iris bright orange."

115. *Lamprocolius chalybeus* Ehr.

♂ Eldoma Ravine, in the Uganda Protectorate, 24/3/98. "Iris bright yellow."

116. *Lamprocolius purpureus* (P. L. S. Müll.)

One specimen, marked "♀," from Wakibara in Unyoro, 24/4/97, is so much smaller than all specimens of *L. purpureus* known to me that I believe it belongs to a different form, but more specimens are desired to decide about it.

117. *Cosmopsarus regius* Rchw.

This finest of all African birds was shot at Kinani, in British East Africa, on the 2nd of May 1898. "Iris is light yellow, feet black, bill black." The female differs from the male only in having the wing 2 or 3 mm. shorter.

118. *Spreo superbus* (Rüpp.)

Ukamba, and Gilgil River, in the Uganda Protectorate. "Iris light yellow."

119. *Spreo fischeri* (Rchw.)

One female of this very rare bird, first described by Professor Reichenow as "*Notauges*," then placed by Sharpe under "*Spreo*," where it belongs, and afterwards by the same author in "*Pholidauges*," was shot at Kinani (British East Africa) in May 1898. "The iris is light yellow, feet and bill black." The bird named *S. fischeri* in the British Museum, and described in Cat. B. xiii. p. 667, is not *S. fischeri*, but a widely different new species. No specimen of *S. fischeri* is in the British Museum.

120. *Dilophus carunculatus* (Gm.)

Campi-ya-Simba, 8/11 96, British East Africa.

(WEAVER-BIRDS.)

121. *Quelea cardinalis* (Hartl.)

Masindi, Unyoro, June and July 1897.

♂ "Iris dark brown, feet light brown, bill black."

♀ "Iris brown, feet light brown, maxilla light brown, mandible brownish-yellow."

122. *Amblyospiza melanotis* (Lafr.)

Masongoleni, British East Africa, 2/11/96. "Iris in both sexes red-brown, bill orange."

123. *Melanopteryx nigerrima* (Vieill.)

Masindi in Unyoro, Magogo in Kavirondo, Kiwalogoma in Uganda.

♂ ad. "Iris yellow, feet brown, bill black."

124. *Hyphantornis bohndorffi* (Rchw.)

Fovira and Fajao in Unyoro; Kampala in Uganda.

♂ ad. "Iris red." ♀ ad. "Iris red." Juv. "Iris hazel-brown."

125. *Hyphantornis bojeri* Cab.

Mombasa Island, British East Africa, 12/10/96. "Iris dark brown."

126. *Hyphantornis fischeri* (Rchw.)

Masindi and Fajao in Unyoro, and Kibero (on the east shore of Lake Albert) in Unyoro. "Iris brown."

Thirteen eggs of *Hyphantornis fischeri* show again the same stupendous variation of colours known to occur in most African weaver-birds. Some are bluish-green, others bluish-green with brown spots, or plain dark rufous-brown, or plain brownish olive-brown, almost like a nightingale's egg; or brown spotted with darker brown. They are all from one colony, in which no other species was observed. These birds, according to Dr. Ansorge, fed chiefly on the "matama" (Kaffre-corn). The males were noticed to be the most vigorous nest-builders, selecting the extreme tip of a branch, on which they fastened the strip of grass they had brought in their beak. The female occasionally came and inspected the work, and the male sometimes left its work unfinished and vigorously began another nest. The female occasionally took part in bringing some softer grass for the inner lining of the nest. When the nest was finished, the male most viciously persecuted every other bird that ventured to alight on his chosen twig, but it never came to any real fighting between them. In other species of *Hyphantornis* both sexes were observed to be equally busy in building.

127. *Hyphantornis vitellinus* (Licht.)

"Mto-ya-mkuyuni," in Ukamba, British East Africa. (This specimen is, I think, the true *vitellinus*, and *not reichardi*.)

128. *Sitagra ocularia crocata* (Hartl.)

Masindi, Unyoro, May 1897.

129. *Hetcryphantes emini* (Hartl.)

Masindi, Unyoro.

130. *Ploceus pachyrhynchus* Rchw.

Masindi, Unyoro. (Probably a sub-species of *superciliosus*.)

131. *Dinemellia dinemelli* (Rüpp.)

Taru desert and Kinani, British East Africa.

132. *Pyromelana franciscana* (Isert.)

Kafu River, Unyoro; Kibero; Naruangu, a short day's march from Mruli on the Kafu River.

133. *Pyromelana flammiceps* (Swains.)

♂ ad. Mtibua, Usoga country, Uganda Protectorate, 19/12/96.

134. *Pyromelana ansorgei*, sp. nov. (Plate II. fig. 2.)

This evidently very distinct new species seems to be nearest to *P. friedrichseni* Fisch. and Rchw. from Masai Land, but differs in being very much larger, in having a narrower scarlet band across the lower throat, and apparently also in having the back and rump black, not scarlet. The upper part of the back (the interscapulary region) only is orange, all the remainder of the back is black with pale buff edges to the feathers. It is a question whether these feathers are those of the fully adult bird, but there is no sign of their not being so. Under tail-coverts black with whitish-buff tips. Wing 90 mm., tail 66, culmen 19, tarsus 25 mm. "Iris dark brown, feet chocolate-brown, bill black." ♂, Masindi, Unyoro, 17/6/97.

135. *Urobrachya phœnicea* (Heugl.)

Mtibua, Usoga country, Uganda Protectorate. The bill of this specimen is smaller than in one from "Mtoni," collected by Bohndorff.

NEW SPECIES OF AFRICAN BIRDS

1. See page 350, No. 180.
2. „ 344, No. 134.

136. *Penthetriopsis macrura* (Gm.)

Ntuti (Singo), Uganda, and Eldoma Ravine (Uganda Protectorate). A young bird from Masindi (Unyoro) probably belongs to this species as well.

137. *Penthetria eques* (Hartl.)

Muani and Mto-ya-mkuyuni (Ukamba), British East Africa. "Bill light blue."

138. *Coliuspasser ardens concolor* Cass.

Specimens from Masindi in Unyoro (wing 75 to 76 mm.) have no sign of a red patch on the foreneck.

139. *Lagonosticta brunneiceps* Sharpe.

Four adult males, one immature male, and one female, from Masindi (Unyoro), Kibero (Unyoro), Kampala (Uganda), and Kibwezi (British East Africa), must, geographically, belong to *L. brunneiceps*; on the other hand, however, some of them are as red above as *L. senegala*. It is possible that even among the forms from N.E. Africa to Transvaal, to all of which Sharpe applies the name *L. brunneiceps*, there exist several forms. Unfortunately Dr. Sharpe did not say which of all these he would have regarded as the type, no specimen being marked type (see Cat. B. xiii. pp. 277, 278). In Nov. Zool. v. p. 72 I named the form from the Upper Shiré River *L. Senegala rendalli*, but I now doubt its distinctness from *L. brunneiceps* Sharpe (in his wide sense). By a mistake the length of the wing of *rendalli* has been given as 42 mm., it should have been 47. The wings of Dr. Ansorge's males measure 49 to 50 mm.

Dr. Sharpe and Prof. Reichenow are apparently also at variance with regard to *L. brunneiceps*, the former restricting *L. senegala* to Senegambia, the latter calling specimens from Kakoma, Udjiji, and Bukoba *L. senegala*, others from Kakoma (?), Kingani, Bagamoyo, Tabora, Usambara, Karema, &c., *L. brunneiceps*. This can hardly be right; for it is, in my opinion, most unlikely that *L. senegala* and *L. brunneiceps* are well defined species, they are probably sub-species. My *rendalli* is perhaps a smaller and somewhat brighter form, if separable from *brunneiceps*.

140. *Zonegastris melba* (L.)

Makindos River, British East Africa, 4/11/96.

141. *Philæterus arnaudi* (Bp.)

Campi-ya-Simba, British East Africa, 8/11/96.

142. *Estrilda bengala* (L.)

Mtoto Ndei and Kibwezi (British East Africa), and Kibero (Unyoro).

143. *Estrilda nonnula* Hartl.

(= *E. tenerrima* Rchw.) A fine series from Masindi (Unyoro) and Kampala (Uganda). *E. tenerrima* is the adult of *E. nonnula*. "Bill black with a red streak on each side of maxilla and mandible."

144. *Estrilda paludicola* Heugl.

Masindi in Unyoro; Kampala in Uganda. It seems from these specimens that the adult male has an orange-red bill, the female and young a brownish-black one.

145. *Estrilda astrild minor* (Cab.)

Campi Mbaruk, Kampala, Masindi (Uganda Protectorate). Young birds have a blackish bill. Typical *astrild* from South Africa is larger and with much darker throat and sides of the head.

146. *Estrilda rhodopyga* Sundev.

♂ ♂ ♂ Kibero, Unyoro, 13/10/97. The males have the "bill chocolate-brown;" the female "chocolate brown with a pink patch at each corner of mandible and pink edge to maxilla."

147. *Granatina ianthinogaster* (Rchw.)

One pair from Mto-ya-mkuyuni in Ukamba, British East Africa, 13/11/96. "Iris red, bill red, feet slate." Narrow red ring round eye.

148. *Spermestes cucullata* Sw.

Mahaji in the Lur country, on the west shore of Lake Albert; Masindi in Unyoro; Kampala in Uganda.

BIRDS

149. *Spermestes stigmatophora* Rchw.

One male of this rare bird from Fajao, on the left bank of the Victoria Nile, just below the Murchison Falls, 8/12/07. "Iris dark brown, feet black, bill light blue." (See Reichenow, Vögel Deutsch-Ost-Afrika's, p. 154.)

150. *Vidua vidua* (L.)

This is one of the commonest African birds, generally called *Vidua principalis* or *serena*, the proper name of which, however, seems to be as above.

A series from Masindi, Hoima, and Kampala, Uganda Protectorate.

(FINCHES.)

151. *Serinus reichenowi* Salvad.

Kikuyu, British East Africa.

152. *Serinus icterus* (Bonn. and Vieill.)

Evidently common in Masindi, Unyoro. On January 21, 1898, a nest was found with one normally coloured young and one albino ("Iris pink, feet pale flesh-colour, bill pale yellow") of a canary-yellow colour with white wings.

153. *Serinus flaviventris* (Sw.)

Masindi (Unyoro) and Campi-ya-Banda (Uganda Protectorate).

154. *Passer swainsoni* (Rüpp.)

A series of sparrows from Unyoro and Uganda seem to be rather *swainsoni* than *diffusus*.

(WAGTAILS.)

155. *Motacilla flava* L.; and 156. *Motacilla campestris* Pall.

Yellow Wagtails, of these two species, were frequently met with at different places in Uganda and Unyoro from October to March. It is possible that one or two belong to a third form of Yellow Wagtails, but this cannot be decided with certainty, as the specimens in question are young birds.

157. *Motacilla alba* L.

Common at Fajao and Fovira in Unyoro from November to January.

158. *Motacilla vidua* Sundev.

Fajao and Masindi in Unyoro; Kampala in Uganda.

(PIPITS.)

159. *Macronyx tenellus* Cab.

♂ ad. Taru, British East Africa, 21/10/96. "Iris dark brown, feet dark brown, bill brown."

This beautiful and rare Pipit has first been described as a *Macronyx*, from which it differs in its smaller size and more gracile form; but in the "Catalogue of Birds," vol. xiii., it was removed to the genus *Anthus*, while later on Dr. Sharpe created for it the new genus *Tmetothylacus*.

160. *Macronyx croceus* (Vieill.)

This common gigantic form of Pipit was shot at Mruli on the Kafu River in Unyoro, and at Mtibua in the Usoga country, Uganda Protectorate.

161. *Anthus trivialis* (L.)

♀ Masindi in Unyoro, January 1898.

(LARKS.)

162. *Mirafra fischeri* (Rchw.)

♀ Samburu (fourth camp from Mombasa *en route* to Uganda), British East Africa, 20/10/96. "Iris dark orange-brown, feet flesh-colour, bill brown."

163. *Mirafra africana* A. Smith.

♂ Kiboko River, Ukamba, British East Africa, 25/4/98. "Iris ochre."

164. *Mirafra intercedens* Rchw.

♂ ♀ Kiboko River, British East Africa, April and November.

BIRDS

165. *Mirafra hypermetra* (Rchw.)

This rare Lark was shot on the Voi River in British East Africa on 25/10/96. "Iris chocolate-brown, feet flesh-colour, bill slate-brown, maxilla much darker."

Reichenow has created the new genus *Spilocorydon* for this bird, but I see no reason for removing it from *Mirafra*.

166. *Mirafra pœcilosterna* (Rchw.) (1879.)

This rare Lark was procured at Kinani and on the Tsavo River, British East Africa, in October. "Iris, feet, and bill brown."

The narrow and long soft bill remove this species very much from all *Mirafræ*, and it will probably be necessary to create a new genus for it.

(BULBULS.)

167. *Pycnonotus nigricans minor* Heugl.

♂ ad. Masindi, Unyoro, 12/6/97, and Ukamba (British East Africa).

168. *Pycnonotus dodsoni* Sharpe.

Makindos River, British East Africa, 4/11/96.

This skin agrees with one of the co-types of *P. dodsoni* in the Tring Museum.

169. *Andropadus eugenius* Rchw.

♀ ad. Eldoma Ravine, Uganda Protectorate. "Iris dark brown, feet yellowish-brown, bill black." A young bird from Rau (Nandi), Uganda Protectorate.

170. *Andropadus flavescens* Hartl.

Mombasa Island, British East Africa. "Iris yellow."

171. *Phyllostrephus strepitans* Rchw.

Mombasa Island, British East Africa, 10/10/96.

(SILVER-EYES.)

172. *Zosterops stuhlmanni* Rchw.

A series of this rare bird from Masindi and Fajao in Unyoro. "The iris is orange-red, feet and bill blackish."

(A specimen from Kiwalogoma in Uganda is deeper yellow and seems to belong to another species.)

173. *Zosterops kikuyensis* Sharpe (?)

A female from Eldoma Ravine (Uganda Protectorate) seems to belong to this species. Its iris is "sepia brown." With a series one might be able to find differences from typical *kikuyensis*. The yellow mark on the forehead seems to be larger in extent.

(SUN-BIRDS.)

174. *Cinnyris verticalis viridisplendens* Rchw.

Masindi in Unyoro, May and June. "Iris dark brown."

175. *Cinnyris osiris suahelicus* Rchw.

Kampala, Uganda.

176. *Cinnyris cupreus* (Shaw.)

Common at Masindi (Unyoro).

177. *Cinnyris falkensteini* Fisch. and Rchw.

Masindi in Unyoro. "Iris dark brown."

178. *Cinnyris mediocris* Shell.

♂ ad. Subugo Forest, Uganda Protectorate, 6/12/96. "Iris chocolate-brown, bill and feet black."

179. *Cinnyris reichenowi* Sharpe.

The considerably shorter bill and the deep purple upper tail-coverts and breast-band distinguish this bird without difficulty from *mediocris*. Rau, Nandi country, Uganda Protectorate, 12/12/96.

180. *Cinnyris ansorgei*, sp. nov. (Plate II. fig. 1).

An adult male, shot at Nandi Station in the Uganda Protectorate on March 16, 1898, differs from *C. reichenowi* Sharpe in the great extension of the somewhat deeper red colour of the breast, which occupies an area of about 23 mm. in length, while in *C. reichenowi* it extends for about 17 mm., and in the beak being still shorter than in *C. reichenowi*. Wing 53 mm., tail 40 mm., tarsus 20, culmen (from end of feathering on forehead) 18.3 mm., against fully 20 mm. in *C. reichenowi*. The belly and lower abdomen seem to be a little darker than in *C. reichenowi*.

It is not without hesitation that I describe a third form, in addition to *C. mediocris* and *C. reichenowi*, from almost the same localities; yet, on the other hand, it seems to be about as distinct from *C. reichenowi* as the latter is from *C. mediocris;* and Prof. Reichenow and Mr. Neumann, both authorities in East African Ornithology, pronounced it to be an undescribed species when they saw it at Tring.

181. *Cinnyris acik* (Antin.)

A good series from Masindi in Unyoro. The wings of the males measure from 68 to 71 mm.

182. *Cinnyris senegalensis lamperti* Rchw.

(See Journ. f. Ornith. 1897, p. 196.) A male from Mtoto Ndei in British East Africa belongs to this form, described as a sub-species of *senegalensis*, from which it differs in being much larger (wing 77 mm.), and more brownish on the back.

(Specimens of *C. gutturalis* from East Africa differ also considerably from those of South Africa in being much smaller, and must be separated sub-specifically. I propose for them the name *Cinnyris gutturalis inaestimata* subsp. nov.)

183. *Cinnyris hunteri* Shelley.

Kinani and Tsavo River, British East Africa, October 1896. "Iris very dark brown, feet and bill black."

The females differ from the females of *C. acik* in being paler and more greyish above, lighter below and almost whitish on the abdomen.

184. *Nectarinia kilimensis* Shelley.

Kiketi (British East Africa); Campi Mbaruk (Uganda Protectorate); and Masindi in Unyoro. "Iris dark brown; feet and bill black."

185. *Nectarinia pulchella* (L.)

Kibero, on the east shore of Lake Albert, Unyoro.

186. *Anthotreptes hypodila* (Jard.)

Samburu; Masongoleni; Taru desert; British East Africa.

(TITMICE.)

187. *Parus niger* Bonn. and Vieill.

Fajao on the Victoria Nile, below the Murchison Falls, Unyoro, 13/8/97. "Iris light yellow, almost white. Feet blue-black. Bill black."

188. *Parus albiventris* Shelley

Taru, British East Africa, 22/10/96. "Iris deep brown; feet and bill black."

(BABBLING-THRUSHES.)

189. *Argya rufula* Heugl.

Mombasa Island, British East Africa. "Iris yellow."

190. *Dryodromas rufidorsalis* Sharpe

Kinani, British East Africa, 31/10/96. "Iris yellow."

191. *Prinia mystacea* (Rüpp.)

Mruli and Masindi in Unyoro. "Iris golden-orange, bill black, feet light brown."

192. *Cisticola dodsoni* Sharpe (?).

♂ Voi River in British East Africa, 25/10/96.

This specimen differs from *C. dodsoni* in being washed with rufous-brown on the back, but this character may be seasonal.

193. *Cisticola lateralis* (Fras.)

Kampala in Uganda, 14/1/97. "Iris yellow."

194. *Cisticola subruficapilla* (A. Smith.)

Muani (British East Africa) and Kibero (Unyoro). "Iris dark brown." According to Dr. Sharpe this species occurs nearly all over tropical Africa. The names of *cantans* Heugl. and *fischeri* Reichenow are perhaps both belonging to the same northern form which may be a sub-species.

195. *Cisticola cinerascens* (Heugl.)

♂ ad. Masindi (Unyoro), 14/4/97. "Iris red-brown, feet flesh-colour. Bill black."

196. *Cisticola lugubris* Rüpp.

♂ Masindi (Unyoro), 26/4/97. "Iris orange-brown. Feet flesh-colour. Maxilla black, mandible light brown."

197. *Cisticola strangei* (Fras.)

♂ ad. Kafu River, Unyoro, 4/9/97. "Iris yellow."

198. *Cisticola erythrogenys* Rüpp.

♂ First Swamp, Kikuyu, British East Africa, 23/11/96. "Iris orange."

199. *Melocichla orientalis* (Sharpe.)

Masindi in Unyoro, 25/6/97. "Iris orange-gold, feet light slate-blue, maxilla blackish, mandible light blue-grey."

200. *Euprinodes schistaceus* Sharpe.

Mau, in the Uganda Protectorate. "Iris red, feet flesh-colour, bill black."

201. *Calamonastes simplex* (Cab.)

Tsavo River, British East Africa.

202. *Erythropygia leucoptera* (Rüpp.)

Tsavo River, British East Africa, 29/10/96.

203. *Erythropygia hartlaubi* Rchw.

Masindi, Unyoro. "Iris light brown, feet slate-colour, bill blackish."

z

(THRUSH-LIKE BIRDS.)

204. *Phylloscopus trochilus* (L.)

Eldoma Ravine, Uganda Protectorate, 23/3/98.

205. *Turdus bocagei* (Cab.)

Masindi, Unyoro, 18/4/97.

206. *Turdus deckeni* Cab.

Mau, Uganda Protectorate, 7/12/96.

207. *Monticola saxatilis* (L.)

Eldoma Ravine, Uganda Protectorate, March 1898.

208. *Myrmecocichla cryptoleuca* Sharpe.

Eldoma Ravine, Uganda Protectorate, March 1898. "Iris dark brown."

209. *Myrmecocichla nigra* (Vieill.)

Fort Hoima, Unyoro, October. "Iris chocolate-brown."

210. *Saxicola livingstonei* (Tristr.)

Lake Naivasha, Uganda Protectorate, 26/11/96.

211. *Saxicola œnanthe* L.

Kiboko River, and Kinani in British East Africa; Masindi, in Unyoro in winter.

212. *Saxicola isabellina* Cretzschm.

Masindi, Unyoro.

213. *Saxicola pleschanka* (Lepech.)

Eldoma Ravine, Uganda Protectorate, 24/3/98. Fovira in Unyoro, 12/1 98.

214. *Pratincola rubetra* (L.)

In winter everywhere in Unyoro and Uganda.

215. *Pratincola rubicola* (L.)

Kikuyu (British East Africa) and Nandi (Uganda Protectorate), March and November.

216. *Pratincola emmæ* Hartl.

Rau (Nandi) in Uganda Protectorate in March, and First Swamp, in Kikuyu, British East Africa. "Iris dark brown, feet and bill black."

I believe that *P. emmæ* is different from *P. albofasciata* Rüpp. from Abyssinia in having a rufous band across the chest; while in *P. albofasciata* this band is absent in the fully adult bird. It is nevertheless strange that Hartlaub, when describing *P. emmæ*, did not mention its close affinity to the former.

Printed by BALLANTYNE, HANSON & Co.
Edinburgh & London

www.ingramcontent.com/pod-product-compliance
Lightning Source LLC
Chambersburg PA
CBHW051743300426
44115CB00007B/675